Virginia Genealogies
and
Family Histories

A BIBLIOGRAPHY
OF BOOKS
ABOUT
VIRGINIA FAMILIES

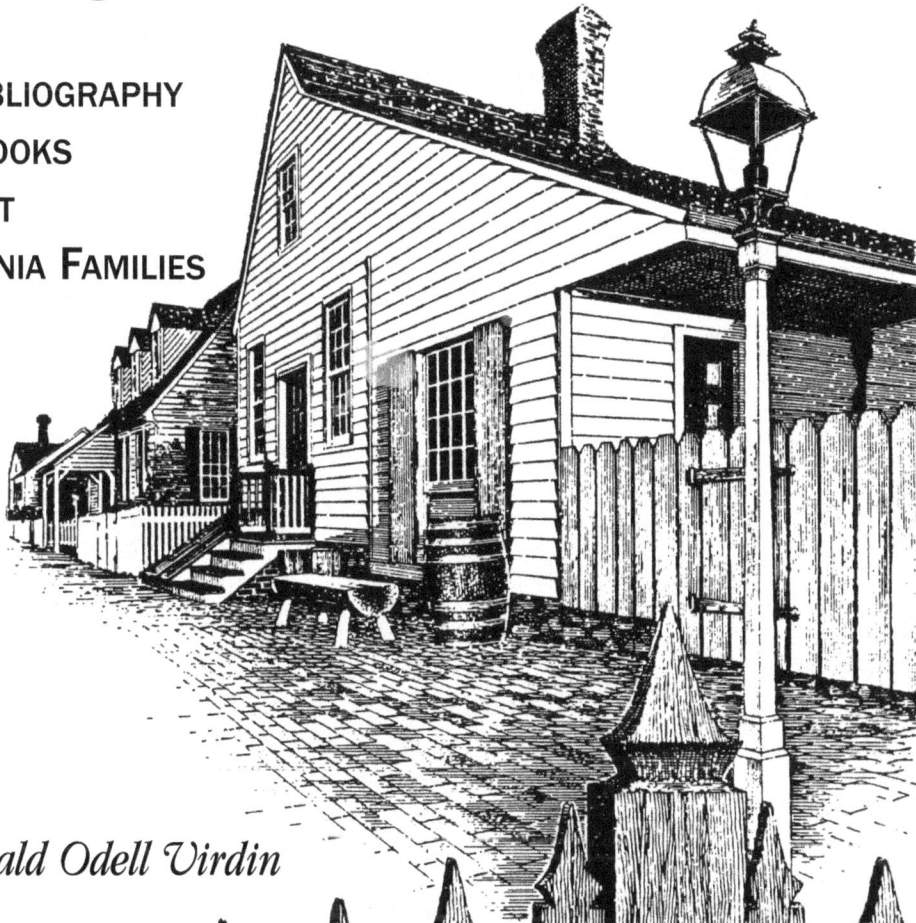

Donald Odell Virdin

HERITAGE BOOKS
2017

HERITAGE BOOKS
AN IMPRINT OF HERITAGE BOOKS, INC.

Books, CDs, and more—Worldwide

For our listing of thousands of titles see our website
at
www.HeritageBooks.com

Published 2017 by
HERITAGE BOOKS, INC.
Publishing Division
5810 Ruatan Street
Berwyn Heights, Md. 20740

International Standard Book Numbers
Paperbound: 978-1-55613-404-3

TABLE OF CONTENTS

INTRODUCTION

All of the books in this bibliography (about 2,500 total) deal with families who have some connection to Virginia, including what is now West Virginia. Most of the books (over 2,000) can be found at the Library of Congress in Washington, D.C., the Daughters of the American Revolution (DAR) Library in Washington, D.C., the National Genealogical Society (NGS) Library in Arlington, Virginia, or the library known as Lloyd House (devoted to Virginia history) in Alexandria, Virginia. If you should want to examine one of the family histories listed here, you should first contact one of these libraries (see addresses below) to see if they have the book. You could also ask your own public library to see if they can obtain the book on inter-library loan.

In some cases, titles listed here are not available in the Washington, D.C. area, so you might also want to contact one of the large metropolitan libraries that have genealogical collections, such as the New York Public Library, the Allen County Public Library (Fort Wayne, Indiana), the St. Louis Public Library, the Sutro Library (San Francisco), or the Los Angeles Public Library. Another location to check is the LDS Family History Library in Salt Lake City.

Keep in mind that no bibliography of this kind can ever be complete. Many family histories are privately printed and never turn up in large libraries. At the same time, there will be new family histories published too late for inclusion in this book.

If you find a family name listed here, do not assume the family was primarily or exclusively associated with Virginia. There may be other published material on the same name or the same family in another area. Many of the books cited here include references to other states.

Library of Congress
Local History and Genealogy Room
Washington, D.C 20540
(202) 707-5537

DAR Library
1776 D Street N.W.
Washington, D.C. 20006
(202) 879-3229

NGS Library
4527 17th Street North
Arlington, VA 22207
(703) 525-0050

Lloyd House
220 North Washington St.
Alexandria, VA 22314
(703) 838-4577

ABBOTT -- Southall, James P.C.
Memoirs of the Abbotts of Old Bellevue. Charlottesville: University
Press, 1955.

ABBOTT -- Turner, David Anderson
The Abbotts of West Virginia. Madison, W. Va., 1981.

ABERNETHY -- Abernethy, Thomas Perkins
The antecedents of the Abernethy family in Scotland, Virginia and
Alabama. Charlottesville, 1966.

ADAMS -- Adams, Elizabeth H.
Adams - Va., Md., Pa., Del., etc. 19--.

ADAMS -- Adams, Katherine K.
Adams genealogy; Addams-Adams of Maryland ..., Gannaway of Virginia,
Concklin of New York, Kellogg of Mass., Williams-Love ..., Brownlow
of Virginia and Kentucky. Chicago, 1925.

ADAMS -- Adams, Thomas Tunstall
Biographical genealogies of the Virginia Adams families, with notes
of some collateral branches. Richmond: Richmond Press, Inc., 1928.

ADAMS -- Baldwin, Emma
An Adams-Goolsby genealogy, some descendants of Robert Adams of
Virginia, Georgia, and Texas, 1624-1982, and a Shirley genealogy,
some descendants of Thomas Shirley of Virginia, South Carolina,
Georgia, and Texas, 1612-1982. Tenaha, Texas, 1983.

ADAMS -- Campbell, Julia Anna Francis (Courtenay)
De(s)cendants of Joel Adams and Grace Watson of "The Fork,"
Richland County, South Carolina. Charlottesville, 1959.

ADCOCK -- Lawless, Blanche E. A.
Family history; Adcock, John, of Buckingham, Virginia, some of his
descendants, with collateral lines: Christian, McMurty, Robertson,
Ingersoll, etc. Astoria, Ill.: Stevens Pub., 1973.

ADDINGTON -- Addington, Hugh M.
History of the Addington family in United States and England.
Nickelsville, Va., 1960.

AGEE -- Agee, Louis N.
The Agee register: a genealogical record of the descendants of
Mathieu Agee, a Huguenot refugee to Virginia. Baltimore: Gateway
Press, 1982.

AKERS -- The Akers family of Franklin County, Virginia; combined with the
Boone, Cannaday, Hickman, and Pridgen families. Roanoke Rapids, N.C.,
1953.

ALBEMARLE -- Woods, Edgar
   Albemarle County in Virginia, etc. Charlottesville: The Michie Co.,
   1901.

ALBRITTAIN -- McSwain, Eleanor Davis
   Some descendants of Francis Albrighton (1609-1667), Mathew Jones of
   Mulberry Island, Virginia (1643-1712), and Ralph Albritton of York
   County, Virginia (1656-1701), and connecting families. Macon, Ga.,
   1984.

ALEXANDER -- The Alexander Family; Virginia, Princeton-New York branch.
   New York, 1914.

ALEXANDER -- Alexander Family Records, First American Settlers and Early
   Colonial Families. New England and Virginia Records.

ALEXANDER -- Melson, John W.
   Ye Albemarle County Alexander Family. 1962.

ALFRED THE GREAT -- Watson, Annah W.
   A royal lineage; Alfred the Great, 901-1901. Richmond: Whittet &
   Shepperson, 1901.

ALLEGHANY -- Morton, Oren F.
   A centennial History of Alleghany County, Virginia. Dayton, Ohio:
   J. K. Ruebush Co., 1923.

ALLEN -- Alen, Maud B.
   Allen-Easter families of Virginia. Salt Lake City, Utah.

ALLEN -- Allen, Maud Bliss
   Allen-Easter families of Virginia. 1954.

ALLEN -- Allen, Robert M.
   The genealogy of Robert Allen, Sr. of Augusta County, Virginia (17--
   1791). San Jose, Calif., 1981.

ALLEN -- Allen, Robert M.
   The genealogy of Robert Allen, Sr. of Augusta County, Virginia (17--
   1791). San Jose, Calif., 1983.

ALLEN -- Allwn, Littlebury W.
   "Family sketch" written in 1837 ... Being a history of the early Allan
   family of Henrico County, Va. Hinsdale, Ill., 1963.

ALLEN -- Baldwin, Alma H.
   Genealogy of the Allen family from Shenandoah county, Virginia, to
   Ohio, Indiana, Wisconsin, Iowa and Kansas.

ALLEN -- Ancestors and descendants of Moses Allen, born Virginia, 1815;
   pioneer settler of Bonham and Ector, Fannin County, Texas, 1827.
   Bonham, Tex., 1971.

ALLEN -- Bell, Landon C.
   The old Free state; a contribution to the history of Lunenburg County
   and southside Virginia. Richmond: The William Byrd Press, Inc., 1927.

ALLERTON -- Greenwood, Isaac J.
   Allertons of New England and Virginia. 1890.

ALLEY -- Allen, Maud B.
   Alley-Osbourne genealogy ... of Va., Ky., Tennessee and Indiana.

ALLEY -- Carey, Virginia Miller
   Alley highlights: yesterday for tomorrow. Prichard, W. Va.: G. A.
   Hampton, 1983.

ALTAFFER -- Altaffer, Maurice W.
   The Altaffer family; a short chronicle of the Altaffer family of
   Virginia and Ohio. London: Favil Press, 1968.

AMBLER -- Nelson, Thomas Forsythe
   American historica. Richard Ambler, the Ambler family in Virginia,
   and those who carry the blood of the migrant in 1716. Washington,
   1907.

AMES -- Edwards, Lucy Ames and Nannie Ames Mears
   Ames, Mears and allied lines; the American ancestors of Samuel
   William Ames and Sarah Anne Edmunds Mears of Accomack County, Virginia.
   Accomack, 1967.

AMISS -- Ray, Laura Collison
   The Amiss family of Amissville, Rappahannock and Culpeper County,
   Virginia. Washington, 1952.

AMMERMAN -- Ammerman, Charles Richard
   Historical and biographical record of the antecedents and descendants
   of Anson Leonard and Ida (Bryan) Ammerman. St. Petersburg, Fla., 1953.

AMMONET -- Bransford, Clifton Wood
   Jacob Ammonet, of Virginia, and a part of his descendants.

AMORY -- Autobiography of Otis Taylor Amory, M.D. Richmond: Guardian Pub.,
   1946.

ANDERSON -- Andersons. This chart is prepared for Alexander F. Anderson of
   Cincinnati, Ohio, from the chart of Edward Lowell Anderson, prepared
   in 1912, by William Clayton Torrence from the scattered records available
   in the Virginias; amplified from the "Anderson family records," compiled
   by W. P. Anderson in 1936, and from current data by Luke S. Murdock.
   Cincinnati: Gibson-Perin Co., 1936.

ANDERSON -- Anderson, A. S. (Arnett Sooy)
   Allen M. Anderson, Abraham B. Grimes, and John Hamrick families and
   descendants. Parsons, W. Va.: McClain Print Co., 1983.

ANDERSON -- Anderson, Charles
Ye Andersons of Virginia and some of the descendants, bye one of ye
Famile. New York, 1908.

ANDERSON -- Anderson, Edward
Andersons of Gold Mine, Hanover Co., Va. Chicago.

ANDERSON -- Anderson, Edward Lowell
The Andersons of Gold Mine, Hanover County, Virginia. Cincinnati, 1913.

ANDERSON -- Anderson, Grant James
Genealogy, in part, of the Anderson-Owen-Beall families. Richmond:
Whittet & Shepperson Printers, 1909.

ANDERSON -- Anderson-Overton; a continuation of Anderson family records,
published 1936, and The early descendants of Wm. Overton & Elizabeth
Waters of Virginia, and allied families, published 1938, by W. P.
Anderson. Cincinnati: The Gibson and Perin Co., 1945.

ANDERSON -- McCsrthy, Lynette Nolen
Jacob Anderson of Pulaski, Virginia, 1758-1842, and related families.
Normal, Ill., 1981.

ANDERSON -- Anderson, Rual P.
Genealogy: Spaid, Anderson, Whitacre, and a number of allied families.
Strasburg: Shenandoah Pub. House, 1975.

ANDERSON -- Genealogy of the Peyton family, embracing the lineage of Virginia
immigrant (I) Thomas Anderson, of Northumberland, England and Frances
Jones (Anderson) of Virginia, first in Gloucester County, permanent
in Louisa County at "Laurel Branch," covering descendants of their 10
children. Charlottesville, 1963.

ANDERSON, Wise, Jennings Cropper
Genealogical record and chart of the family of Elizabeth Lydecker
Anderson (Anderson-Lydecker). Richmond, 1916.

ANDREWS -- Andrews, James Ray
The Andrews family; descendants of Varney Andrews, Virginia soldier
of the American Revolution. Dallas, Tex., 1963.

ANDREWS -- Andrews, James Ray, Sr.
Genealogy of the Andrews, Maxey and related families of Henrico
County in colonial Virginia; Bondurant, Ford (Faure), Salle, Sampson.
Dallas, Tex., 1965.

ANDREWS -- Andrews, L. W.
Genealogical Tree of the descendants of Isham Andrews who went from
Virginia to Georgia about 1760.

ANDREWS -- Jester, Annie Lash with Martha Woodroof Hiden
    Adventurers of purse and person, Virginia, 1607-1625. Princeton,
    N.J., 1956.

ANDREWS -- LeBlanc, Kittie
    Andrews family: descended from James Andrews of Old Rappahannock County,
    Virginia, showing miscellaneous branches. Los Angeles, Calif., 1981.

ANGLE -- Angle, Eula Ferguson
    Peter Angle, 1754-1968 and related families: Wills Lee Moorman.
    Richmond, 1969.

ANTHONY -- Swain, Frederic A.
    Mark and Joseph Anthony families of Virginia, with contributory data
    on Capt. Christopher Clark and Moorman families. Sarasota, Fla., 1933.

ANTIQUARY -- James, Edward Wilson
    The Lower Norfolk County, Virginia, Antiquary. Baltimore: The
    Fredinwald Co., Printers, 1895-1906.

ANTRIM -- Bird, R. Byron
    An Antrim family history: ... pertaining to descendants of John Antram
    and Frances Butcher of Burlington County, New Jersey, Aaron Antram and
    Cahrlotta King of Culpeper County, Virginia, and Joseph Antrim and Mila
    America Edwards of Marion County, Indiana. Madison, Wisc., 1977.

ARCHER -- Randolph, Wassell
    George Arthur I of the Umberslade Archers of Henrico County, Virginia,
    and his descendants. Memphis, Tenn., 1865.

ARCHER -- Archer and Silvester families; a history written in 1870, by Dr.
    Robert Archer ... (with notes by Rev. E. L. Goodwin, a grand-son).
    Richmond: The William Byrd Press, Inc., 1937.

AREW -- Rhue, George N. and Elizabeth C.
    Descendants of John Arew of Accomac County, Virginia, who now spell
    their family name: Rew, Rue and Rhue. Los Angeles, 1955.

ARLINE -- Wynn, Louise Tomkins
    Jeremiah Arline of Nansemond Co., Va., 1695, and descendants in North
    Carolina, Georgia, and Florida: including a short account of the
    Kittrell family. Decorah, Iowa: Anundsen Pub. Co., 1983.

ARMENTROUT --Armentrout, Russell S.
    The Armentrout family in America, 1739. Falls Church, 1962.

ARMENTROUT -- Armentrout, Russell S.
    Armentrout family history, 1739-1978. Reston, 1980.

ARMISTEAD -- Appleton, William Sumner
The family of Armistead of Virginia. Boston: D. Clapp & Son, 1899.

ARMISTEAD -- Cash, Betty C.
Line of John Armistead of Cumberland County, Virginia. 1942.

ARMISTEAD -- The Family of Armistead of Virginia. Boston, 1899.

ARMISTEAD -- Garber, Mrs. Virginia Armistead
The Armistead Family, 1635-1910. Richmond: Whittet & Shepperson
Printers, 1910.

ARMSTRONG -- Jones, Lizzie E. Boice
Ancestry and descendants of Catherine Weas of West Virginia. Des
Moines, Iowa, 1920.

ARNAUDO -- Arnaudo, David
History of the Arnaudo, Alexander, Gordon, and allied families.
Alexandria, 1983.

ARNOLD -- Leach, Charles B.
The Arnold family of Virginia.

ARNOLD -- MacIvor, Hazel A.
Some ancestors and descendants of Benjamin Arnold, King William
County, Virginia, and Greenville, S.C. Lake Grion, Mich., 1974.

ARRINGTON -- Arrington, Mary Marie Koontz
"Lest we forget": a genealogy of Elder R. A. Arrington. Harrisonburg:
Park View Press, 1974.

ARRINGTON -- Word, Mary Florence Arthur
Absalom Arrington: some descendants, Virginia, Georgia, Alabama,
1798-1984: down from the hills. Cullman, Ala.: Gregath Pub. Co.,
1984.

ARTHUR -- Arthur, Robert L.
The William Arthur family. Parsons, W. Va.: McClain Printing Co.,
1982.

ASHE -- Willis, Betsy L.
Genealogy and letters of the Strudwick, Ashe, Young and allied
families. Alexandria, 1971.

ASHMORE -- Davis, Mary Jane Irwin
Ashmores in early America: with some of their descendants. Norfolk,
1983.

ASTOR -- Gates, John D.
The Astor family. Garden City, N.Y.: Doubleday, 1981.

ASTOR -- O'Connor, Harvey
The Astors. New York: A. A. Knopf, 1941.

ATKINS -- Snezek, Mae
  The family of Jacob Adkins and Hesekiah Adkins of Wayne County, West
  Virginia. 1984.

AUGUSTA -- Vandeventer, Rev. J. N.
  History of Augusta Church, from 1737 to 1900. Staunton: The Ross
  Printing Co., 1900.

AUGUSTA CO. -- Waddell, Jos. A.
  Waddell's Annals of Augusta Co. Annals of Augusta County Virginia from
  1746 to 1871. Staunton. 1902.

AUTIN -- Widener, Ralph W., Mrs.
  A history of my Austin-Anderson family in Virginia and West Virginia.
  Dallas. 1977.

AVERY -- Avery, Carrie White
  Genealogical Records-gathered from graveyards, public monuments and
  family papers, etc. Washington. 1925.

AYERS -- Donaldson, Florence
  Ayers family: 500 descendants of Matthias Ayers and Elizabeth Hale who
  came to Virginia in 1740. 1984.

AYLETT -- Junkin, Francis T. A.
  The Aylett letters, being four letters written in the 17th century to
  the cavalier Captain John Aylett of Virginia, by his brothers Sir
  William, and Sir Benjamin Ayloffe, from the family seat, Braxted Magna.
  Essex, England. Chicago, Ill.: The Guntborp-Warren Press, 1908.

BACON -- Townsend, C. H.
  Bacons of Virginia and their English ancestry.

BACHMAN -- Phlegar, Cornelia Ellen Backman
  Backman. Radford: Commonwealth Press, 1970.

BACHMANN -- Phlegar, Cornelia Ellen Backman
  Backman; a record of some of the descendants of Samuel Bachman (1739-1814)
  and his wife Rachel Owen (1744-1823). Radford: Commmonwealth Press, 1970.

BADGER -- Kilham, Austin D. and Francis M. Clark
  Badger and Tankard families of the Eastern Shore of Virginia.
  Charlottesville: Bailey Printing, 1973.

BAGBY -- Bagby, Bathurst Browne
  Recollections. West Point, Va. 1950.

BAGBY -- Bagby, Rev. Alfred, D.D.
  Bagby Family Tree. Richmond. 1897.

BAGBY -- Bagby, Rev. Alfred, D.D.
King and Queen County, Va. Washington. 1908.

BAGLEY -- Bagley, Ernest Griffen
The Bagley family, 1066-1958. Raleigh, N.C. 1958.

BAGLEY -- Bell, Landon C.
The old Free state; a contribution to the history of Lunenburg County
and southside Virginia. Richmond: The William Byrd Press, Inc., 1927.

BAILEY -- Washburn, Mabel Thatcher Rosemary
The Virginia Bailey genealogy together with related families. Lewiston,
Idaho. 1946.

BAILEY -- Willis, Betsy Lawson (and) Martha Barksdale Craddock
Sketches and genealogy of the Bailey-Craddock-Lawson families of
Virginia and North Carolina; with notes on the families of Coleman,
DuVal, Scott, Easley, Madison, Lanier, Allen, Hunt, Wimbish, Traynham,
Ragland, and Barksdale. Alexandria. 1974.

BAKER -- Genealogy of the Baker family; descendants of John Nicholas Baker,
1708-63 (a native of Germany, he came to the United States in 1754)
with some connecting lines. Strasburg. 1955.

BAKER -- Baker, Robert Helsley
Genealogy of the Baker family. Strasburg. 1955.

BAKER -- Baker, William Thompson, Sr.
The Baker family of England and of central Virginia, their many related
families and kin. 1974.

BAKER -- Johnson, Katherine Baker
The forebears and descendants of Caleb Baker of Prince Edward County,
Virginia. 1940.

BAKER -- Maxwell, Raymond C.
The history and genealogy of Frederick Baker, Jr. 1775-1862 ...
Farmville: Press of the Farmville Herald, 1965.

BALDWIN -- Baldwin, Karl F.
Baldwin genealogy notes. Fort Monroe: Coast Artillery Journal, 1928.

BALDRIDGE - Shepard, Clarence E.
A small twig from the Baldridge tree: the descendants of William Baldridge
of Russell County, Virginia. Dayton, Ohio. 1984.

BALL -- Supplement to The Balls of Fairfax and Stafford in Virginia, 1961.
Provo, Utah. 1971.

BALL -- Ball family; of Saxon derivation, a power in Virginia and New England
from the first ... New York. 1921.

BALL -- Ball, Bonnie S., James Elihu Ball (and) Estella Ball Brady
The Balls of Fairfax and Stafford in Virginia. Provo, Utah:
J. G. Stevenson, 1961.

BALL -- Ball, Palmer R.
The Ball family of southwest Virginia; a genealogy of some of the
descendants of Moses Ball of Fairfax County, compiled from court,
Bible and church records and gravestone inscriptions. Big Laurel.
1933.

BALL -- Ball, William Lee
Genealogy of William Ball born 1812, Loudon County, Virginia. Honolulu,
Hawaii. 1974.

BALL -- Barker, Nina Ball
The Ball family of Boone County, West Virginia. Jeffrey, West Virginia.
1980.

BALL -- Heck, Earl L. W.
Colonel William Ball of Virginia, the Great-grandfather of Washington.
London: S. M. Dutton, 1928.

BALL -- Hiday, Nellie E.
Ball lines: Col. William Ball of Virginia. Salem. 1939.

BALL -- Hoskins, William W.
John Ball of Lee County, Virginia, and his descendants; Bell County, Ky.,
Harland County, Ky. Radford: Commonwealth Press, 1975.

BALL -- Masnata, David E.
Colonel William Ball of Lancaster County, Virginia, and his descendants.
New York. 1966.

BALL -- Noble, Chas. N.
Ball family of Virginia. New York. 1932.

BALL -- Throckmorton, C. Wickliffe
Descendants of Colonel William Ball of "Millenbeck," Lancaster Co., Va.
1931.

BALLARD -- Blackwell, Lyle M.
A Ballard-Brown ancestry. Parsons, W. Va.: McClain Print, 1979.

BANKS -- Storey, Mary Frances Banks
Grandpap's family: a Banks family genealogy; descendants of James Banks
of the Northern Neck of Virginia. Newnan, Ga. 1984.

BARB -- Bard family of Germany, New Jersey, Shenandoah County, Va., and
Ohio. 1973.

BARBEE -- Stone, Kathryn Crossley
Supplement to: A study of the Barbee families of Chatham, etc., (Boulder
Colo. 1971). Supplement consists of corrections and additions, including
A study of the Virginia ancestors of the Barbee families of Chatham,
Orange and Wake counties in North Carolina. Boulder, Colo. 1976.

BARBER -- <u>Several famous families of Orange County, Virginia; genealogical</u>
<u>charts of several famous Orange county families</u>, collected by D. N.
<u>Davidson</u> ... Orange. 1934.

BARBOUR CO., W. VA. -- <u>History of Barbour County, Western Virginia.</u>
Morgantown, W. Va.: Acme Publishing Co.

BAREKMAN -- Barekman, June B.
<u>Some Bible records on a family named Barackman, Barickman, Barkman,</u>
<u>Barrackman, Barrickman, Bergman; from Germany to the Colonies: Va.,</u>
<u>W. Va., Ind., Penns., Ky., Ill., Md., and Ohio</u> ... Chicago, Ill. 1967.

BARGER -- <u>The Barger journal; a publication devoted to the genealogy and</u>
<u>history of the Bargers and allied kindred</u> ... Charlottesville: A. L.
Barger, 1924.

BARGER -- Barger, Fred Hugh
<u>Family tree, in time scale chart (of the family of Adam Barger, son and</u>
<u>8th child of Philip Barger - Eve Clements of Blacksburg, Va.)</u> Washington.
1962.

BARGER -- Barger, Gervase J. P.
<u>Natural Bridge, Va., Bargers.</u> Washington. 1956.

BARHAM -- Barham, Charles, Jr.
<u>Barham family.</u> Charlottesville. 1958.

BARHAM -- <u>The pedigree of the family Barham of England and Virginia.</u>
Extracted from the records of the College of Arms. New York: Salisbury
Press, 1963.

BARHAM -- Barham, Robert Young
<u>The family of Barham.</u> Orange. 1963.

BARKELY -- Barkley, Richard Warren
<u>Barkley, Henley, Fleet, Randolph and allied families.</u> Petersburg. 1981.

BARKER -- Hager, Janet Barker
<u>The Barker family of southern West Virginia: Barker--Hager--Dolin.</u>
Hewett, W. Va. 1978.

BARKER -- Pullen, Wm. E.
<u>Barkers of Virginia; Captain John Barker, English ship master of Surry</u>
<u>County, Va., his descendants and their kin.</u> Hollywood, Fla. 1971.

BARKSDALE -- Barksdale, Captain John A.
<u>Barksdale family history and genealogy (with collateral lines).</u> Richmond:
William Byrd Press, Inc., 1940.

BARNES -- Rev. I. A.
The Barnes family in West Virginia; being a brief account of this branch of the family in West Virginia. Scottsdale, Pa.: Mennonite Publishing House, 1920.

BARNES -- Barnes, Ralph Mosser
Early days in Clifton Mills. Parson, W. Va.: McClain Print Co., 1985.

BARNES -- Bates, Robert L., with Harry H. Bates
The story of Smithfield (Middleway), Jefferson County, West Virginia. Endicott, N.Y. 1958.

BARNETT -- Lester, Anne Jopling
My Virginia cousins and ancestors. 195-.

BARNETT -- Martin, J. R.
Our family ties; descendants of John and Thomas Barnett of Virginia-Ohio-Missouri-Iowa. 1957.

BARNHART -- Barnhart, Nat G., Katie Ellen (Rea) Barnhart
Barnhart family history: Augusta County, Virginia, 1767-1967; the 200th anniversary of our family in America. New Hope. 1967.

BARRETT -- Chappelear, George Warren
Families of Virginia. Harrisonburg: Cavalier Press, 1934.

BARRETT -- Claypool, Edward A.
Rev. Robert Barret of Virginia, and his descendants. Chicago, Ill. 1901.

BARRETT - Claypool, Edward A.
The Rev. Robert Barrett of Virginia and his descendants. Chicago, Ill. 1907.

BARROWS -- North, Mae Belle Barrow
The Barrow family of Virginia, 1620-1972. Summerfield, N.C. 1972.

BARTLETT -- Bartlett, James Vincent
The descendants of Thomas Bartlett Sr. (1730-1806) of Fauquier Co., Va. and Harrison Co., W. Va. Springfield. 1977

BARTON -- Barton, Jason E.
Barton family; descendants of John Barton, coast of Virginia. 1968.

BARTON -- Barton, William Bayard
A genealogy of the descendants of Anthony Barton; the First American Barton of this record, an emigrant from England to America 1825. 1956.

BARTON -- Kaye, Ruth Lincoln
Barton-Green and related families. Alexandria. 1969.

BASHAM -- Hatcher, Charles Silas
Historical genealogy of the Basham, Ellison, Hatcher, Lilly, Meadows, Pack, Walker, and other families. Lynchburg. 1968.

BASHAM -- Hatcher, Charles Silas
Historical genealogy of the Basham, Ellison, Hatcher, Lilly, Meadows, Pack, Walker, and other families. Lynchburg. 1980.

BASKERVILLE -- Baskervill, Patrick Hamilton
Genealogy of the Baskerville family and some allied families, including the English descent from 1266 A.D. ... Richmond: W. E. Jones' Sons, Inc., 1912.

BASKERVILLE -- Baskerville, P. Hamilton
Additional Baskerville genealogy; a supplement to the author's Genealogy of the Baskerville family of 1912; being a miscellany of additional notes and sketches from later information, including a study of the family history in Normandy. Richomnd: W. E. Jones' Sons, Inc., 1917.

BASKIN -- Bell, Raymond M.
The Baskins-Baskin family, Pennsylvania, Virginia, South Carolina. Washington, Pa. 1957.

BASSETT -- Bassett, Mary Henrian
The Bassett family in Henry County, Virginia, with stories, mainly of the Woodsen Bassett branch. Martinsville. 1976.

BATES -- Bates, Onward
Bates, et al, of Virginia and Missouri. Chicago: Pettibone & Company, 1914.

BATES -- Bates, Robert L. with Harry H. Bates
The story of Smithfield (Middleway), Jefferson County, West Virginia. Endicott, N.Y. 1958.

BATES -- Chapman, Thomas Wilson
Bates et al. of Culpeper & Madison Counties. Richmond. 1969.

BATES -- Graham, Virginia W.
Ancestral lineage: Mildred Olive Bates McCann, Adair County, Iowa; Prince George County, Va. Hopewell. 1964.

BATES -- Lanphere, Edward Everett
Descendants of Bates ancestors who lived in Virginia. Chapel Hill, N.C. 1973.

BATH CO. -- Morton, Oren F.
Annals of Bath County, Virginia. Staunton: The McClure Co., Inc., 1917.

BATSON -- Bornemann, Vivian Davis
  The Batson family in Virginia, North Carolina, and Georgia, Mississippi, Louisiana and Texas. Related families: Dale, Hatten, Culpepper, Price, Smith, Lott, Longino, Daughdrill, Davis, Terrell. New Orleans. 1959.

BATTEY -- Battey, George Magruder, III
  Batteys of England or Wales, Rhode Island and Georgia. Bealls of Scotland and Maryland. Carrs of England and Rhode Island. Deitrichs (Deadericks) of Germany, Virginia and Tennessee. Magruders of Scotland, Maryland and Georgia. Nixons of Delaware, Van Dykes of Holland, Delaware and Tennessee. Washington. 1940.

BAUGH -- Personal genealogy, containing data on Baugh, Blair, Crawford, Hammer, Mitchell, Simpson. Abingdon.

BAUGH -- Baugh, Minnie L.
  Ancestors of Miss Minnie I. Baugh, including the Hammer, Crawford, McMahon and Simpson families of Tennessee and Virginia. Abingdon. 1910.

BAUGHMAN -- Baughman, Urbanus E.
  Genealogy of Urbanus E. Baughman, Jr., and son William Edmund Baughman and wife, Ruth Yessel Baughman. Arlington. 1965.

BAYLIS -- Blum, Willetta Baylis and William Blum, Sr.
  The Baylis family in Virginia. Supplements on the Chunn, Fawcett, Hawkins, and Turner families, and a Baylis family in England. Washington. 1958.

BAYNE -- Bane, F. J.
  John Bane of Short Creek, West Virginia, and his descendants as of 1956. Fairview, W. Va. 1956.

BAYTOP -- Stubbs, William Carter
  A history of two Virginia families transplanted from County Kent, England. New Orleans, La. 1938.

BAXTER -- Baxter, Miss Frances
  The Baxter family, descendants of George and Thomas Baxter, of Westchester County, New York, as well as some West Virginia and South Carolina lines. New York: T. A. Wright, 1913.

BEAL -- Beale, B. DeRoy
  The Beale family of Halifax County, Virginia. Richmond. 1978.

BEALL -- James, Jerry Preston
  A history and genealogy of the Beall family as traced through the Prestons of Maryland, the Bealls of Maryland, and the Bealls of Oklahoma. Springfield. 1966.

BEAN -- Lochary, Clara Eleanor Henry
An appendage to the Bean family, Hardy County, Virginia line, now
West Virginia. Pomery, Ohio. 1973.

BEAN -- Seitzer, Francis A.
Biehen, Young, and Nonnenmacher families from Alsace, France: a
genealogical history. Arlington. 1982.

BEAN -- Wilson, Josephine Bean
The Bean family Hardy County, Virginia line, now West Virginia.
Athens, Ohio. 1917.

BEATON -- Beeton, Robert D.
History of the Beeton family of Virginia. Sterling: F&L Printing,
1979.

BECKER -- Hodge, Robert A.
Notes on the Becker, Muzzy and Vogt families. Fredericksburg. 1965.

BECKHAM -- Beckham, Annie L.
Beckham family, Virginia, North Carolina, Georgia and Texas. Dallas,
Texas. 1957.

BECKHAM -- Beckham, James Madison
Genealogy of the Beckham family in Virginia and the branches thereof
in Kentucky, Tennessee, Pennsylvania and West Virginia with family
sketches ... Richmond: O. E. Flanhart Printing Company, 1910.

BEDFORD COUNTY -- Ackerly, Mary Denman and Lula Eastman Peter Parker
"Our Kin," being historical and genealogical sketches of old families
of Bedford County, Virginia, etc. Bedford.

BEDFORD -- Wight, Florence B.
Virginia Bedfords, North, South, West. West Springfield, Mass. 1963.

BEDFORD -- Wight, Florence B.
Bedford from Virginia to Maryland to Delaware (some Pennsylvania).
W. Springfield, Mass. 1966.

BEDWELL -- Bedwell, Mary Elizabeth
Our Bedwell line: a history of twelve generations from Robert Bedwell,
the immigrant. Blacksburg. 1977.

BEDWELL -- Bedwell, Mary Elizabeth
Our family history. Blacksburg. 1980.

BEESON -- Shaw, S. C.
Historical sketches of the life and character of the Hon. Jacob Beeson,
an early pioneer of Wood County, Virginia, now West Virginia, and his
descendants. Parkersburg, W. Va. 1881.

BEHEATHLAND -- Gray, Violet Noland
Genealogy history of Robert Beheathland, gentleman, one of the founders
of James Towne, 1607, and his descendants through his daughter Mary,
covering the years from 1607 to 1976. Baltimore: Gateway Press, 1978.

BELFIELD -- Lyman, John
The Belfield family; a record of the descendants of Dr. Joseph Belfield,
immigrant to Virginia about 1700. Washington. 1960.

BELL -- Bell, James Pinkney
Our Quaker Friends of Ye Olden Time. Lynchburg: J. P. Bell Company,
1905.

BELLIS -- Bellis, Tom
Bellis ancestors and cousins. Arlington. 1983.

BENNETT -- Bennett, Benjamin Hugh
A history of Richard Bennett family of Westmoreland County, Virginia
and Iredell County, N.C. Washington. 1960.

BENNETT -- Bennett, Carmen Taylor
The Bennetts: Italy, France, England, Virginia. Georgia, Texas,
1501-1982. Lubbock, Tex.: Duncan Press, 1982.

BENNETT -- Kozee, William Carlos
Early families of eastern and southeastern Kentucky and their
descendants. Strasburg: Shenandoah Pub. House, 1961.

BENSON -- Grant, Howard B.
William Benson of Barbour County, Virginia. Philippi, W. Va. 1934.

BENTON -- Benton, Jesse W.
Portrait: Joseph Pinkney Benton, 1777-1966. Danville. 1967.

BERKEY -- Berkey, William Albert
The Berkey book. Arlington. 1984.

BERKHEIMER -- Lontz, Mary
The Berkheimer family in Pa., Va., W. Va., and other States, plus
other lines. Milton, Pa. 1970.

BERNARD -- Bernard, William Dallas
The John Bernard and Mary Abney genealogy, Fluvanna County, Virginia.
Lascassas, Tenn. 1975.

BERRY -- Hamilton, Lynn Berry
Berry-Berrey family: the family of Elijah Berry, Va., Ga., Ala.,
and Tex., 1700-1980. Harlingen, Tex. 1980.

BERTRAND -- Bartram, Violet W. (Violet Wiggs)
Bartram branches: genealogy of the families of West Virginia,
Connecticut, and Pennsylvania. Baltimore: Gateway Press, 1984.

BEVERLEY -- McGill, John
    The Beverley family of Virginia; descendants of Major Robert Beverley, 1641-1687, and allied families. Columbia, S.C.: R. L. Bryan Co., 1956.

BEVILLE -- Tedcastle, Agnes Benville Vaughn
    The Beville family of Virginia, Georgia, and Florida, and several allied families, north and south. Boston. 1917.

BEWLEY -- Collected Works
    Bewley roots in Virginia and Kentucky. Rineyville, Ky. 1980.

BICKERS -- Bickers, Joseph Edward
    Robert Bickers of Virginia and his descendants. 1945.

BIGGS -- Hathaway, Bernice FitzSimmons
    Biggs - McGrew and allied lines (Swartwout, Hall, Munday, Howell, Finley, McFerran). Many of the ancestors and descendants of Llewellyn Biggs and Martha McGrew, married 16 July, 1827; early New York, New Jersey, Maryland, Virginia, and Pennsylvania lines. Denver. 1963.

BINFORD -- Bruner, Mary L.
    Binford Family Genealogy. Greenfield, Ind.: Wm. Mitchell Printing Co.

BIRDSALL -- Birdsall, George A.
    The Birdsall family; genealogy and history of interest to every living descendants and their posterity. Annandale. 1958.

BIRDSALL -- Birdsall, George A.
    The Birdsall family. Annandale. 1964.

BIRDSALL -- Perry, H. G. and C. M. B.
    The descendants of James Birdsall. Arlington. 1962.

BIRNIE -- Birnie, Joseph Earle
    The Earles and the Birnies. Richmond: Whittet & Shepperson, 1974.

BISHOP -- Bishop family. Former residents of Fauquier and Loudon Counties, Virginia, Clark County, Ohio and Elkhart County, Indiana.

BLACK -- Black, Howard C.
    William Black and his descendants ... of Augusta County, Va., and Clark County, Ky. Cincinnati. 1973.

BLACK -- Black, Natalie K.
    Pioneer preacher: descendants to 1980 of the Rev. Samuel Black (1700-1770) of Pennsylvania and Albemarle County, Virginia. Madison, Tenn. 1981.

BLACK -- Porter, Nannie Francisco
    Blacks and other families. Richmond. 1954.

BLACK -- Weiland, Florence Black
    Fifty New England colonists and five Virginia families. Boothbay Harbor, Maine. 1965.

BLACKBURN -- <u>Blackburn family in records of Essex and Caroline Counties,</u>
<u>Virginia.</u> 1950.

BLACKBURN -- Ranke, Vinnetta Wells
<u>The Blackburn genealogy; with notes on the Washington family through</u>
<u>inter-marriage. Containing historical facts on Virginia lore and</u>
<u>Mount Vernon, including records of allied families.</u> Washington. 1939.

BLACKWELL -- Blackwell, Edward Maurice
<u>Blackwell genealogy.</u> Richmond: Old Dominion Press, 1948.

BLACKWELL -- Blackwell, Judith G.
<u>With the Blackwells, from Chesterfield-Halifax-Bedord-Floyd Counties,</u>
<u>Va., 1755-1973.</u> Roanoke. 1973.

BLACKWELL -- Blackwell, Lyle M.
<u>My fathers: the Elk River ancestry of James Elvin Blackwell with a</u>
<u>brief genealogy of the Morris family.</u> Gauley Bridge, W. Va. 1979.

BLACKWELL -- Jones, Mrs. Sallie Orgain Blackwell
<u>Sketch of John Blackwell, by his daughter.</u> Richmond: Whittet &
Shepperson, 1916.

BLAIN -- Hooker, Ruth N.
<u>The Blain family of Albemarle County, Virginia and Tennessee.</u>
Memphis. 1948.

BLAIN -- Tennessee DAR, G.R.C.
<u>The Blain family of Albemarle County, Virginia and Tennessee.</u> 1948.

BLAIR -- <u>Blairs of Richmond, Virginia; the descendants of Reverend John</u>
<u>Durburrow Blair and Mary Winston Blair, his wife.</u> Richmond: William
Byrd Press, Inc., 1933.

BLAKE -- Lindsay, Joyce H.
<u>The Virginia ancestry of Alice Upshaw Blake, wife of John Daniel</u>
<u>Baker.</u> 1963.

BLAKEMORE -- Blakemore, John A.
<u>Known descendants of Edward Blakemore, Junior, of Lancaster County,</u>
<u>Virginia.</u> Abingdon. 1963.

BLAKEMORE -- Blakemore, Maurice Neville
<u>The Blakemore family and allied lines.</u> Richmond. 1963.

BLAKEY -- Blakey, Bernard Buckner
<u>A Blakey book: being an account of those believed to be descended</u>
<u>from Thomas and Susannah Blakey of Christ Church Parish, Middlesex</u>
<u>County, Virginia.</u> Little Falls, Minn. 1977.

BLANKENBECKLER -- Blankenbeckler, William P.
    Blankenbeckler family of southwest Virginia and related families.
    Nickeslville: Service Printery, 1941.

BLEVINS --Blevins, Laccie W.
    Jonathan Blevins, Sr. of Virginia and his descendants. Powell,
    Tenn. 1982.

BLEVINS -- Privett, Harriett Kinnaird
    Glimpses of the Blevins family (Virginia - Tennessee - Alabama).
    1964.

BLEW -- Slinner, Pauline Kimball
    The ancestry of John Blew, Hampshire Co., Va., will 1770, from
    John Blew Sr., Somerset Co., New Jersey and possible descent from
    the famous Bleau family of Printers, Holland. Newark, Del. 1973.

BLOYD -- Nichols, Edna Bloyd
    William Bloyd-Bloyed of Maryland, Virginia, North Carolina, and Green
    County, Kentucky and his descendants. Baltimore: Gateway Press, 1980.

BLUE -- Haney, Alice Blue
    John Blew (Blue) of Hampshire County, Virginia and some of his
    descendants. Columbus, Ohio. 1967.

BLUE -- Hornsby, Lillie S.
    Descendants of John Blue, Virginia. Detroit, Mich. 1969.

BLUM -- Blum, William
    The Blum family of Waldmohr, Pfalz, Germany and United States of
    America. Strasburg: Shenandoah Pub. House, 1968.

BLUNT -- Crocker, James Francis
    The Blunts of Isle of Wight County, Virginia, and their descendants.
    Portsmouth: Whitson & Shepherd Printers, 1914.

BLY -- Bly, Daniel W.
    History of the Bly family of Virginia, 1771-1972. Harrisonburg.
    1975.

BOAZ -- Boaz, T. D., Jr.
    The family of R. H. Boaz: a record of the descendants of Richard
    Harris Boaz (1845-1918). McLean. 1973.

BOAZ -- Boaz, T. D.
    Zephaniah Henry Tait Boaz, 1825-1889. McLean. 1980.

BOAZ -- Boaz, T. D.
    Joshua Boaz (1810-1890) and his descendants. McLean. 1981.

BOAZ --Boaz, T. D.
   David Boaz (1806-1876) and his descendants. McLean. 1982.

BOHNER -- Lewis, Dorothy R.
   Genealogy of John Michael Bohner. Alexandria. 1967.

BOISSEAU -- Boso, James L.
   The Boso family (Boisseau), 1757-1977. Parson, W. Va.: McClain Print,
   1978.

BOITNOTT -- Boitnott, John W.
   Boitnott and related families; a history and genealogy of the descendants
   of Just and Susannah (Dishong) Boitnott. Harrisonburg: Park View
   Press, 1971.

BOLEN -- Boling, Marion
   Genealogy of the Boling family of Sullivan County, Tennessee and
   Washington County, Virginia. 1982.

BOLEN -- Bolling, Robert
   A memoir of a portion of the Bolling family in England and Virginia.
   Ann Arbor, Mich. 1979.

BOLEN -- Brown, Stuart E.
   Pocahontas' descendants: a revision, enlargement, and extension of the
   list as set out by Wyndham Robertson in his book Pocahontas and her
   descendants (1887). Berryville. 1985.

BOLLING -- Bolling, Robert
   Memoirs of the Bolling Family. Chellowe, Buckingham Co., Va., etc.
   1803.

BOLLING -- Bolling, Robert
   A memoir of a portion of the Bolling family in England and Virginia.
   Richmond: W. H. Wade & Co., 1868.

BOLLING -- Thurber, Mary Carter
   The Genealogy of the Descendants of Thomas Tabb Bolling and Seignora
   Peyton. Published by Roberta Bolling Blake, MDCCCIX.

BOLLING -- Wynne, T. H.
   A Memoir of the Bolling Family in England and Virginia. Richmond:
   W. H. Wade & Co., 1868.

BOLLING -- Wynne, Thomas H.
   A memoir of a portion of the Bolling family in England and Virginia.
   Berryville: Chesapeake Book Co., 1964.

BOLTON -- Evans, Cleo H.
   Curtis Edwin Bolton, pioneer, missionary. Fairfax. 1968.

- 20 -

BONAR -- Brown, Dorothy E.
    Bonar genealogy; Bonar, Boner, Bonnar, Bonner, Booner, Bowner.
    Wheeling, W. Va. 1969.

BOOGHER -- Boogher, Wm. F.
    Gleanings of Virginia History. Washington. 1903.

BOOGHER -- Reed, Avery H.
    Boogher family; later genealogy embracing the lineage of 13 Boogher
    children, descendants of Nicholas Boogher and Rebecca Davis Coombs
    (Boogher). Charlottesville. 196-.

BOOHER -- Booher, Emma R.
    Rich Hill, Westmoreland County, Virginia, 1740 to Rich Hill, Noble
    County, Ohio, 1880. 1976.

BOOKER -- Kentucky DAR, G.R.C.
    Family of Richard Maret Booker, (1751-1805) of Charlotte County,
    Virginia, and his Bible records. 1949.

BOOTH -- Booth, Lucian D.
    Descendants of George Boothe, 1737-1813, Montgomery County, Va.
    Roanoke. 1948.

BOOTH -- Massie, Evelyn Booth
    Charles Booth (1774-1821) pioneer settler in what is now Wayne
    County, West Virginia, who married Elizabeth Ferguson in 1798,
    and descendants. Wayne, W. Va. 1978.

BORDER SETTLERS -- McWhorter, Judge J. C.
    The Border Settlers of Northwestern Virginia from 1768 to 1795, etc.
    Hamilton, Ohio: The Republican Publishing Co., 1915.

BOSO -- Boso, James L.
    The Boso family (Boisseaux), 1757-1977. Parsons, W. Va.: McClain
    Print Co., 1978.

BOSWELL -- Buswell, Frederic Grant
    Henry Lee Buswell: his descendants and ancestors. Culpeper. 1985.

BOSWELL -- Pippenger, Jean Boswell
    Descendants of Edward Boswell: Prince William County, Virginia and
    Orange County, North Carolina. Baltimore: Gateway Press, 1986.

BOTTNER -- Felder, Paula S.
    Ludwig Bottner and his sons: the beginning of the Bottner family in
    America. Fredericksburg: Historic Publications of Fredericksburg,
    1985.

BOTTS -- Baer, Mabel Van Dyke
    Botts families of Virginia and other states. 1973.

BOULWARE -- Bradley, Frank E., Jr.
   A short history of the Boulware family of Essex Co., Va., 1973.

BOURN -- Stone, May
   Bourne family and connecting lines of Virginia and Kentucky,
   1607-1943. Kansas City, Mo. 1947.

BOURNE -- Katz, Gertrude M. P.
   Old letters, old biographies, and old family trees of the Bourne,
   Morton and allied families of Virginia, Kentucky and other states.
   Valley Stream, N.Y. 1973-4.

BOURNE -- Katz, Gertrude P.
   Old letters, old biographies, and old family trees of Bourne, Carr,
   Darden and allied families of Virginia, Tennessee and other states.
   Allied families: Gardner, Wilkerson, Polk and many others. Tampa,
   Fla. 1976.

BOWEN -- Grady, Jamie Ault
   Bowens of Virginia and Tennessee; descendants of John Bowen and
   Lilly McIlhaney. Knoxville, Tenn. 1969.

BOWEN -- Bayliss, Ada Wheatley
   Descendants of John Bowen of old Rappahannock County, Virginia.
   Richmond. 1924.

BOWLES -- Bowles, Inez M.
   Thomas Bowles, Hanover County, Va. ... Gilliam, Mo. 1947.

BOWMAN -- Davis, Lillian Virginia Ludwig
   Silon James Bowman family; early Bowman history and descendants, a
   short sketch of the ancestry of Silon James Bowman and the records
   of his lineage. Strasburg. 1970.

BOWMAN -- Manley, Iva Bowman
   Origins of the Bowmans of Carroll County, Va.: the Bowman family
   history. 1984.

BOWMAN -- Wayland, John W.
   The Bowmans, a pioneering family in Virginia, Kentucky and the
   Northwest Territory. Staunton: The McClure Company, Inc., 1943.

BOYKIN -- Boykin, Edward M.
   History of the Boykin family, from their first settlement in Virginia,
   1685, and in South Carolina, Georgia, and Alabama, to the present
   time. Camden, S.C.: Colin Macrae, 1876.

BOYKIN -- Murphy, Anne Jacobs Boykin
   History and genealogy of the Boykin family. Richmond. 1964.

BRACEY -- Bracey, Carstairs and Verna
   Bracey; (primarily a history of the Bracey family of Mecklenburg
   County, Virginia). Norfolk. 1955.

BRADFORD -- French, Marline R.
   The Bradford and Kirkpatrick ancestry of Virginia, Tennessee and
   Texas, and some of their descendants. 1959.

BRADFORD -- LeCato, Charles Beauregard
   Original Bradford grants: Bradford-LeCato home, "Atlantic View,"
   Accomack County, Virginia. Haddonfield, N. J. 1965.

BRADFORD -- White, Mrs. Nelle Rhea
   The Bradfords of Virginia in the revolutionary war, and their kin.
   Richmond: Whittet & Shepperson, 1932.

BRAHAN -- Lane, Elsie
   Documentary evidence concerning John Brahan (1725-1775) of Fauquier
   County, Virginia and some of his descendants. San Antonio, Tex.
   1946.

BRANCH -- Cabell, James Branch
   Branchiana; being a partial account of the Branch family in Virginia.
   Richmond: Whittet & Shepperson, 1907.

BRANCH OF ABINGDON -- Cabell, James Branch
   Being a partial account of the ancestry of Christopher Branch of
   "Arrowhattocks" and "Kingsland", in Henrico County, and the founder
   of the Branch family in Virginia. Richmond: William Ellis Jones'
   Sons, Inc., 1911.

BRAND -- Bailey, R. G.
   The Virginia Brand-Meriweather genealogy. Lewiston, Idaho: R. G.
   Bailey Printing Co., 1948.

BRAND -- Brand, Franklin Marion
   The Brand family of Monongalia County, Virginia, now West Virginia.
   Charleston, W. Va.: Tribune Printing Co., 1922.

BRANDER -- Meigs, Return Jonathan
   A record of the descendants of James Brander, who settled in Virginia
   about 1780. Westfield, N.J. 1937.

BRANNER -- Branner, John Casper
   Outline of the genealogy of the first four generations of the Branner
   family in Virginia . New Market. 1904.

BRANNER -- Branner, John Casper
   Casper Branner of Virginia and his descendants. San Francisco, Calif.
   Stanford University. 1913.

BRANSFORD -- Lewis, Edward Simmons
   Bransford family. Williamsburg. 1928.

BREEGLE -- Breegle, Daniel
   History of the (Breegle, Briggle). Alexandria. 1977.

BRENNEMAN -- Breneman, Charles D.
   A history of the descendants of Abraham Breneman, born in Lancaster
   County, Pennsylvania, December 3, 1744, and settled near Edom,
   Rockingham County, Virginia, in 1770, or soon after, and a complete
   genealogical register with biographies of many of his descendants,
   from the earliest available records to the present time, giving
   dates in three centuries. Elida, Ohio. 1939.

BRENT -- Brent, Chester Horton
   The descendants of Hugh Brent, immigrant to Isle of Wight County,
   Virginia, 1642 and some allied families, Curd, Doggett, Edmonds,
   Fleet, Lawson, Nutt & Wale. Rutland, Vt. 1936.

BRENT -- Brent, Chester Horton
   The descendants of Col. Giles Brent, Capt. George Brent and Robert
   Brent, gentl. immigrants to Maryland and Virginia. Rutland, Vt.:
   Tuttle Publishing Conpany, 1946.

BRENT -- French, David M.
   The Brent family. Alexandria. 1977.

BRESSIE -- Baer, Mabel Van Dyke
   Three earlier Virginia families. 1963.

BREWSTER -- William B. Brewster: Virginia-Tennessee, 1793-1853; (notes,
   comments, and observations). Provo, Utah. 1966.

BRICKEY -- Brickey, Raymond Luther
   The Brickey heritage. Radford: Commonwealth Press, 1983.

BRIDGES -- Feigley, Dorothea Gwinn
   Bridges family history, 1780-1953. Vienna. 1956.

BRIGGS -- Mansfield, Dolorus Briggs
   History of the Briggs-Bridge family, since its settlement in America
   (Virginia) in 1752, with genealogy as found in early church record,
   government documents, wills, and family correspondence. Edmonds, Wash.
   1960.

BRISTOL PARISH -- Slaughter, Rev. Philip, D.D.
   A history of Bristol Parish, etc. Richmond: J. W. Randolph, 1879.

BRISTOW -- Bristow, Emmett Albion
   Descendants of John Bristow of Middlesex County, Va., & William
   Bristow of Orange and Randolph Counties, N.C., 1650-1919. Bel Air,
   Md. 1971.

BRISTOW -- Woolley, Gordon Byron
John Bristow of Middlesex County, Virginia and descendants through
ten generations. New York: Vantage Press, 1969.

BROCK -- Brock, Dr. R. A.
Virginia and Virginians, etc. Richmond: H. H. Hardesty, 1888.

BROCK, Robert Alonzo
Documents, chiefly unpublished, relating to the Huguenot emigration to
Virginia and to the settlement at Manakin-Town, with an appendix of
genealogies, presenting data of the Fontaine, Maury, Dupuy, Trabue, Marye,
Chastain, Cocke, and other families. Edited and published for the
Virginia Historical Society. Baltimore: Genealogical Pub. Co., 1962.

BROCK -- Zirkle, Franklin A.
Brief outline of Brock family of Shenandoah Valley of Virginia. New
Market: Henkel Pr., 1971.

BROCKMAN -- Brockman, William Everett
Virginia wills and abstracts; Brockman, Bell, Bledsoe, Burris, Collins,
Durrett, Graves, Henderson, and Tatum families. Minneapolis: Burgess
Pub. Co., 1948.

BROCKMAN -- Davidson, D. N.
Several famous families of Orange County, Virginia; genealogical
charts of several famous Orange County families. Orange. 1934.

BROOKS -- Edwards, Bruce Montgomery
The Brooks of Virginia. Baltimore: Gateway Press, 1985.

BROUN -- Broun, Virginia M.
The Broun Family and their Kindred. Chart of the descendants of
William Broun the Immigrant to Virginia.

BROWDER -- Genealogy of David Browder, of Virginia and his descendants.
Nashville, Tenn.: Folk & Browder, 1902.

BROWDER -- Browder, Nathaniel C. and Blanche
Notes on the Browder family of Tidewater, Virginia, 1704-1850.
Hayesville, N.C. 1970.

BROWDER -- Browder, Blanche Penland
Notes on the Browder family of Tidewater, Virginia, 1695-1850.
Raleigh, N.C. 1984.

BROWN -- Brown, James Edgar
Genealogy of the Brown family, of Prince William County, Virginia;
being a history of William Brown and seven generations of his
descendants. Chicago: G. E. Brown & Co., 1898.

BROWN -- Brown, James Edgar
Genealogy of the Brown family of Prince William County, Virginia,
and the following group of families allied by marriage: Bland,
Buckner, Byrne, Fairfax, Morgan, Tebbs, Watson, Zinn and others.
Strasburg: Shenandoah Publishing House, Inc., 1930.

BROWN -- Brown of Scotland and Virginia.

BROWN -- Brown, Dakota Best
Data on some Virginia families. Berryville: Virginia Book Co.,
1979.

BROWN -- Reverend Daniel Brown of Culpeper County, Virginia, and allied
families: Webster, Finnell, McCain, Pemberton. Tuscaloosa, Ala.
1954.

BROWN -- Brown, Hollis
Austin Brown and his descendants. Conicville. 1978.

BROWN -- Brown, John R.
Browns of Albemarle County, Va. 1963.

BROWN -- Broun, Thomas L.
The Ball, Conway, Gaskins, McAdam and other kindred of William and
Janetta Broun of Northern Neck, Va. Charleston, W. Va. 1911.

BROWN -- Chart of the descendants of William Broun, the immigrant to
Virginia from Scotland. Constructed by Virginia M. Broun for her
uncle Thomas L. Broun, from family records collected by him.
Washington: The Norris Peters Co., 1914.

BROWN -- DeHuff, Elizabeth Willis
Brown family of Virginia and South Carolina. 1964.

BROWN -- Martin, John R.
Berryman Brown of Roanoke County, Virginia, and Clinton, Dade, and
Ozark Counties, in Missouri (a record of his descendants, St. Joseph,
Mo.). St. Joseph, Mo. 1957.

BROWN -- Mead, Edward C.
Broun family of Virginia. Richmond. 1904.

BROWN -- Merrill, Eleanor Brown
A Virginia heritage. Richmond: Whittet & Shepperson, 1968.

BROWN -- Parker, Albertina Brown
The history of John Francis Deane Brown and members of his family in
Virginia, Montana, and California in relation to the Harrison, Reade,
Cary, Digges, and Cabell families of Colonial Virginia. Missoula,
Mont. 1963.

BROWN -- Strasburger, Arthur K.
The Descendants of William Brown of Virginia, 1740-1965. Baltimore:
John Hopkins University School of Medicine, Division of Medical
Genetics. 1966.

BROWNING -- Carter, John Denton
The Virginia ancestors of Captain Francis Browning, 1753-1855,
revolutionary soldier of Russell County, Virginia. Alexandria. 1962.

BROWNING -- Davidson, D. N.
Several famous families of Orange County, Virginia; genealogical charts
of several famous Orange County families. Orange. 1934.

BRUCE -- Bruce, John Goodall
The Bruce family: descending from George Bruce, 1650-1715. Salem.
1977.

BRUCE -- Bruce, Philip Alexander
History of Virginia. Chicago: The American Historical Society. 1924.

BRUMBACH -- Brumbaugh, Gaius Marius, M.S., M.D.
Genealogy of the Brumbach Families, etc. New York: Genealogical
Publishing Co.

BRUMBACH -- Vann, Elizabeth Chapman Denny and Margaret Collins Denny Dixon
Brumbach-Hotsinpiller genealogy; some of the descendants of Melchoir
Brumbach of the 1714 Germanna Colony of Virginia through his daughter
Elizabeth who married Stephen Hotsinpiller, and allied families of
Afflick, Anderson, Bunger, Burns, Campbell, Coffman, Cornwell, Denny,
Dotson, Graham, Jennings, Kessler, Kincaid, Knapp, Knox, La Rue,
Lemley, Lewis, Livesay, McCutcheon, Neal, Nichols, Pollock, Powell,
Ransberger, Rector, Rudolph, Sharp, Surbaugh, Tuckwiller, Watts,
Williams, and others. Englewood, N.J. 1961.

BRUNK -- Brunk, William C.
The progeny of Christopher Brunk. Harrisonburg: Park View Press.
1981.

BRUTON CHURCH -- Goodwin, William A. R.
Historical Sketch of Bruton Church. Williamsburg. 1903.

BRYAN -- The Bryan and Stewart families, descendants of John Randolph Bryan
of Eagle Point, Gloucester Co., Va., ... and of John Stewart of Brook
Hill, Henrico County, Va. ... Washington. 1969.

BRYAN VALLEY OF VIRGINIA -- Bryan, Dr. J. D.
The Boone-Bryan History. Frankfort, Ky.

BRYANT -- Lane, Annabel W.
History of the Bryant family of Virginia, Kentucky and Missouri.
Littleton, Colo. 1966.

BUCHANAN -- Trimble, David B.
Southwest Virginia families. San Antonio, Tex.: Trimble, 1974.

BUCK -- The Bucks of Wethersfield, Connecticut, and the families with which
they are connected by marriage, a biographical and genealogical sketch.
Roanoke: Stone Printing and Manufacturing Co., 1909.

BUCK -- Buck, Walter H.
The Buck family of Virginia. Baltimore: Schneiderith & Sons, 1936.

BUCK -- Buck, Walter Hooper
The Buck family and its kin. Baltimore. 1956.

BUCKNERS OF VA. -- Crozier, W. A.
The Buckners of Virginia and Allied Families of Strother and Ashby.
New York. 1907.

BURGESS -- Burgess, James A.
Burgess, Mullins, Browning, Brown, and allied families. Parsons,
W. Va.: McClain Print, 1978.

BURGESS -- Reginald, R.
The House of the Burgesses: being a genealogical history of Edward
Burges of King County and Stafford Counties, Virginia. San
Bernardino, Calif.: Borgo Press, 1983.

BULLOCK -- Aker, Mary Bullock
Bullocks of Virginia and Kentucky and their descendants. Parkville,
Mo. 1952.

BURGESS -- Burgess, Louis A.
Virginia Soldiers of 1776. Richmond: Richmond Press, Inc., 1927 and
1929.

BURKE -- Kelly, John A.
Burk(e) family of southwest Virginia and the valley. Haverford, Pa.
1944.

BURKE -- Kelly, John A.
Burk(e) family of Southwest Virginia and the valley. Roanoke. 1973.

BURKE -- Sherwood, Mary B.
Nicholas Burke (1838-1878) Margaret Shannon (1838-1916): their
descendants and a few ancestors. Falls Church: Great Oak Press of
Virginia, 1985.

BURKHOLDER -- Hess, Nancy B.
By the grace of God. Harrisonburg: Hess Book Co., 1979.

BURNLEY -- Bentley, Elizabeth B.
   Some ancestors and descendants of Dr. Hardin Burnley of Mississippi
   and Virginia, 1827-1894. 1970.

BURNETT -- Burnette, Earl E.
   Burnett-Parsons ancestral line; with some collateral branches; also ...
   newspaper clippings, abstracts of wills and deeds in Va. and Tenn.;
   data on kindred families of Atchley, Baker, Boyd, Cameron, Clark,
   Evans, Franklin (and others). Sebastopol, Calif. 1964.

BURNETT -- Burnet, Isabella Neff
   Dr. William Burnet and his sons Jacob, Isaac and David, a chart of the
   forefathers and descendants in America, 1640-1938 ... Charlottesville.
   1938.

BURNETT -- Burnet, Isabella Neff
   War records and experiences beginning with World War 2, of the
   Burnet and Neff kin. Charlottesville. 1953.

BURNETT -- Gass, Francis
   A Burnett family of the South: Thomas Burnett, 1755-1780, of Virginia
   and North Carolina and his descendants. Washington: National Pub.
   Co., 1964.

BURNSIDE -- Clark, Betha Lewis
   The Burnside - Byrnside family of Augusta and Rockingham Counties, Va.
   and Monroe and Pocahontas Counties, W. Va. 1947.

BURR -- Long, John D.
   Benjamin Burr, of Hartford, Connecticut and Thomas Owsley, of
   Stafford County, Virginia and their respective descendants, Hollister
   Harvey Burr and William Anthony Owsley of Cherokee County, Kansas.
   1954.

BURR -- Peter Burr of Berkeley County, Va. and Warren and Clinton Counties,
   Ohio. Muncie, Ind. 1975.

BURROWS -- Burough, Howard Duane
   The Burrow family: descendants of Henry and Lucy Burrow, from Virginia
   to North Carolina and beyond: Allison, Amick, Bowman, Buckles, Burough,
   Burrough, Burroughs, Burrow, Embler, Gombie, Goodman, Lane, McCarry,
   Moore, Robinson, Stout, Warren, Yergin, York, and related families.
   Augusta, Ga. 1981.

BURT -- Mathis, Robert B.
   The Mathew Burt family of Virginia and Deep South. Killeen, Tex.
   1976.

BURTLE -- Burtle, John Paul
    American Burtles: descendants of William Burtles of Charles County, Maryland. Reston. 1983.

BURTON -- Harrison, Francis Burton
    Burton chronicles of colonial Virginia; being excerpts from the existing records, particularly relating to the Burtons of the valley of the James and Appomattox; with especial references to the ancestry of Jesse Burton of Lynchburg, 1750-1795. Darmstadt: L. C. Wittich, 1933.

BURTON -- Harrison, Francis Burton
    Burton chronicles of colonial Virginia: being excerpts from the existing records, particularly relating to the Burtons of the valley of the James and Appomattox, with especial references to the ancestry of Jesse Burton of Lynchburg (1750-1795). Hartford, Ky.: Cook & McDowell Pub., 1979.

BURWELL -- Brown, Stuart E.
    Carter Hall. Berryville: Virginia Book Co., 1978.

BURWELL FAMILY -- Burwell, Rev. Robt.
    Record of the Burwell Family, copied in part from the manuscript by the Rev. Robt. Burwell. Revised 1908 by George H. Burwell and others of Millwood, Clarke County, Va.: Whittet & Shepperson.

BURWELL -- John, Paul
    Burwell residents of King's Creek, a plantation in York County, Colonial Virginia, and descendants of William Cocke: also the families of Armistead, Bacon, Ball, Emmerson, Jones, Latane, Waring, and others of England and Virginia. Baytown, Tex. 1982.

BUSBY -- Riggs, Dorothy I. B.
    Compilation of facts regarding the family of Isaac Busby of Monroe County, W. Va. and some of his descendants. Anderson, Ind. 1971.

BUTLER -- Butler, Julia Mae
    Further Butler history: starting two generations earlier with Col. Thomas Butler, born ca. 1745, Virginia (or Europe), died 1806 on Gulf Coast of yellow fever. St. Louis. 1977.

BUTTERS -- Butters, George
    The genealogical registry of the Butters family ... including the descendants of William Butter, of Woburn, Mass., 1665 and the families of New York, Pennsylvania, West Virginia, Ohio, Iowa and others bearing the name, who settled in America. Chicago: D. Oliphant, Printer, 1896.

BUTTERWORTH -- Ball, Walter V.
    The Butterworth family of Maryland and Virginia. Chevy Chase, Md. 1960.

BUTTON -- Button, William Garland
A part of the Button family of Virginia and its westward migration to Kentucky, Texas, Oklahoma, and California from 1666 to 1959. Waco, Tex. 1959.

BYRD -- Byrd of Westover, Virginia. Copy of entries in the old family Bible in the possession of Miss Mary Armistead Byrd of Westchester.

BYRD -- Bassett, John Spencer
The writings of Colonel William Byrd in Virginia. New York: Doubleday, Page & Co., 1901.

BYRD -- Byrd, Colwell Patterson
History and genealogy of the Byrd family, from the early part of 1700, when they first settled at Muddy Creek, Accomack County, Virginia, down to 1907. Pocomoke City, Md. 1908.

BYRD -- Harrison, Constance Cary
Colonel William Byrd of Westover, Virginia.

BYRD -- Harton, Marilyn K. Byrd
Byrds and Sonners of Shenandoah Valley, Virginia and their migration to Wells County, Indiana. Worthington, Ohio. 1983.

BYRD -- Hatch, Alden
The Byrds of Virginia. New York: Holt, Rinehart and Winston, 1969.

BYRED -- Bassett, J. D.
The Writings of Colonel William Byrd of Westover in Virginia, Esqr. New York. 1901.

BYROM -- Byron, Mark Bennett
Descendants of Henry Byrom of Virginia. Westbury, Conn.: Hemingway Press, 1956.

CABELL -- Brown, Alexander
The Cabells and their kin, a memorial volume of history, biography, and genealogy. Richmond: Garrett & Massie, 1939.

CAIN -- Cain, Stith Malone
A history of our Cain family of Virginia, Alabama and Tennessee Whitewater, Wisc. 1970.

CALE -- Sislter, Janice Cale
Christopher Cale's family of Preston County, West Virginia, 1841-1973. Parsons, W. Va.: McClain Print. Co., 1973.

CALHOUN -- Dundas, F. de S.
Calhoun settlement, District of Abbeville, South Carolina. Staunton.
1950.

CALLAWAY -- Hart, Mrs. A. E.
The Callaway family of Virginia, and some Kentucky descendants. Los
Angeles, Calif. 1928.

CALLAWAY -- Hart, A. E.
The Callaway family of Virginia, and some Kentucky descendants. Los
Angeles, Calif. 1929.

CALLAWAY -- Hart, Jessie W.
Richard Callaway family of Va. and Ky. Los Angeles, Calif. 1933.

CALVERT -- O'Gorman, Ella Foy
Descendants of Virginia Calverts. Los Angeles. 1917.

CAMP -- Carter, Nell Jones
Camp, Jones, and related families of Connecticut, Illinois, Missouri,
Virginia, Carolina, Georgia, Alabama, Mississippi, Louisiana, Texas,
and points west. Tallahassee, Fla. 1977.

CAMPBELL'S HISTORY OF VIRGINIA -- History of the Colony and Ancient Dominion
of Virginia. Philadelphia: J. B. Lippincott & Co., 1850.

CAMPBELL -- Campbell, Arthur Price
Campbell family history, 1715-1973; descendants of Thomas Campbell, Sr.
1973.

CAMPBELL -- The Campbell's of Virginia and E. Tennessee, with special
reference to one of the several David Campbells of revolutionary days.
By the great-grandson of Judge David Campbell (1750-1812), of
Washington, Rhea Co., Tenn. George Magruder Battey III. Washington.
1940.

CAMPBELL -- Campbell, Henry R.
A history of the William Campbell family, Timberville, Virginia: about
1850 to December, 1983. Harrisonburg. 1984.

CAMPBELL -- Campbell, Leslie Lyle
The Campbell Clan in Virginia. Lexington. 1954.

CAMPBELL -- Campbell, Thomas
The Campbell family chart and distaff line. Charlottesville. 1955.

CAMPBELL -- Thompson, Elizabeth Campbell
Descendants of Captain James Campbell of Scotland, Maryland, and
Virginia. Detroit: King-Smith, Inc., 1961.

CAMPBELL CO. -- Early, H. R.
Campbell Chronicles and Family Sketches embracing the History of
Campbell Co., Va., 1782-1926. Lynchburg. 1927.

CANFIELD -- Kyle, Hailie Canfield
Canfield family history. Parsons, W. Va., McClain Print, 1979.

CANTRILL-CANTRELL -- Christie, Susan Cantrill
The Cantrill-Cantrell Genealogy. New York: The Grafton Press, Fifth
Ave., 1908.

CAPERTON -- Caperton, Bernard M.
The Caperton family. Charlottesville. 1973.

CARDWELL -- Cardwell, Robert
Robert Cardwell of Campbell County, Virginia. El Paso, Tex. 1980.

CARDWELL -- Pendergraft, Allen
The Cardwells of Virginia: Thomas Carwell of Henrico County, his
descendants, and allied families Osborne, Farrar, Spencer, Worsham,
Royal, Perrine, Lockett, Thweat, Barkley, Crews, West and Butler.
Sedona, Ariz. 1973.

CAREY -- Toennies, Dorothy Carey
Branches of the John Carey family of Buck's County, Pennsylvania,
to Virginia, Ohio and on West. Toennies & Matthews, 1969.

CAREY -- Vollertsen, Arthur H.
The Careys and the Peirces: Mulberry Island families: papers.
Yorktown: Citizen Pub., 1983.

CARLTON -- Bowman, Frances Dunn
The Carl(e)ton story. Lynchburg. 1977.

CARLYLE -- Carlyle, Gayla Rae
Descent of Gayla Rae Carlyle through Catherine Diggs, through
fourteen of the Magna Charta Sureties one hundred thirty-five ways,
and through five of the original knights of the garter eight ways.
Danville. 1970.

CARLYLE -- Spencer, Richard Henry
Carlyle family and descendants of John and Sarah (Fairfax) Carlyle.
The Carlyle House and its associations. Richmond: Whittet &
Shepperson, 1910.

CARLYLE-WHITING -- Spencer, Richard Henry
Descendants of John and Sarah (Fairfax) Carlyle. Richmond: Whittet
& Shepperson, 1910.

CAROLINE COUNTY -- Wingfield, Marshall
A History of Caroline County, Va., etc. Richmond: Trevvett-Christian
& Co., Inc., 1924.

CARPENTER -- Carpenter, Samuel V.
Descendants of Samuel Carpenter of Virginia; Iowa branch. Centerville,
Iowa. 1967.

CARPENTER -- Wilson, Barr
Family history: Nicholas Carpenter, Christopher Carpenter. Toll Gate, W. Va. 1971.

CARRINGTON -- Hopkins, Garland E.
Colonel Carrington of Cumberland. Winchester. 1942.

CARTER -- Carter, General William Giles Harding
Giles Carter of Virginia - Genealogical Memoir. Baltimore: The Lord Baltimore Pres, 1909.

CARTER -- Carter, F. R. Nicholas
Genealogy of William R. Carter of the state of Pennsylvania, of Loudoun Co., Virginia, of Preble, Co., Ohio and Clinton Co., Ind. South Bend, Ind. 1974.

CARTER -- Carter, R. R.
The Carter family tree ... Additions ... by his daughter. Richmond. 1897.

CARTER -- Genealogy of William R. Carter of Pennsylvania of Loudoun Co. Va., of Preble County, Ohio and Clinton County, Indiana, with genealogy of the following allied families: Byers, Richards, Jury, Thomas, Douglass, Hughes, McCulloch, and Smiley. South Bend, Ind.

CARTER -- Cam (pseud.)
The Carter family of Virginia. An extended genealogy of its representatives. Richmond. 1888.

CARTER -- Carlton, Florence Taylor
A genealogy of the known descendants of Robert Carter of Corotoman. Irvington: F. T. Carlton, 1982.

CARTER -- Currer-Briggs, Noel
The Carters of Virginia: their English ancestry. Chichester, England. 1979.

CARTER -- Dillon, Ruth
Carter miscellanae from the State of Virginia, 1669-1834. 1962.

CARTER -- Foster, Carolyn Agnes (Mrs. Edgar M. Marbourg)
Carter family of North Carolina; descendants of Robert Carter of Bertie County. Richmond: Whittet & Shepperson, Printer, 1914.

CARTER -- Hartshorn, Edwin Simpson
The genealogy of certain descendants of John Carter of Corotoman, Lancaster Co., Va. Washington. 1949.

CARTER -- Jones, Christine
The early Thomas Carters of Lancaster County, Virginia. Lancaster: Mary Ball Washington Museum & Library, 1982.

CARTER -- Liddell, Charles Marcus
Those who were and would be named "Carter": the first 300 years in America (1682-1982). Torrance, Calif. 1982.

CARTER -- Miller, Joseph Lyon
... The descendants of Capt. Thomas Carter of "Barford," Lancaster County, Virginia, with genealogical notes of many of the allied families. Thomas, W. Va. 1912.

CARTER -- Miller, Joseph Lyon
The descendants of Capt. Thomas Carter. Bridgewater. 1912.

CARTER -- Morton, Louis
Robert Carter of Nomini Hall. Williamsburg: Colonial Williamsburg, Inc., 1941.

CARTER -- Newman, Harry Wright
Carter - Mitchell - Weir - Willcoxon and related families of Virginia and Maryland. 1969.

CARTER -- Ravenscroft, R. T.
Supplement to: Descendants of Captain Thomas Carter of "Barford," Lancaster County, Va., by J. L. Miller, 1912. Colorado Springs, Colo. 1912.

CARTER -- Rowland, Kate M.
The Carters of Virginia.

CARTER -- Schroeder, Lyra
The Carters of Virginia and some of their descendants. Roanoke. 1976.

CARTER -- Stewart, Charles Leslie
Raymond Arthur White ancestry, Illinois, Virginia and Europe. Urbana, Ill. 1865.

CARTER -- Sutton, Rita K. (Rita Kennedy)
Early Carters in Scott County, Virginia. 1981.

CARTER -- Turner, Avis Carter
The Carter family tree. 1984.

CARTER -- Wallace, George Selden
The Carters of Blenheim. Huntington, W. Va. 1955.

CARTER -- Wallace, George S.
The Carters of Blenheim; a genealogy of Edward and Sarah Champe Carter of "Blenheim" Albemarle County, Va. Richmond: Garrett & Massie, 1955.

CARTER -- Warner, Charles Willard
Thomas Carter II of Corotoman, Lancaster County, Virginia; his ancestry and descendants, and sketches on certain families with whom Carter descendants have married: Garnett, Roy and Hoskins. Richmond: Expert Letter Writing Co., 1957.

CARTER -- Wulfeck, Dorothy F.
Carter of Virginia; queries from the Virginia gazette, queries from other periodicals, abstracts of wills and deeds, etc. Naugatuck, Conn. 1962.

CARTMELL -- Cartmell, T. K.
Shenandoah Valley Pioneers and their descendants. A History of Frederick County, Va. Winchester: Eddy Press Corporation, 1909.

CARTWRIGHT -- Walter, Alice G.
Cartwright and Shipp families of Lower Norfolk, Princess Anne & Surry Counties, Va. & North Carolina. Lawrence, N.Y. 1968.

CARY -- Toal, Helen C.
Cary families from Virginia. Manteca, Calif. 1969.

CARY -- The Virginia Carys. An Essay in Genealogy. New York: The De Vinne Press, 1919.

CASKIE -- Caskie, J. A.
The Caskie family of Virginia. Charlottesville: Conway Printing Company, Inc., 1928.

CASON -- Smith, Winfred Broadus
Some Virginia Casons in the Revolution. Houston, Tex. 1971.

CASPER -- Stoutner, Barbara S.
The American ancestry of Harriet Matilda Merchant. Arlington. 1978.

CATCHINGS -- Catchings, T. C. and Mrs. M. C. Torrey
The Catchings and Holliday families and various related families, in Virginia, Georgia, Mississippi and other southern states. Atlanta, Ga.: A. B. Caldwell Pub. Co., 1919.

CATLETT -- Stubbs, Dr. and Mrs. William Carter
A history of two Virginia families transplanted from county Kent, England. Thomas Baytop, Tenterden, 1638, and John Catlett, Sittingbourne, 1622. New Orleans, La. 1918.

CAUTHORN -- Phillips, R. C.
Record of the Cauthorn Family. Richmond: The Dietz Printing Co., 1909.

CAVE -- Davidson, D. N.
    Several famous families of Orange County, Virginia; genealogical
    charts of several famous Orange county families. Orange. 1934.

CHADWICK -- Kilham, Austin D.
    Notes on the descendants of John and Joan Chadwick and related
    families. Charlottesville: Bailey Print, 1966.

CHAMBERS -- McCullough, Rose Chambers Goode
    Yesterday when it is past. Richmond: William Byrd Press, 1957.

CHANCE -- Chance, Hilda
    Chance of Ohio, Virginia, North Carolina, Georgia, Texas, Tennessee,
    Kentucky, Delaware, Maryland, Pennsylvania, Michigan, California,
    Indiana, New Jersey. Liberty, Pa. 1970.

CHANCE -- Supplement to Chance of Ohio, Virginia, etc. Liberty, Pa. 1970.

CHANDLER -- Hazelwood, Myrtle Cochran
    "Us" from England to Virginia, 1468 A.D. - 1983 A.D.: descendants of
    Thomas Chandler. 1983.

CHAPLINE -- Dare, Maria J. Liggett
    Chaplines from Maryland and Virginia. Washington: Franklin Print,
    1902.

CHAPMAN -- Chapman, Berlin B.
    The Chapman family, a study in the social development of central
    West Virginia. Tulsa, Okla.: Mid-west Printing Company, 1942.

CHAPMAN -- Chapman, Sigismunda Mary Frances
    A history of Chapman and Alexander families. Richmond: Dietz Printing
    Co., 1946.

CHAPMAN -- Edmonds, Elsie Chapman
    John Chapman of Spotsylvania County, Virginia, Thomas Powe of Cheraw,
    South Carolina, and related families. Newton, Miss. 1971.

CHAPMAN -- Machir, Violette S.
    Some Chapman, Jolly, Rayburn and Smith families in W. Va. & Ohio.
    Middleport, Ohio: Quality Print Shop, 1965.

CHAPPELEAR -- Chappelear, George Warren
    Chappelear. Dayton, Va.: Shenandoah Press, 1932.

CHAPPELEAR -- Chappelear, George Warren
    Families of Virginia. Harrisonburg. 1932.

CHAPPELL -- Chappell, Philip E.
    A genealogical history of the Chappell, Dickie, and other kindred
    families of Virginia. Kansas City, Mo.: Tiernan-Havens Print., 1895.

CHAPPELL -- Chappell, Philip E.
A Genealogical History of Chappell, Dickie and other Kindred Families of Virginia, 1635-1900. Kansas City, Mo.: Hudson Kimberley Publishing Company, 1900.

CHARLES -- Charles, Clell E.
History of Charles family in eastern Kentucky, southwest Virginia. Erwin, Tenn. 1960.

CHAUMIERE PAPERS -- Peet, Henry J.
Containing matters of interest to descendants of David Meade of Nansemond County, Va. Chicago.

CHEATHAM -- Moseley, Lucille Cheatham
Descendants of Thomas Cheatham of Chesterfield County, Virginia. Richmond: Dietz Press, 1981.

CHENOWETH -- Chenoweth, Alex Crawford
Genealogy and chart of the Chenoweth and Cromwell family of Maryland and Virginia. New York: Redfield Press, 1894.

CHERRY -- Sieferman, Lucile M.
Jesse Cherry family, allied families of Long & Cole with additional records on the Cherry, Ramsey, Ingold and Longworth-Longwith families of N.J., Ohio and Va. Washington: Sieferman & Baer, 1965.

CHEW -- Chew family of Virginia and Maryland.

CHEW -- Chew, Dorothy Clendenin
John Chewe, some descendants in Virginia, Maryland, and Ohio. Dalton, Ga. 1982.

CHILTON -- Chilton, Mary Tarr
A genealogical history of the Chilton family. Charleston, W. Va.: Jarrett Printing Company, 1941.

CHINN -- Chinn, Walter Neal
An autobiography of Walter Neal Chinn, Jr., his relatives and friends. Fredericksburg: Fredericksburg Press, 1976.

CHRISMAN -- Christman, Glen
A Chrisman/Christman genealogy: the descendants of Jacob Christman I, of Frederick County, Virginia. 1983.

CHRIST CHURCH PARISH -- Chamberlayne, C. G.
Vestry Book of Christ Church Parish, Middlesex County, Virginia, 1663-1767. Richmond: Old Dominion Press, 1927.

CHRISTIAN -- Esker, Mrs. Jerome A.
Wood collection of Virginia families. 1945.

CHRISTIAN -- McClanahan, Marshall L.
William Christian, immigrant to Virginia, and some of his descendants.
1958.

CHRISTIAN -- Stacy, Eunie V. Christian
Christian of Charles City: an account of the antecedents and descendants
of Charles Christian of Virginia and allied families, mainly found in
the southern states. Natchitoches, La. 1982.

CLAIBORNE -- Claiborne, G. M.
Claiborne pedigree, a genealogical table of the descendants of
Secretary William Claiborne, of the junior branch in the United
States, with some other tracings in the female line. Lynchburg:
J. P. Bell Company, 1900.

CLAIBORNE -- Claiborne, John Herbert
William Claiborne of Virginia, with some account of his pedigree.
New York: G. P. Putnam Sons, 1917.

CLARK -- Clark, Bertha Lewis
The Clark family of Augusta County, Virginia and Monroe County,
West Virginia. 19--.

CLARK -- Clark, Everett Rankin
Westward ho, from Massachusetts Bay to Oklahoma Short Grass Country:
my colonial and Virginia ancestors from Ayers to Wyeth, including
Clarks, Baldwins, Rogers, Reed, Stacys, Richardsons, Chase, Sanborn,
Dow, and fifty-four others. Tahlequah, Okla. 1979.

CLARK -- Clark, Fred A.
The Clarks of Centroplis and Eight Mile Creek: a genealogical account
of the lives and migration of Jacob and Juliann Huntgate Clark and
their descendants. Fairfax: Classic Print Center, 1976.

CLARK -- Clark, James W.
Richard Clark of Virginia, 1732-1811, with a brief history of his
descendants, and their westward migration through Montgomery County,
Kentucky; Putnam and Montgomery Counties, Indiana; Dallas County, Iowa;
and Jewell County, Kansas. Abilene, Tex. 1971.

CLARK (E) -- Richard Clarke of Virginia, 1732-1811; with a brief history
of some 750 of his descendants, and their westward migration through
Montgomery Co., Ky.; Putnam and Montgomery Co., Ind., Dallas Co., Iowa;
and Jewell Co., Kans. Abilene, Tex. 1971.

CLARK -- Davidson, D. N.
Several famous families of Orange County, Virginia; genealogical
charts of several famous Orange County families. Orange. 1934.

CLARK -- Mulford, William
Banister Lodge: a history of unbaffled Virginians. 1982.

CLARK -- Paul, Gordon W.
  Samuel Clark of Proctor, Wetzel County, West Virginia, and most of
  his descendants. Albuquerque, N.M. 1985.

CLARY -- Rowland, Ralph Shearer
  Clary genealogy. Fairfax. 1980.

CLAY -- Clay, Clifford Charles
  The Colonial Clays of Virginia and some of their descendants. Atlanta,
  Ga. 1943.

CLAY -- Rigsby, L. W.
  The Georgia branch of the Virginia Clays and their celebrated cousins;
  with Harden and Jones genealogies and notes of related families. 1926.

CLAYTON -- Ferguson, Frances L.
  William Clayton family from "Clayton Hall," England to "Clayton Hall,"
  Loudoun Co., Va. Lagrange, Ind. 1969.

CLEEK -- Cleek, George Washington
  Early western Augusta pioneers, including the families of Cleek, Gwin,
  Lightner, and Warwick, and related families of Bratton, Campbell,
  Barlile, Craig, Crawford, Dyer, Gay, Givens, Graham, Harper, Henderson,
  Hull, Keister, Lockridge, McFarland, and Moore. Staunton. 1957.

CLEMENS' WILLS -- Clemens, William Montgomery
  Virginia Wills, before 1790. A complete abstract of all names
  mentioned in over six hundred recorded wills from courthouse records
  of Amherst, Bedford, Campbell, Loudoun, Prince William and Rockbridge
  counties. Pompton Lakes, N.J.: The Biblio Co., Inc., 1924.

CLEVELAND -- Cleveland, James Butler
  A genealogical register of the descendants of Moses Cleveland of
  Woburn, Mass., an emigrant in 1635 from England, with a sketch of
  the Clevelands of Virginia and the Carolinas. Albany, N.Y.:
  Munsell Printer, 1881.

CLEVER -- Clever, Donald Goodhart
  My ancestors. Springfield. 1966.

CLIFFORD -- Clifford, Robert L.
  Family histories: Clifford family, January 1946, updated April 1977,
  Kikendall family, January 1946, Lambert family, January 1946, Laning
  family, December 1967, Short family, January 1946. Williamsburg. 1977.

CLOPTON -- Erwin, Lucy Lane (Mrs. William Whitehead Erwin)
  The ancestry of William Clopton of York County, Virginia, with records
  of some of his descendants, to which are added royal lines; Magna Carta
  sureties; charters; wills; deeds, etc. Also, notes on certain English
  families, viz: Acworth, Basset, Belhous, Calthorpe, Chastelyn, D'Arcy,
  Despenser, Drury, Echyngham, Howard, Jenny, Jolye, Knevet, Lunesford,
  Maydstone, Players, Stapleton, Sutcliffe, Waldegrave, Wentworth.
  Rutland, Vt.: Tuttle Publishing Co., 1939.

COBB -- Cobb, John E.
Cobb and Cobbs, early Virginians. Alexandria: Durant Pub. Co., 1976.

COBB -- Cobb, John Edward
Cobb chronicles: an overview of the clan. Alexandria: Durant Pub. Co., 1985.

COBB -- Edwards, Bruce Montgomery
The Cobbs of the Tidewater. Knoxville, Tenn.: Montgomery Pub. Co., 1976.

COBB -- Montgomery, Horace
Johnny Cobb, Confederate aristrocrat. Alexandria: Durant Pub. Co. 1981.

COBB -- Prince-Tharp, Barbara
Thrice blessed. Parsons, W. Va.: McClain Print, 1981.

COBURN -- Coburn, Raymond H.
Ancestors and descendants of James William Coburn, 1850-1929. Parsons, W. Va.: McClain Print, 1982.

COCHRANE -- Hunter, Miriam M.
The Cochrane family of Virginia and Kentucky. Fresno, Calif. 1943.

COCKE -- Cocke, Wm. Ronald, Jr.
The founding of a Virginia family. Richmond: Southern Stamp & Stationery Co., 1931.

COFFEY -- Coffey, Laurence H.
Thomas Coffey and his descendants, with a brief sketch of the life of Thomas Coffey, a pioneer in North Carolina from Virginia, and of Reuben Coffey, a pioneer in Indiana from North Carolina, and others. Chattanooga. 1931.

COGHILL -- The family of Coghill continued; a supplement to and continuation of "The family of Coghill," by James Henry Coghill, (The Riverside Press, Cambridge, 1879), and setting forth the genealogy of the Coghill family, with particular emphasis upon the Virginia descent of Frederick Coghill, and the Illinois descent of Benjamin Coleman Coghill, and family trees. Richmond: Dietz Press, 1956.

COLAVITA -- Colavita, Philip
History of the Colavita family of Richmond, Virginia. Richmond. 1979.

COLE -- The Coles of Virginia: its numerous connections from the emigration to America to the year 1915. New York. 1931.

COLE -- Leiter, Fay C.
Cole history and genealogy, from Wythe County, Virginia to Cooper County, Missouri. Sedalia, Mo. 1962.

COLE -- Cole, Robert Franklin
Some male descendants of Richard Cole of Louisa County, Virginia.
Washington. 1935.

COLES -- Coles, William B.
The Coles family of Virginia: its numerous connections from the
emigration to America to the year 1915. New York. 1931.

COLLIER -- Collier, Thomas Cleatin, with assistance of Clara McGrath Hill
Collier, Fassitt, White & Hill: Virginia, Maryland & Missouri. Silver
Spring, Md. 1958.

COLLIER -- Collier, Thomas Cleaton
Presidents of Virginia ancestry. Silver Spring, Md. 1964.

COLLINS -- Collins, Herbert Ridgeway
History and genealogy of the Collins family of Caroline County, Va.,
and related families, 1569-1954. Richmond: Dietz Press, 1954.

COLEMAN -- Coleman, James P.
The Robert Coleman family, from Virginia to Texas, 1652-1965.
Ackerman, Miss. 1965.

COLEMAN -- Coleman, James W.
The Robert Coleman family from Mobjack Bay, Virginia to Reno, Nevada
and Hollywood, California,1638-1970. Reno, Nev. 1970.

COLEMAN -- Reddy, A. W.
Coleman family from Caroline County, Virginia. 1940.

COLONIAL CHURCH -- Rev. Edward Lewis
The Colonial Church in Virginia, etc. London: Morehouse Publishing
Company, 1927.

COMER -- Walker, Anne Kendrick
Braxton Bragg Comer; his family tree from Virginia's colonial days.
Richond: Dietz Press, 1947.

COMPTON -- Blalock, Delton D.
British and American Comptons from the colonial era to the modern day
in New York, New Jersey, Virginia, Tennessee, Alabama, and Texas,
1634-1984. Hanceville, Ala. 1984.

CONARD -- Bowen, Amy Metcalf
The descendants of John Conard of Loudoun County, Virginia. San
Antonio, Tex.: Darley Duplicating Co., 1939.

CONAWAY -- Conaway, Orrin Bryte
The Conaways of Marion and Tyler Counties, West Virginia. Middlebourne,
W. Va. 1951.

CONDIT -- The Conditt family: an outline genealogy of the descendants of
  Fielding Conditt, who was born in Virginia in 1771. Blooming Grove,
  N.Y.: Condit Family Association, 1978.

CONNELL -- Uhrbrock, Richard S.
  Brooke Co., W. Va., Connells, McCrackens, and Gatewoods. Palo Alto,
  Calif. 1974.

CONNELLY -- Connelley, William Elsey
  Eastern Kentucky papers: the founding of Harman's Station, with an
  account of the Indian captivity of Mrs. Jennie Wiley and the exploration
  and settlement of the Big Sandy Valley in the Virginias and Kentucky ...
  to which is affixed a brief account of the Connelly family and some of
  its collateral and related families in America. New York: The Torch
  Press, 1910.

CONNER -- Stapleton, Harriet L.
  Conner/Connor family: John K. Conner and his descendants, 1820-1973.
  Arlington. 1973.

CONRAD -- Bowen, Amy M.
  Descendants of John Conrad of Loudoun County, Virginia. San Antonio,
  Tex. 1939.

CONRAD -- Coffman, Floyd Wilmer
  The Conrad clan; family of John Stephen Conrad, Sr., and allied lines.
  Harrisonburg: Joseph A. Ruebush Company, 1939.

CONWAY -- Conway family of Virginia. Richmond. 1904.

CONWAY -- Conway, Byrd Taliaferro
  William Buchanan Conway, M.D.: ancestors and descendants, 1640-1976.
  Alexandria. 1976.

CONWAY -- Price, W. Conway
  Some descendants of Captain Catlett Conway, Revolutionary soldier and
  Justice of Orange County, Virginia. 1979.

CONWAY -- Price, W. Conway
  Some descendants of Captain Catlett Conway, Revolutionary soldier and
  Justice of Orange County, Virginia: Conway family in America, 1640-1980.
  1980.

COOK -- Order of first families of Virginia, 1607-1620. Milwaukee, Wisc.:
  Specialty Press, 1928.

COOK -- Shaw, S. C.
  Captain Joseph Cook of Wood County, western Virginia, and his descendants.
  Parkersburg, W. Va. 1879.

COOK -- Stubbs, William Carter
Descendants of Mordecai Cooke, of 'Mordecai's Mount' Gloucester County, Virginia, 1650. New Orleans, La.: L. Graham & Son, 1895.

COOK -- Turner, David Anderson
Genealogy of the Floyd Cook family of Boone County, West Virginia. Madison, W. Va. 1980.

COOKE -- Stubbs, Dr. and Mrs. William Carter
Decendants of Mordecai Cooke, of "Mordecai's Mount," Gloucester Co., 1650, and Thomas Booth, of Ware Neck, Gloucester Co., Va., 1685. New Orleans, La. 1923.

COOKE -- Turner, Stephen Roscoe
A genealogy of one branch (King and Queen County) of the Cooke family descended from Mordecai Cooke. 1965.

COOKE -- Cooke, Charles G.
Many Cooke's and their broth; a genealogical outline of the Cooke family of Virginia, North Carolina, Georgia, and Alabama. Alexandria. 1967.

COOKE -- Beatty, John O.
John Esten Cooke, Virginia. New York: Columbia University Press, 1922.

COOKE-BOOTH -- Stubbs, Dr. and Mrs. Wm. Carter
Descendants of Mordecai Cooke, of "Mordecai's Mount," Gloucester Co., Va., 1650, and Thomas Booth, of Ware Neck, Gloucester Co., Va., 1685. New Orleans. 1923.

COOPER -- Cooper, Homer C.
Cooper, McKenny, Ferrell/Farrell, Wooddell, Gothard, Wilson & Patton families of Augusta & Rockbridge counties, Virginia; York & Adams Counties, Pennsylvania; Blount, Knox & Roane Counties, Tennessee; Pocahontas, Gilmer & Ritchie Counties, West Virginia; Wayne County, Kentucky; Vigo & Sullivan Counties, Indiana; York County, South Carolina. Athens, Ga. 1969.

COOPER -- Cooper, Murphy Rowe
The Cooper family. Richmond. 1931.

COPELAND -- Coplen, Herman L.
The Copeland/Coplen and allied families: immigrants to Virginia. Baltimore: Gateway Press, 1983.

COPENHAVER -- Canfield, Clifford Robert
The Copenhaver family of Wythe County, Virginia. Pasadena, Calif. 1958.

COPPEDGE -- Manahan, John E. and A. Maxim Coppage
The Coppage-Coppedge family, 1542-1955. Radford: Commonwealth Press, 1955.

CORBIN -- Meigs, Return Jonathan
    The Corbins of Virginia; a genealogical record of the descendants of
    Henry Corbin who settled in Virginia in 1654. Westfield, N. J. 1940.

CORDELL -- Humphreys, Allan S.
    Cordell records; a Virginia family. Ann Arbor, Mich.: Edwards Brother,
    Inc., 1940.

CORDER -- Franklin, Eleaner M.
    John Corder of Virginia and descendants, 1761-1961. Mattoon, Ill.
    196-.

CORDER -- Grant, Howard B.
    William Corder of Barbour County, West Virginia. Philippi, W. Va.
    1934.

CORDY -- Cordy, Eugene Allen
    Descendants of Virginia, Kentucky, and Missouri pioneers. Bunceton,
    Mo. 1973.

CORLEY -- Corley, Dewitt Clinton
    A genealogy of Corleys beginning with Caniel Corley of Bedford County,
    tracing all lineal descendants of his son, Jonathan Cheatham Corley.
    Decatur, Ill. 1927.

COUGHENOUR -- Evans, Robert Lee
    History of the descendants of Jacob Gochenour. Arlington. 1977.

COUNCILL -- Councill, Judson
    Hodges Councill of Virginia, and descendants. Baltimore: J. H. Furst
    Company, 1941.

COUNTS -- Proceedings ... of the descendants of John Counts of Glade
    Hollow. Charlottesville: Jarman's Inc., 1936.

COUNTS -- Sutherland, Elihu Jasper
    Some descendants of John Counts of Glade Hollow (southwest Virginia):
    including the families of Artrip, Carter, Colley, Counts, Deel, Dyer,
    Edwards, Fuller, Grizzle, Jessee, Kiser, Long, Mattox, Owens, Rasnick,
    Skeen, Smith, Stinson, Sutherland, Willard, Yates, and many others.
    1978.

COURTENAY -- Courtenay, William Ashmead
    The Courtenay family; some branches in America. Charlottesville:
    J. C. Campbell, 1964.

COURTNEY -- Ritchie, Ruth
    Genealogy of some east Tennessee families of the early nineteenth
    century. Charlottesville. 1945.

COVEY -- Covey, Winton Guy
Revised notes on the family of Samuel Covey (1761-1840) and Elizabeth of present Pulaski County, Virginia. Athen, W. Va. 1977.

COWAN -- Cowne, Jonathan Augustine
The Virginia Cowne family: from its origins in the Isle of Man to England and America. Richmond. 1981.

COWAN -- Lamb, Frank A.
The Henry Cowan family of Virginia. Waterford, Penn. 1949.

COWGILL -- Nees, John
Ancestors and descendants of John Tilden Coughill of Frederick Co., Va., 1682-1984, also related families. Greenup, Ill. 1985.

COWLES -- Cowles, Eugene
Branches of Virginia Cowles Family. 1903-1904.

COWNE -- Cowne, Jonathan Augustine
The Virginia Cowne family. Ashland. 1963.

COX -- Cox, Laura C.
Cox and related families of Virginia and Maryland ... Washington.

COX -- Cox, Opal London
One branch of the Cox family of Virginia. Enid, Okla. 1978.

COX -- Cox, W. E.
Descendants of Solomon Cox of Cole Creek, Virginia (1730-1812); and other Cox ancestry of the Cole Creek Coxes. Wytheville, Calif. 1955.

COX -- Jones, Maben
Genealogical chart of Mary Louisa Jones Forbes of Buckingham and Cumberland Counties, Virginia. 1956.

COX -- Miller, Anne V.
A lineage in the Cox family and the Gilley family of Henry County, Virginia, Ridgeway Township, 1776-1985. Sterling: Old Mill Printers, 1985.

COX -- Morell, Louise Cox
Jamestown to Washington; little biographies of twelve generations from Beheathland to Cox, 1607-1950. Baltimore: Gateway Press, 1974.

COX -- Ray, Laura Collison
The Cox and related families of Virginia and Maryland. 1955.

COX -- Speck, Grace Croy
Genealogy of the Cox families of Virginia and Ohio. Concord, Ohio. 1955.

COX -- Staats, Mary H.
Genealogy of the Samuel and Elizabeth Cox family of Virginia and Ohio.
Ann Arbor, Mich. 1975.

CRABILL -- Crabill, Robert Louis
How we came to be--: a history of the Crabill family in the Shenandoah
Valley of Virginia and their migration westward. Baltimore: Gateway
Press, 1983.

CRABTREE -- Fritz, Arah Miller
The Crabtrees of southwest Virginia. Pecos, Tex.: Fritz & McProud, 1965.

CRABTREE -- Fritz, Arah Miller and Margaret Milam McProud
The Crabtrees of southwest Virginia; abstracts of historical information,
census and service records, genealogies and legends. Pecos, Tex.: Hawks
Print Co., 1965.

CRAIG -- Craig, Mrs. William
Taliaferro Craig family of Virginia and Kentucky. Hartford City, Ind.

CRAWFORD -- Crawford, Robert Leighton
Laurus Crawfurdina, memorials of that branch of the Crawford family
which comprises the descendants of John Crawford of Virginia, 1660-1883,
with notices of allied families. New York: Vanderbilt & Crawford, 1883.

CRAWFURDIANA -- Crawfurdiana, Laures
Descendants of John Crawford of Virginia. New York. 1883.

CRAWFORD -- Crawfurdiana, Laurus
Memorials of that branch of the Crawford family which comprises the
descendants of John Crawford, of Virginia, 1660-1883. With notices
of the allied families. New York: E. O. Jenkins Printer, 1883.

CRAWFORD -- Vanderbilt, Mrs. Frank A. C.
Laurus Crawfurdiana: Memorials of that branch of the Crawford family
which comprises the descendants of John Crawford, of Virginia, 1660-
1883. New York. 1883.

CREECY -- Peffer, Mary L.
300 years of Creecy-Creasy and allied families from Virginia to Oregon.
Corvallis, Oreg. 1974.

CREECY -- Peffer, Mary Lines
300 years of Creecy-Creasy and allied families from Virginia to Oregon.
Portland, Oreg. 1960.

CRITCHER -- Critcher, Catherine Carter and Henry
Descendants of John Critcher of Waterview, Westmoreland County, Virginia.
Denver. 1946.

CROCKER -- The maternal ancestors and kindred of Margaret Jane Crocker.
Portsmouth. 1914.

CROCKER -- Crocker, James Francis
Our Crocker ancestors. Portsmouth: Whitson & Shepherd. 1914.

CROCKETT -- Hill, Dorothy V.
The Crockett, Davidson (Davison), Graham, Montgomery, Stockton and
allied families of Virginia, Kentucky and Missouri, also the Taylor -
Hill and March-Cureton families of Virginia - Ohio - New England -
Alabama - California. 1969.

CROCKETT -- Montgomery, Robert H.
Robert Crockett of Great Calpasture, Augusta Co., Va.

CRONIN -- Cronin, Daniel W.
Descendants of Michael Cronin and Pricillah Pulley Cronin.
Strasburg: Shenandoah Pub., 1972.

CROOM -- Wood, Lillian F.
Daniel Croom of Virginia, his descendants in North Carolina; data
compiled for the North Carolina society of the descendants of the
Palatines. New Bern, N.C. 1943.

CROOM -- Wood, Lillian F.
Daniel Croom of Virginia, his descendants in North Carolina. 1945.

VROSS -- Cross, John Newton and Mary Cross Cole
William Cross of Botetourt Co., Va., and his descendants, 1733-1932;
also a record of the related families of McCown, Gentry-Blythe, Cain-
Robertson, Harris-Martin, and Conner, of Virginia, Kentucky, Illinois
and Missouri. Columbia, Mo.: E. W. Stephens Publishing Co., 1932.

CROSS -- Tucker, Helen E.
Descendants of John Cross, 1761-1847 and Elizabeth Hardwick, 1769-1842
of Virginia representing five generations of Daughters of the American
Revolution. 1954.

CROSSEN -- Taylor, Dorothy Russ
Crossen. Alexandria. 1975.

CROW -- Crow, James Homer
The history of the Jacob Crow family in Greene County, Pa. and in
Marshall County, W. Va. Cameron, W. Va. 1977.

CROW -- Crow, James Homer
The fireside stories of the Jacob Crow family. Parsons, W. Va.: McClain
Print, 1979.

CROWE -- Crow, Jewell Lofland
    History of William Crow of Virginia and his descendants in America,
    and related families: their settlements, migrations, marriages,
    military achievements. Dallas. 1961.

CROZIER -- Crozier, W. A.
    Virginia County Records. Hasbrouck, N.J. 1910.

CRUM -- Lybarger, Donald Fisher
    The Crum family, notes concerning the descendants of Anthony Crum, Sr.,
    of Frederick County, Virginia. Cleveland. 1963.

CRUMLEY -- Haunschild, Ormal Crumley
    The Crumleys of Frederick Co., Va., and Green Co., Tenn., and their
    descendants. Ada, Okla. 1975.

CRUTCHER -- McNamara, Elizabeth W.
    Descendants of Thomas Crutcher, died 1772, Essex County, Virginia.
    Baltimore: Gateway Press, 1985.

CULPEPER -- The proprietors of the Northern Neck. Chapters of Culpeper
    Genealogy. Richmond: The Old Dominion Press, 1926.

CULPEPER -- Notes on Culpeper County, Va., embracing a revised and
    enlarged edition of Dr. Philip Slaughter's History of St. Mark's
    Parish. Culpeper. 1900.

CULPEPPER -- Culpepper, C. L.
    A brief gist of the history of the Culpepper family from 1475 to
    present. 1970.

CULPEPER -- Harrison, Fairfax
    The proprietors of the Northern Neck, chapters of Culpeper genealogy.
    Richmond: Old Dominion Press, 1926.

CUMBERLAND PARISH -- Bell, Landon C.
    Lunenburg Co., 1746-1816. Contains genealogies of Cameron (Rev. John),
    Bacon, Ballard, Betts, Billups, Bouldin, Blagrove, Brodnax, Buford,
    Caldwell, Chappell, Claiborne, Clay, Cureton, Cox, Delony, Dixon, Edloe,
    Ellidge, Embry, Farmer, Ferth, Fontaine, Garland, Davis, Gee, Hall,
    Hardy, Hawkins, Hobson, Howard, Jackson, Macfarland, Marrable, Martin,
    Nash, Neblett, Parrish, Pettus, Phillips, Ragsdale, Red, Robertson,
    Smith, Speed, Stevenson, Stokes, Street, Tabb, Talbott, Taylor,
    Tomlinson, Tucker, Twitty, Winn. Richmond: The William Byrd Press,
    1930.

CUNARD -- Conard, Erik P.
    Edward Cunard, Junior, of Loudoun County, Virginia; his ancestry and
    descendants. Pittsburg, Pa. 1966.

CURD -- Curd, Thomas H. S.
    Supplement to The Curd family in America. Roanoke. 1981.

CURD -- Curd, H. S.
  1982 addendum and index to the 1981 supplement of The Curd family in America. Roanoke. 1982.

CURD -- Fuller, Frank D. and Thomas H. S. Curd
  The Curd family in America, a genealogy of some of the descendants of Edward Curd of Henrico County, Virginia, 1704, with brief notes on the allied families of Price and Watkins. Rutland, Vt.: Tuttle Publishing Co., Inc., 1938.

CURRY -- Lawler, Truman Barton
  History of the Currey family of West Virginia. 1950.

CURTIS -- Curtis, Theodore M.
  The Curtis family. Richmond. 1980.

CURTIS -- King, Mable LeVert
  Descendants of Michael Curtis, Elisha Felton, John Fennel, Richard King, Jr., Virginia and North Carolina to Lawrence County, Alabama. Memphis, Tenn. 1982.

CUSHMAN -- Burt, Alvah Walford
  Cushman genealogy and general history, including the descendants of the Fayette county, Pennsylvania, and Monongalia county, Virginia, families. Cincinnati, Ohio. 1942.

CUSTIS -- Lowther, Minnie Kendall
  Mount Vernon, Arlington and Woodlawn; history of these national shrines from the earliest titles of ownership to the present, with biographical sketches, portraits, and interesting reminiscences of the families, who founded them. Washington: C. H. Potter & Co., Inc., 1922.

CUSTIS -- Rubincam, Milton
  The royal ancestry of George Washington Parke Custis. Richmond. 1957.

DABNEY -- The John Blair Dabney manuscript ... "Written with his own hand for his children, A.D. 1850." Richmond. 19--.

DABNEY -- Dabney, William H.
  Sketch of the Dabneys of Virginia, etc. Chicago, Ill.: Press of S. D. Chiles & Co., 1888.

DABNEY -- Johnson, Thomas Cary
  Life and Letters of Robert Lewis Dabney. Richmond: The Presbyterian Committee of Publication, 1903.

DAGIT -- Adams, Henry Walton
The Dagit family genealogy: American branch, 1837-1985: the guide to the relationship and present location of all the descendants of Josephine Leonide Dandurand & Charles Dagit. Fairfax. 1985.

DAINGERFIELD -- A Virginia Plantagenet, royal descent of Sarah Vowell Daingerfield; records and other matter dating from 741 to 1949. Alexandria. 1959.

DAINGERFEILD -- McRae, Lawrence
Descendants of John Daingerfield and his wife. New Kent, Va. 1640.

DAINGERFIELD -- MacRae, Lawrence
Descendants of John Daingerfield and his wife, New Kent County, Virginia, 1640, including descendants of Elizabeth Meriweather of Essex Co., Va., Apphia Fauntleroy of Richmond Co., Va., Elizabeth Parker of West Moreland Co., Va., and their husbands, also Thomas Deaderick and his wife, of Frederick Co., Va., and Dora Virginia Deaderick and her husband, Robert Strange MacRae of Orange County, N. Carolina. Descendants of George Parker and his wife, Accomac Co., Va., 1650. Greensboro, N.C. 1928.

DALE -- Daniels, Almon E.
A work book on the Dale families of Virginia, with particular reference to the branch which moved from the northern neck of Virginia to Woodford County, Kentucky, and with notes on the related families of Dodson, Goad, Hanks, Phillips, Sydnor, etc. Arlington. 1958.

DALTON -- Horton, Lucy H.
Daltons of Virginia. Franklin, Tenn.

DALTON -- Troyer, Madeline Heitzman
The descendants of William McThais Dalton. Arlington. 1978.

DAMERON -- Dameron, Alfred Speer
Historical and genealogical sketch of the Dameron family of England and Virginia. Newport, Ky. 1940.

DAMERON -- Snow, Helen Foster
The Dameron-Damron genealogy; the descendants of Lawrence Dameron of Virginia, with notes on the related Northumberland County families of Gaskins, Harvey, Bledsoe, Tignor, Ball, Coppedge-Coppage, Waddy, Taylor, Smith and the John Ladd family, originating in lower Norfolk County, Virginia. Madison, Conn. 1953.

DANCE -- Campbell, L. L.
Dance family in Virginia. Lexington. 1952.

DANCE -- McKinney, R. T.
Name and family of Dance; genealogical and historical sketch. Parkersburg, W. Va. 1971.

DANIEL -- Gee, Christine South
John Daniel, Sr., 1724-1819, of Essex County, Virginia, and Laurens
County, South Carolina; his Virginia ancestry and some of his
descendents. Columbia, S.C.: McDonald Letter Shop, 1970.

DANIEL -- Grant, Howard B.
John Daniels; copyright by Howard B. Grant ... Philippi, W. Va. 1936.

DANIEL -- Heinemann, Charles Brunk
Daniel families of the southern states, a compilation covering one
hundred thirteen Daniel families. Washington, D.C. 1934.

DANIEL -- Mann, Robert Neville and Catherine Cleek Mann
Middlesex, Virginia, Daniel descendants ... Cedar Bluff, Ala. 1959.

DANIELS -- Daniel, Denzil R.
The Nehemiah Daniel family. Norfolk. 1976.

DANIELS -- Jones, Daniel Wesley
The house of Daniel: John Daniel the immigrant (sic), York County,
Va., through 1975. Decorah, Iowa: Anundsen Pub., 1976.

DAEDEN -- Baer, Mabel Van Dyke
Darden-Lassiter Lineage of Isle of Wight and Nansemond Counties,
Virginia. 1965.

DARDEN -- Darden, Newton Jasper
Darden family history, with notes on ancestry of allied families:
Washington, Lanier, Burch, Strozier, Dodson, Pyles, McNair, Barnett;
a memorial of Dearden-Durden-Dardens of the United States of America,
particularly in Virginia, Georgia, Tennessee, Alabama, Mississippi,
and Texas. Edited by Leroy W. Tilton. Washington. 1957.

DARDEN -- Darden, Gordon Wallace
Dardens of Williams Creek (antecedents and descendants), a record of
the Dardens, including their antecedents and descendants, who moved
from Virginia to Wilkes County, Georgia and settled on Williams Creek,
now a boundary between Taliaferro and Warren Counties, Georgia. Athens,
Ga. 1963.

DARST -- Darst, Henry Jackson, Jr.
A genealogy of the Darst family of Virginia. Detroit, Mich. 1943.

DARST -- Darst, Henry Jackson
The Darsts of Virginia: a chronicle of ten generations in the Old
Dominion, with sketches of the Cecil, Charlton, Glendy, Grigsby,
Larew, Miller, Trolinger, Welch, Wygal, and Wysor families.
Williamsburg. 1972.

DARST -- Gladden, Sanford C.
   The Darst family in the Shenandoah Valley of Virginia. Oxford, Miss.
   1946.

DARTER -- Darter, Oscar H.
   The Darter-Tarter family. Richmond. 1965.

DASHER -- Dasher, N. Seymour
   Christian Dasher of Virginia: a family genealogy, 1757-1924. Moss
   Beach, Calif. 1985.

DAUGHHETEE -- Heinemann, Charles Brunk
   The Daughhette family of Frederick, Shenandoah, and Monongalia counties,
   Va.; Clark and Estill counties, Ky.; Cape Girardeau county, Mo.; and
   other locations indicated in the compilation. Washington. 1935.

DAUGHHETTE -- Heinemann, C. S.
   Descendants of AhDaughhette, Daughetee, Daughity, O'Dogherty, etc.
   families of Northumberland county, Virginia. Washington. 1942.

DAUGHHETEE --Heinemann, Charles Brunk
   The Daughhetee family of Estill County, Kentucky. Big Laurel. 1934.

DAVENPORT -- Davenport, Henry Bedinger
   Genealogy of the Davenport family and connections. Charleston,
   W. Va. 1947.

DAVENPORT -- Davenport, Kevan Edward
   The Davenports of Berkeley County, West Virginia, and Wells County,
   Indiana, includes Simms, Romey, Widmer, Bonahoom, and Richardson: a
   genealogical, biographical, and historical perspective. Durham, N.C.
   1984.

DAVIS -- Bates, Robert L. in collaboration with Harry H. Bates
   The story of Smithfield (Middleway), Jefferson County, West Virginia.
   Endicott, N.Y. 1958.

DAVIS -- Davis, Thomas Frederick
   A genealogical record of the Davis, Swann and Cabell families of North
   Carolina and Virginia. Jacksonville, Fla. 1934.

DAVIS -- Davis and Wakefield families; some descendants of Travis Davis (1780)
   of North Carolina and Franklin Co., Ind.; and some descendants of
   Thomas Wakefield who came to Virginia in 1635. Oakland, Calif. 1952.

DAVIS -- Davis family records from the Bible of the Reverend William Davis,
   1770-1836. Newport News. 1971.

DAVIS -- DeVerter, Ruth Henricks
   The genealogy of the Davis family, Middlesex County, Virginia, and
   Montgomery County, Kentucky. Baytown, Tex. 1957.

DAVIS -- <u>Genealogy of Jefferson Davis and of Samuel Davis</u> ... New York
and Washington: Neale Publishing Company, 1910.

DAVIS -- <u>William Davis family; a short sketch of the ancestry of William
Davis and the records of his lineage and a brother, Samuel Davis.</u>
Front Royal. 1972.

DAVIS -- Heinemann, Charles Brunk
<u>Davis families of the southern states</u> ... Chicago, Ill. 1938.

DAVIS -- Hurst, Anne Davis
<u>Matthias Willoughby Davis, 1752-1829.</u> Bristol, W. Va. 1975.

DAVIS -- Morris, John S.
<u>Davis, Spencer, and Gillespie families of Prince Edward County, Virginia.</u>
Richmond. 1983.

DAVIS -- Nicholson, Susie Davis
<u>Davis: "the settlers of Salem, West Virginia" (their ancestors and
some of their descendants).</u> Strasburg, Ohio: Gordon Print, 1979.

DAVIS -- Whitsitt, William H.
<u>Genealogy of Jefferson Davis; address delivered October 9, 1908,
before Lee camp, No. 1, confederate veterans, Richmond, Va.</u>
Richmond: Everett Waddy Co., Printers, 1908.

DAVIS -- Whitsett, William H., A.M., D.D., LL.D.
<u>Genealogy of Jefferson Davis and of Samuel Davies</u> . New York: The
Neale Publishing Co., 1910.

DAVIS -- Wingfield, Marshall
<u>Pioneer family of Franklin County, Virginia.</u> Berryville: Chesapeake
Book Co., 1964.

DAWKINS -- Prewitt, Lela Wolfe
<u>The Dawkins and Stewart families of Virginia and Kentucky.</u> Fairfield,
Iowa. 1968.

DAWSON -- Dawson, Leslie Davis
<u>History of the Dawson-Davis family and related families of Fairfax
and Prince William Counties, Virginia.</u> Plainfield, N.J. 1974.

DEACON -- Diehl, George West
<u>The Deacons of Virginia and some collateral lines.</u> Staunton: Deacon
Family Association, 1963.

- 54 -

DEADERICK -- ... The pioneering Deadericks of Virginia & Tennessee. From
data in the possession of Lyon Childress of Nashville and John
Williams Childress of Nashville and John Williams Childress of
Washington. Presented by George Magruder Batey III. Washington. 1940.

DEAKINS -- Perry, Alyce Rebecca Pulliam
Deakins-Pulliam & allied families of America. Keyser, W. Va. 1957.

DEAN -- Deane, Frank Putnam
A family tree in America: being a genealogical story of the families
of Deane, Putnam, Boynton, Gager, Bull, and allied families from the
year 1630. Richmond. 1979.

de GRAFFENRIED -- de Graffenried, Thomas P.
The de Graffenreid family scrapbook . Charlottesville: University of
Virginia Press, 1958.

deGRAFFENRIED -- deGraffenried, Thomas P.
History of the deGraffenried family from 1191 A.D. to 1925. 1925.

de GRAFFENRIED -- Reynolds, Katherine
Some descendants of Tscharner de Graffenried of Va. (1722-1794),
1722 - 1961. 1961.

DENNISON -- Joyner, Peggy S.
Jordan Dennison (-1806), some of his ancestors and descendants and
"Beechwood," Denson-Pretlow-Darden ancestral home, Southampton County,
Virginia. Portsmouth. 1978.

DENNY -- Denny, William Murdock
Richard Denny of Philadelphia, Pennsylvania, and Richmond, Virginia,
and his descendants. Schenectady, N.Y. 1973.

DENT -- Newman, Harry Wright
The Maryland Dents. Richmond: Dietz Press, 1963.

HUNT-DENTON -- Brown, Mrs. Herbet (Immogene Hannan Brown)
Hunt-Denton families of Va., Tenn., Ky., Ind., and Western States.
Alaxandria, Ind. 1969.

DETWEILER -- Gehman, I. G.
Ancestors and descendants of Anna Detweiler. Harrisburg. 1967.

DE VAULT -- Gillmore, William Bruce
A De Vault genealogy, with Gillmore and Hunt supplements. Arlington.
1954.

DEW -- White, Ernestine Dew
Genealogy of some of the descendants of Thomas Dew, colonial Virginia
pioneer immigrant, together with genealogical records and biographical
sketches of families in Virginia, Maryland, North Carolina, South
Carolina, West Virginia and Tennessee ... Greenville, S.C. 1937.

DEWEY -- Leger, P. D.
Josiah Dewey, son of Thomas Dewey, the settler and illustrious
descendants of Josiah; including Admiral George Dewey. Falls Church.
1953.

DICKERSON -- Cox, Carlyle E.
Dickerson, a Kentucky-Virginia family. Chicago, Ill. 1938.

DICKERSON -- Dickerson, Florence Smith
Dickerson and Walden families. Richmond: Dietz Press, 1961.

DICKEY -- Dickie family (of Virginia). Richmond.

DICKINSON -- Dickinson, Richard J.
A Dickinson family of Virginia and Illinois. Eureka, Ill. 1955.

DICKINSON -- Shaw, Frederick Benjamin
History of the Dickinson family and descendants of Nathaniel Dickinson,
the first American ancestor who arrived in 1630. Arlington. 1942.

DIEHL -- Genealogy of the descendants of Samuel Diehl and Margaretha Ritchey,
his wife, of Loudoun County, Va. and Bedford County, Pa., 1740-1828.
Holidaysburg, Pa. 1976.

DIGGES -- Rowe, Anna Mae
The genealogy of Henry Arthur i.e. Arthur Henry Diggs, Jr. family
connections. Norfolk. 1977.

DILS -- Johnson, M. M.
Dils family of Wood County, W. Va.

DINWIDDIE -- The official records of Robert Dinwiddie, lieutenant governor
of the colony of Virginia, 1751-1758, now first printed from the
manuscript in the Collections of the Virginia historical society, with
an introduction and notes by R. A. Brock ... Richmond. 1883-84.

DINWIDDIE -- Holladay, Elizabeth Dinwiddie
Dinwiddie family records, with especial attention to the line of
William Walthall Dinwiddie, 1804-1882. Charlottesville: King
Lindsay Print. Corp., 1957.

DIXON -- Ramsey, Glenn Virgil
Descendants of George Dixon, Virginia frontiersman, Revolutionary War
soldier and spy (and) Warren County, Indiana, pioneer. Peoria, Ill.
1955.

DIXON -- Sample, Trixie Dixon
Dixons, from Virginia to Texas. Owensboro, Ky.: Cook-McDowell Pub.,
1981.

DOANE -- Enderton, Marian D.
Our father's family ... giving data on the following families: Carter,
Doane, De Money, Kinnear, Murray, Ogelsby, Violett, and the Wells
family of Virginia. San Jose, Calif. 1970.

DOBYNS -- Dobyns, Kenneth W. and Margaret S. Thorpe
Daniel Dobyns of Colonial Virginia; his English ancestry and American
descendants. Arlington. 1969.

DODRILL -- Dodrill, Charles Tunis
Heritage of a pioneer, being the story of William (English Bill
Doddridge) Dodrill and his wife, Rebecca (Lewis) Daugherty, their
family, the times in which they lived, and a genealogy of the families
of their sons. Huntington, W. Va. 1967.

DODSON --Callahan, Mary Lee Dodson
Genealogy of Charles Dodson of Southwest Virginia and Watkins H.
Dodson and his wife, Jerusha Ann Blakemore of West Tennessee. 1953.

DODSON -- Callahan, Mary Lee Dodson
Genealogy of the Dodson families of Pittsylvania and Halifax County,
Virginia, from the diary of the Reverend Elias Dodson. 1956.

DODSON -- Sloan, Emma I.
Charles Dodson family of Richmond County, Va. Nashville, Tenn. 1940.

DOGGETT -- Lynch, Pauline Jones
The Doggett family: generations of Miller, Doggett (1789-1841) from
Virginia to Tennessee 1809. Lewisburg, Tenn. 1978.

DOOLEY -- Cline, Laura Smith
Dooley and Scobee families in Virginia, Kentucky, and Missouri. Los
Altos, Calif. 1982.

DORSEY -- Dorsey, Maxwell, J., Jean Muir Dorsey and Nanny Ball Nimmo
The Dorsey family: descendants of Edward Darcy-Dorsey of Virginia and
Maryland for five generations, and allied families. Urbana, Ill. 1947.

DOSTER -- Doster, Elizabeth A. M.
The Doster genealogy. Richmond: William Byrd Press, 1945.

DOSTER -- Doster, Wadsworth
The Doster genealogy, by Mrs. Ben Hill Doster, in memory of her
husband. Richmond: William Byrd Press, 1945.

DOUGHERTY -- Dougherty, William C.
    Family history of James Dougherty and lineage of descent.
    Nickelsville: Service Printery, 1930.

DOUGLAS -- A branch of the Douglas family, with its Maryland & Virginia
    connections. Garden City, N.Y.: Doubleday, 1967.

DOUGLAS -- Harris, Ruthe Eleanor Poole
    Ruth Eleanor Douglas journal: with genealogies of Douglas, Noell,
    Callaway, Clemens, Moorman, and other related Bedford County, Virginia
    families: also genealogies of Douglas families of Tennessee, Kentucky,
    Missouri. Nashville, Tenn. 1979.

DOUGLAS -- Jones, W. Mac.
    The Douglas Register, being a detailed record of Births, Marriages and
    Deaths, together with other interesting notes as kept by the Rev.
    William Douglas, from 1750 to 1797. Richmond: J. W. Ferguson & Sons,
    Printers and Publishers, 1928.

DOUGLAS -- Newman, Harry Wright
    A branch of the Douglas family with its Maryland and Virginia
    connections. Garden City, N.Y.: Doubleday, 1967.

DOIUGLS -- Wise, John Sergeant
    The family of Douglass or Douglas of Garrallan in Virginia. New
    York. 1894.

DOWNMAN -- Fleming, Clarissa Walton
    William Downman of Plymouth, England, and Virginia, October 1608, and
    some of his descendants. The Plains, Va. 1958.

DREW -- Emison, James W.
    Drew, Hart, Kerby, Dutton families of Virginia, North and South
    Carolina, Georgia, Florida. 1969.

DROMGOOLE -- Dromgoole and Lou Allie Heath
    Canaan; home of the Edward Dromgoole family built 1780-84, Brunswick
    County, Virginia. Richmond, Calif. 1972.

DRYER -- Schneider, Lottie May Dyer
    A chronicle of the Dryer-Johnson family. Radford. 1963.

DU BELLET -- Du Bellet, Louise Pecquet
    Some Prominent Virginia Families. Lynchburg. 1907.

DUDLEY -- Dudley, Clause William
    The Dudley family. Richmond. 1971.

DUFF -- Barnett, James D.
    John Duff of North Ireland, Virginia and Kentucky and his descendants.
    1955.

DUKE -- Notebook concerning Revolutionary pensioners and relating principally
to the Duke family of North Carolina and Virginia.

DUKE -- Duke, Walter Garland
Henry Duke, Councilor, his descendants and connections.   Richmond.   1949.

DUKE, ETC. -- Smythe, S. G.
A genealogy of the Duke-Shepherd-Van Metre Family.   Lancaster, Pa.:
Press of the New Era Printing Co.,   1909.

DULANY (DULANEY) -- Dulaney, B. L.
Something about the Dulaney (Dulany) Family and the Southern Cobb
Family.   Washington.

DULANEY -- Furlong, Roland Dulany
Dulany-Furlong and kindred families.   Parsons, W. Va.: McClain Print.
Co., 1975.

DUNAWAY -- Clendening, A. Elizabeth
The Dunaways of Virginia.   Oqunquit, Maine.   1958.

DUNCAN -- Darrett, Linnie Wright
Duncan families of Virginia ... their descendants and some allied
families ... Dallas, Tex.: McGraw Publishing Co., 1940.

DUNCAN -- Vick, Velma B.
The Duncans of Culpeper County, Virginia to Logan County, Kentucky.
1954.

DUNLAP -- Caraway, William Oates
Genealogy, descendants of Alexander Dunlap including Hodge - Atchison -
Crockett - Rice - Bailey - Hazelrigg - Richard - Wyatt and allied
families - early Virginia and Kentucky pioneers.   Sugar Land, Tex.
1956.

DUNNING -- Dunning, M. B.
Descendants of William Dunning of Nelson County, Virginia.   1953.

DU PUY -- Dingley, Celene DuPuy
Ancestors of William Atherton DuPuy and his wife Ada Lee Orme.
Arlington.   1952.

DU VAL -- Buchanan, Margaret Gwin
DuVals of Kentucky from Virginia, 1794-1935; descendants and allied
families.   Lynchburg: J. P. Bell Company, Inc., 1937.

DU VAL -- Grabowski, Bessie Berry
The Du Val family of Virginia, 1701; descendants of Daniel Du Val,
Huguenot, and allied families.   Richmond: Dietz Print. Co., 1931.

DYER -- Dyer, Watson B.
Dyer family from England to America, 1600's to 1980: Virginia and
Southern Dyer families, their descendants and connecting families.
Cedartown, Ga.   1980.

DYER -- Talbot, Mary Lee Keister
The Dyer Settlement; the Fort Seybert massacre, Fort Seybert,
West Virginia. 1937.

EADS -- Eads-Leach, Margaret Janes
Family history including lines of Charles Eads of Virginia, Jesse
Richardson of Virginia, John Cundiff of Virginia. Maroa, Ill. 1970.

EANES -- Eanes, Richard Henry
The descendants of Edward Eanes of Henrico and Chesterfield counties
In Virginia. 1968.

EARLE -- Birnie, Joseph Earle
The Earles and Birnies. Richmond: Whittet & Shepperson, 1974.

EARLY -- Early, R. H.
The family of Early, which settled upon the eastern shore of Virginia
and its connection with other families. Lynchburg. 1920.

EARLY -- Hampton, Margaret Woods
Descendants of John Early of Virginia (1729-1744). Fort Worth, Tex.:
Miran Publishers, 1973.

EARLY -- Hatcher, Samuel Stockwell
A history of the family of Early in America: being the ancestors and
descendants of Jeremiah Early, who came from the county of Donegal,
Ireland, and settled in what is now Madison County, Virginia, early
in the eighteenth century. Albany, N.Y.: J. Munsell's Sons, 1896.

EARLY -- Holden, Katherine Kent Early
The Earlys of southwest Virginia. Keysville. 1981.

EASLEY -- DeMarce, Virginia Easley
Supplement to A tentative outline of U.S. Easley lines primarily to
the year 1800. Arlington. 1978.

EDGEWORTH -- MacDonald, Edgar E.
The American Edgeworths; a biographical sketch of Richard Edgeworth
(1764-1796) with letters and documents pertaining to the legacy of
his three sons. Richmond. 1970.

EDMINSTER -- Edminster, Frank Custer
The Edminster family in America. Arlington. 1965.

EDMISTON -- Cole, Redmond S.
The ancestry and life of Colonel William Edmiston of Washington County,
Virginia. Tulsa, Okla. 1937.

EDMISTON -- Edmiston, Prentess P.
A branch of the Edmiston family tree from Ireland to North Carolina
to Pennsylvania to Virginia to Tennessee to Arkansas and to Texas,
A.D. 1700 to 1964. Harlingen, Tex. 1964.

EDMUNDS -- Thompson, Alice Chapman
The Edmunds and Barton families of Virginia and Kentucky. 1978.

EDWARDS -- Dixon, Elizabeth Williamson
Col. Nathaniel Edwards family of Brunswick Co., Va., Col. William
Eaton family of Granville, N.C. 1958.

EDWARDS (Northern Neck) -- Edwards, G. H.
Historical Sketch of the Edwards and Todd Families. Springfield,
Ill. 1894.

EDWARDS -- Edwards, Richard Laurence
Ancestors and descendants of the Edwards-Mathis, Delozier, and
related families that pioneered through Virginia, Carolinas, Tennessee,
Kentucky, Illinois, Missouri, Kansas, and spread to descendants in
thirty-seven states and two provinces in Canada. Coffeyville, Kans.
1985.

EDWARDS -- Missouri DAR, G.R.C.
Old wills from Virginia, Kentucky, Maryland. 1951.

EICHENBERG -- Ikenberry, Charles S. and W. Lewis Eikenberry
A history and genealogy of Peter Eichenberg family in the U.S.A.
Daleville. 1956.

ELDER -- Donnelly, Mary Louise
Maryland Elder family and kin: William Elder, 1708-1775, Emmitburg,
Md., pioneer. Burke. 1975.

ELIOT -- The Elliott family. Arlington: American Genealogical Research
Institute, 1972.

ELIOT -- Odell, Anne Elliott
Captain George Elliott of the Virginia Navy; and some allied families,
Anderson, Atkins, Baker, Bridgewater, Campbell, Carpenter, Creel,
Dadisman, Diddle, Fry, Grady, Hindman, Hughes, Jones, Lightfoot,
McKay, Nelson, Odell, Pennebaker, Slaughter, Taylor (and) Thomas.
Pasadena, Valif. 1961.

ELIOT -- Odell, Anne E.
Captain George Elliott of the Virginia Navy, and some allied families.
Los Angeles, Calif. 1973.

ELLIOTT -- Chilton, Harriett A.
William Alexander Elliott (1813-1865), his ancestors and descendants:
includes records from four family Bibles (1771-1964). Falls Church.
1978.

ELLIS -- Ellis, Thomas H.
A memorandum of the Ellis family (of Virginia ... 1649). Revised by
Rt. Rev. Beverly D. Tucker. Richmond. 1907.

ELLIS -- McCrary, Dixie L.
The Ellis line from Surry-Sussex in Virginia. St. Petersburg, Fla.
1978.

ELLSWORTH -- Siebert, Harriett E.
Ellsworth genealogy ... of North Carolina and Virginia. Alameda,
Calif. 1955.

ELMORE -- Elmore, William E.
"Elmore papers": concerning the early Elmores in Virginia and North
Carolina, with some information regarding S. C. and Ky. early
Elmores. Phoenix, Ariz. 1983.

ELSWICK -- Elswick, Jeanette
Elswick genealogy: a genealogical record of the Elswick family, 1784-
1900; early settlers of Buchanan County, Virginia, Pike County,
Kentucky and their descendants. Elkhorn City. 1973.

EMERSON -- Emerson, K. C.
Records of Emerson in Virginia, 1618-1699. Arlington. 1979.

EMERSON -- Emmerson, John C.
(The) Emmersons and Portsmouth, 1737-1965. Portsmouth. 1966.

EMISON -- Emison, James Wade
The Emison families, revised; origin and history of the Kentucky
Emisons, with partial genealogies and notes on Emisions (sic) of
Virginia, Tennessee, Long Island and Massachusetts. Also the following
collateral families: Baird, Holmes, Clark, Love, Posey-Wade.
Vincennes, Ind. 1954.

ENGLE -- Grant, Howard B.
The Engle family of Barbour County, West Virginia. Philippi,
W. Va. 1935.

ENSMINGER -- Bell, Raymond Martin
The Ensminger family: Diemeringen, Alsace; Cocalico, Pennsylvania;
Williamsport, Maryland; Cowpasture, Virginia. Washington, Pa. 1958.

ENSMINGER -- Bell, Raymond Martin
The Ensminger family: Pennsylvania, Maryland, Virginia, South Carolina.
Washington, Pa. 1961.

EPPS -- Porter, Bertha Wheatley
Descendants of James Epps, 1783-1869, Sussex County, Virginia, and
wife Jane Larkin Evans, 1795-1867, Morgan County, Georgia, married
1818. Newborn, Ga. 1968.

ESSEX -- Essex, Hiram E.
Descendants of Thomas Essex and Elizabeth Bowen Essex of Maryland,
Virginia and Illinois. Rochester, Minn.

ETCHISON -- Barekman, June B.
  History of Edmund Etchison, Revolutionary soldier of North Carolina,
  and his descendants: including Atchisons--Virginia, Maryland,
  Kentucky--and records of ... kin throughout America. Chicago, Ill.
  1980.

EUBANK -- Bender, Lucy
  The history and genealogy of the Eubank, White, Lewis, Glazebrook,
  Hayslip and collateral families, compiled from court, census, state,
  War department and old family records and account. Langley Field.
  1938.

EVANS -- Albert, Ethel Evans
  Southwest Virginia kin: a genealogical and historical account of the
  Evans, Kelly, Counts, Stinson, and related families. Kingsport, Tenn.
  1977.

EVANS -- Evans, Cleo H.
  Robert Evans family, Virginia and Georgia. Arlington. Babbelonia
  Print, 1966.

EVANS -- Evans, Ellen Good
  Evans family of Virginia and North Carolina, etc. Joplin, Mo. 1931.

EVANS -- Evans, James Daniel
  History of Nathan Evans of Cat Fish Creek, and his descendants.
  Williamsburg. 1905.

EVANS -- Leithold, Esher M.
  Genealogy of the Evans family, the Virginia Biddles and other related
  families. Woodland, Calif. 1956.

EVANS -- Lewis, Virgil A.
  Sketch of the Evans family of Monongalia County, West Va. Charleston,
  W. Va. 1911.

EVERARD -- Haywood, Marshall De Lancey
  Sir Richard Everard, baronet, governor of the colony of North Carolina,
  1725-1731, and his descendants in Virginia. Washington. 1897.

EWELL -- Ewell, Alice Maude
  A Virginia scene; or, Life in old Prince William. Lynchburg: J. P.
  Bell Co., Inc., 1931.

EWING -- Ewing, Elbert William R.
  Clan Ewing of Scotland, early history and contribution to America;
  sketches of some family pioneers and their times ... with genealogies
  and illustrations of family arms. Ballston: Cobden Publishing Co.,
  1922.

EZEKIEL -- Ezekiel, Henry C.
Genealogical record, 1892, of the Ezekiel family of Philadelphia,
Pennsylvania; Richmond, Virginia, and Cincinnati, Ohio.

FAHEY -- Fahey, Andrew P.
Fahey family facets. Annandale. 1985.

FAIRFAX -- An Historical Sketch of the Two Fairfax Families of Virginia.
New York: The Knickerbocker Press, 1913.

FAIRFAX -- The Proprietors of the Northern Neck. Chapters of Culpeper
Genealogy. Richmond: The Old Dominion Press, 1926.

FAIRFAX -- Neill, Edward D.
The Fairfaxes of England and America in the seventeenth and eighteenth
centuries, including letters from and to Hon. William Fairfax, president
of Council of Virginia, and his sons Col. William Fairfax and Rev.
Bryan, eighth lord Fairfax, the neighbors and friends of George
Washington. Albany, N.Y.: J. Munsell, 1868.

FAIRFAX -- Cartmell, Thomas Kemp
An historic sketch of the two Fairfax families in Virginia. New
York: The Knickerbocker Press, 1913.

FAIRFAX -- Journey from Virginia to Salem, Massachusetts, 1799, by Thomas
Fairfax, 9th baron Fairfax of Cameron, in Scotland, and of Belvoir
and Vaucluse in Fairfax County, Virginia ... London. 1936.

FAIRFAX -- Kilmer, Kenton and Donald Sweig; editor, Nan Netherton
The Fairfax family in Fairfax County: a brief history. Fairfax, Va.
Published by the Fairfax County Office of Comprehensive Planning under
the direction of the County Board of Supervisors in cooperation with
the County History Commission.

FAIRFAX -- Slaughter, Philip
Randolph Fairfax. Sketch of his life. 1878.

FAIRFAX -- Sorley, Merrow Egerton
A chart pedigree of the Fairfax family of Belvoir (now Fort Belvoir),
Fairfax County, Virginia. Washington. 1961.

FARISH -- Dorman, John Frederick
The Farish family of Virginia and its forebears. Richmond. 1967.

FARIS -- Flack, Nellie L.
Eight generations of the Virginia branch of the Faris family in the
United States of America. Seaton, Ill. 1918.

FARIS -- Phillips, Wm. H.
Farises in Virginia. Nashville, Tenn. 1952.

FARIS -- Reynolds, Katherine
The Faris family, Virginia, Tennessee and Texas (1607-1950). 1957.

FARLEY -- History of the descendants of Drewry Farley and the community
of River Ridge, Summers County, W. Va. Thornton, Ark.: Cayce Pub. Co.

FARLEY -- Harris, Mayme E. F.
Fairleigh and allied families: Maryland, Pennsylvania, Virginia ...
(and) Illinois. Chicago Heights, Ill. 1971.

FARMER -- Bishop, Rachel Parsons Flynn
Farmer and Field families of Virginia. Columbia, S.C. 1983.

FARMER -- Farmer, Ellery
Descendants of Thomas Farmer who came to Virginia in 1616. Henderson,
N.C. 1956.

FARROW -- Farrow, Audry Doris Goolsby
A genealogical history of the Farrow, Waters, and related families,
with personality profiles and brief sketches of the times and
experiences of two pioneer Virginia, South Carolina, and Mississippi
families. Ripley, Miss. 1973.

FAWCETT -- Fawcett, Thomas H.
Fawcett family of Frederick County, Virginia. Cheyney, Pa. 1938.

FAWCETT -- Fawcett, Thomas Hayes
The Fawcett family of Frederick County, Virginia. Chesterland,
Ohio. 1973.

FAWCETT -- Fawcett, Thomas Hayes
The Fawcett family of Frederick County, Virginia. Berryville: Virginia
Book Co., 1984.

FEARN -- Ferneyhough, Elizabeth Lee Fearn Cabell and Elizabeth Lee Lusk
The Fearns of Virginia and some allied families. Richmond: Expert
Graphics, 1973.

FEATHER -- Rogers, Edna Davis
Genealogy of the Jacob and Mary (Connoly) Feather family of Preston
County, West Virginia. Morgantown, W. Va.: Feather Genealogic Co., 1980.

FENTON -- Bailey, James Henry
A compilation of the descendants of William Fenton of County Limerick,
Ireland, and Petersburg, Virginia, on the one hundreth anniversary of
his death, November 2, 1955. Petersburg. 1955.

FENWICK -- The John's Island stud (South Carolina) 1750-1788. Richmond: Old
Dominion Press, 1931.

FENWICK -- Sellers, Edwin Jackett
    Fenwick Allied Ancestry. Philadelphia, Pa. 1916.

FEREBEE -- Ferebee, Annie A.
    Ferebee family, 1360-1937. Norfolk. 1955.

FERGUSON -- Cox, Marcia Kay Ferguson
    Ferguson-McPherson, 1680-1980: a genealogical search. Virginia, Ill.
    1983.

FERNOW -- Fearnow, Edgar C.
    The Fernow family (also spelled Ferneat, Ferno, Fearnow) written for
    the Fearnow family reunion and 170th anniversary of the birth of
    John Fernow, (1760-1825), who settled near Bath, Va., (now Berkeley
    Springs, West Virginia), in 1784, and emigrated to Ohio in 1814.
    Capitol Heights, Md. 1930.

FESSLER -- Fessler, William T.
    Fessler ancestories: foreign origins and family summaries and briefs
    in Pennsylvania: also briefs in California, Illinois, Indiana, Iowa,
    Kansas, Kentucky, North Carolina, Missouri, Ohio, Virginia: plus
    hundreds of other surnames. Haddonfield, N.J. 1980.

FETTY -- Stickney, Alpheus Beede
    Lucy & Oliver, some West Virginia genealogy. Pittsburgh, Pa. 1953.

FICKLIN -- Ficklin, Joseph Burwell
    A pedigree of the descendants of William Ficklin(ing) (dec. 1756) of
    King George County, Virginia. Pasadena, Calif. 1971.

FIELD -- Field, Charles Kellogg
    A genealogical and biographical history of the Field family of
    Massachusetts and Vermont and the French-Henry families of Virginia
    and Texas: a union of North and South. Baltimore: Gateway Press, 1985.

FIELD -- Hardon, Henry Winthrop
    Some of the ancestors and the children of Anna Hall Field, wife of
    Comfort Hardon, esq., sometime civil justice in Berkeley co. W. Va. ...
    Born December 26, 1797 ... died September 14, 1854 ... 1904.

FIELD -- Pierce, Frederick Clifton
    Field genealogy: being the record of all the Field family in America,
    whose ancestors were in this country prior to 1700. Emigrant ancestors
    located in Massachusetts, Rhode Island, New York, New Jersey, New
    Hampshire, Virginia. All descendants of the Fields of England, whose
    ancestor, Hurbutus de la Field, was from Alsace-Lorraine ... Chicago,
    Ill.: W. B. Conkey Co., 1901.

FINCH -- Sands, John A.
    Finch. Arlington. 1976.

FINCH -- Thompson, Ruby Finch
Finch families of Dixie: 300 years in the South. Arlington. 1972.

FINNEY -- Finney, Howard
Finney - Phinney families in America. Richmond: William Byrd
Press, 1957.

FISHBACK -- Fishback, James
Genealogy of the John Fishback family of Culpeper County, Virginia.
Glasgow, Ky.: Press of the Republican, 1912.

FISHBACK -- Kemper, Willis Miller
Genealogy of the Fishback family in America, the descendants of John
Fishback, the emigrant, with an historical sketch of his family and
of the colony at Germanna and Germantown, Virginia, 1714-1914. New
York. 1914.

FISHER -- The Fisher Family. Arlington: American Genealogical Institute,
1972.

FISHER -- Fisher, Mayme E.
Fisher families of Penn. - Virginia - Kentucky. 1964.

FISHER -- Heinemann, C. B.
Ludwig (Lewis) Fisher family of Virginia and Kentucky. Washington.
193-.

FITCH -- Sharp, Stephen A.
A Fitch hunt. Arlington. 1973.

FITZ -- Leonard, O. B.
The Fitz Randolphs of Massachusetts and Randolps of Virginia.

FITZHUGH -- Elkins, Mary T.
History of Fitzhughes in England and America; Virginia, Kentucky,
Missouri and Oregon. Sherman Oaks, Calif. 1956.

FITZHUGH -- Lawrence, Liza
The vistas at Eagle's Nest; the Fitzhugh-Grymes family home, King
George County, Virginia. King George. 1969.

FITZHUGH -- Woodman, Nannie C.
The Fitzhugh family in America, treating in particular the West
Virginia branch. Charleston, W. Va. 1928.

FITZPATRICK -- Lea, Reba Fitzpatrick
The 'Belfield' Fitzpatricks and 'Elm' Colemans. Lynchburg: Brown -
Morrison Co., 1958.

FITZSIMMONS -- Hathaway, Bernice FitzSimmons
    FitzSimmons and allied linez: Ellis, Lee, Perkins, Radford, Redding,
    Aston, Cocke, Smith, Pierce. Some of the ancestors and all of the
    descendants of Willis FitzSimmons, b. 1854, d. 1930: early Virginia
    and Kentucky lines. Denver. 1963.

FLAGG -- Flagg, Charles Allcott
    Descendants of Josiah Flagg of Berkeley County, W. Va.; with sketches
    of the Flagg, Keyes, Foss, Shively, Hughes, Slemons, and Campbell
    ancestries; a memorail to Henry Gaither Flagg of Tennessee, by his
    son Joseph Walker Flagg. Boston: T. R. Marvin & Son, 1920.

FLATHERS -- Flathers, Jennings H.
    Edward Flathers and his descendants: a genealogical history of nine
    generations in America. McLean. 1973.

FLEET -- Fleet, Maria Louisa Wacker
    Green Mount after the war: the correspondence of Maria Louisa Wacker
    Fleet and her family, 1865-1900. Charlottesville: University Press
    of Virginia, 1978.

FLEMING -- Fleming, William A. and Wallace B.
    A Fleming family with colonial ancestors in Virginia, Maryland and
    Pennsylvania. Charleston, W. Va.: Charleston Print Co., 1947.

FLETCHER -- Anderson, Grant James
    Genealogy, in part, of the Fletcher-Crowder-Tucker family. Richmond:
    Whittet & Shepperson Printers, 1909.

FLINT -- Smith, Alven Martyn
    Thomas Flint and William Flint, of Salem, Mass. and their descendants;
    also of the probably unrelated lines of Lt. Robert Flint of Sproutbrook,
    Montgomery Co., N.Y. and Robert Flint of Virginia and Trenton, N.J.
    Pasadena, Calif. 1931.

FLOURNOY -- Cheek, Menifee Reed
    Flournoys of France and England to America, 1699. Compiled by request
    for the Huguenot Society Founders of Manakin in the colony of Virginia.
    Nashville. 1957.

FLOURNOY -- Rathbone, Bettye S.
    Some of the ancestors of Francis Flournoy, Sr. of Chesterfield County,
    Virginia. Austin, Tex.: Nortex Press, 1985.

FLOYD -- Ambler, C. H.
    Life and Diary of John Floyd. Richmond. 1918.

FLOYD -- Clagett, Brice McAdoo
    A sketch of the Floyd family of the Eastern Shore of Virginia.
    Washington. 1964.

- 68 -

FLOYD -- Floyd, N. J.
     Biographical genealogies of the Virginia-Kentucky Floyd family, with
     notes of some collateral branches. Baltimore: William and Wilkins
     Company, 1912.

FOGG -- Whitten, Phyllis O.
     Samuel Fogg, 1628-1672: his ancestors and descendants. Annandale:
     Mrs. O. H. Whitten, 1976.

FOLSOM -- Fyer, Eleanor Elizabeth Folsom
     Folsoms in the War between the States, 1861-1865, collected and
     compiled in honor of Edward Penhallow Folsom, Pvt. C.S.A. Co. K.,
     3 Bn., 45 Miss. Inf. Alexandria. 1959.

FONTAINE -- Maury, Ann
     Memoirs of a Huguenot family translated and compiled from the original
     autobiography of Rev. James Fontaine; and other family manuscripts,
     comprising an original journal of travels in Virginia, New York, etc.,
     in 1715 and 1716. New York, N.Y.: G. P. Putnam's Sons, 19--.

FOOT -- Foote, Abram W.
     Foote family, comprising the genealogy and history of Nathaniel Foote,
     of Whethersfield, Conn., and his descendants; also a partial record of
     descendants of Pasco Foote of Salem, Mass., Richard Foote of Stafford
     County, Va., and John Foote of New York City. Rutland, Vt.: Marble
     City Press, The Tuttle Company, 1907.

FOOTE -- Davenport, John Scott
     Chronological data of Conrad Foutz, or Johannes Konrad Pfautz, as
     taken from various records and documents. Lexington. 1977.

FOOTE -- Foote, W. H.
     Sketches of Virginia. Philadelphia. 1850. 1856.

FORD -- Cain, Stith Malone
     A history of our Ford family of Virginia, Kentucky, Indiana, Mississippi,
     and Tennessee. Whitewater, Wisc. 1971.

FORD -- Ford and allied families for William Barney Ford of Norton, Virginia.
     1957.

FORD -- Wulfeck, Dorothy F.
     Ford families of Virginia and Kentucky. Naugatuck, Conn. 1974.

FORDON -- Gordon, Armistead C.
     Gordons in Virginia, etc. Hackensack, N.J. 1918.

FORREST'S HISTORY OF NORFOLK, VA. -- Forrest William
     Historical and Descriptive Sketches of Norfolk and Vicinity, etc.
     Philadelphia, Pa.: Lindsay and Blackiston, 1853.

FORSYTH -- de Fronsac, Forsyth
     Forsyth of Nydie, etc. New Market. 1888.

FOTHERGILL -- Fothergill, Augusta B.
    Wills of Westmoreland County, Virginia, 1654-1800. Richmond: Appeals
    Press, 1925.

FOULKE -- Foule, Roy A.
    Foulke family; one branch descended from James Fookes, who was already
    settled in Accomach County, Virginia by the year 1663. Bronxville,
    N. Y. 1972.

FOUST -- Faust, Bertha P. Y.
    Genealogy of the Foust, Grubb, Yeatts, Short and Tucker families of
    Pittsylvania County, Va. Richmond. 1976.

FOWLER -- Fowler, Grover Parsons
    The house of Fowler; a history of the Fowler families of the South,
    embracing descendants of John Fowler of Virginia and branches in
    North Carolina, Georgia, Tennessee, Kentucky, Alabama, Texas; also
    records of allied families ... Hickory, N.C. 1940.

FOWLER -- Arthur, Glenn Dora Fowler
    Annals of the Fowler family with branches in Virginia, North Carolina,
    South Carolina, Tennessee, Kentucky, Alabama, Mississippi, California
    and Texas. Austin, Tex.: Ben C. Jones & Co., 1901.

FOWLKES -- Burton, Violet Sibley
    Virginia was their home. Fort Smith, Ark. 1971.

FOX -- Cocke, Ellen M.
    Some Fox trails in Old Virginia; John Fox of King William County,
    ancestors, descendants, near kin. Richmond: Dietz Press, 1939.

FOX -- Fox, James W.
    Fox family. Richmond: Whittet & Shepperson, 1917.

FOX -- Fox, Jared Copeland
    The family history of Virginia Tortat Fox. Greensboro, N.C. 1968.

FOX -- King, George H. S.
    Memorial to Henry Fox, gentleman of 'Huntington', King William County,
    Virginia and some account of his descendants. Fredericksburg. 1940.

FOX -- Mitchell, Emma Fox
    Fox - Tuttle genealogical record. Alexandria. 1972.

FRAME -- Feighny, R. R.
    William and Susannah Frame of Pennsylvania, Virginia and Kentucky and
    some of their descendants. Topeka, Kans. 196-.

FRANCIS -- Dickson, Lura M.
    Descendants of Joseph Francis of Maryland and Virginia. Montezuma,
    Iowa. 1949.

FRANCISCO -- Port, Nannie F.
(The) romatic record of Peter Francisco "a revolutionary soldier."
Staunton: McClure, 1929.

FRANKLIN -- Thompson, Mrs. J. Frank
Court records of Chesterfield county, Virginia, pertaining to the
Franklin, Brintle, Bridgewater, Nunnally and related families.
Columbia, Mo. 1934.

FRASER -- Frazer, Margaret Gruse and Elva Frazer Shelton
Frazers, Baptists, Beatitues; descendants of James George Frazer
(1799-1878) of Campbell County, Virginia, and Highland County, Ohio.
Vandalia, Ohio. 1972.

FRASER -- Roystone, Agnes Angelica Fraser
The descendants of Benjamin Fraser and Angelica Farguharson.
Warrenton. 1974.

FRAVEL -- Huntsberry, Joanne M. Fravel
Fravel geneology (i.e. genealogy): with families of Hottle, Keller,
Tabler, Bloom, Chaney, & Mong: in Maryland, Virginia, and West
Virginia (Berk Co.). Lodge Forest, Md. 1981.

FREEMAN -- The Freeman family. Arlington: American Genealogical Research
Institute, 1973.

FREEMAN -- Hopkins, Garland Evans
Freeman forebears, being the history, genealogy, heraldy, homes and
traditions of the family of Freeman, and related families originating
in the original shires of James City and Charles River in Virginia.
Winchester. 1942.

FREY -- Lewis, Florence Virginia Fray
A history & genealogy of John Fray (Johannes Frey) of Culpeper County,
Virginia, his descendants & their related families; Aylor, Blankenbaker,
Carpenter, Clore, Crigler, Keyser, Marshall, Spotts, Yager, Weaver, &
many others. San Diego, Calif. 1958.

FRIEND -- Friend, Carter Watkins
The descendants of Captain Thomas Friends, 1700-1760, Chesterfield
County, Virginia. Alexandria. 1961.

FRIEND -- Olsen, Evelyn Guard
Indian blood. Parsons, W. Va.: McClain Print Co., 1967.

FRISTOE -- Alexander, Carrie Jenkins
Amos Fristoe of Stafford County, Virginia and Pettis County, Missouri
and his ancestors and descendants with allied families. Malta Bend,
Mo. 1968.

FRUM -- Stickney, Alpheus Beede
Lucy & Oliver, some West Virginia genealogy. Pittsburg. 1953.

FRY -- Bates, Robert L. and Harry H.
The story of Smithfield Middleway, Jefferson County, West Virginia.
Endicott, N.Y. 1958.

FRY -- Frye, George W.
Colonel Joshua Fry of Virginia and some of his descendants and
allied families. Cincinnati. 1966.

FRY -- Slaughter, Rev. P.
Memoir of Col. Joshua Fry, sometime professor in William and Mary
college, Virginia, and Washington's senior in command of Virginia
forces, 1754, etc., with an autobiography of his son, Rev. Henry Fry,
and a census of their descendants. Richmond: Randolph & English.
1880.

FUDGE -- Clark, Bertha Lewis
The Fudge family of Rockingham County, Wa., Alleghany Co., Va. and
monroe Co., W. Va. 1939.

FUGATT -- Faris, David
The Fugate family of Russell County, Virginia: a genealogy of the
descendants of Francis, Benjamin, Colbert, Zachariah, Henley &
William Fugate, settlers of Moccasin Valley from 1772. Baltimore:
Gateway Press, 1986.

FULENWIDER -- Bell, Raymond Martin
The Vollenweider family in America: Henry Fullenwider--Kentucky,
Jacob Fulle(n)wider--Maryland, Jacob Ful(l)lenwider--North Carolina,
Ulrich Ful(len)wider--Virginia. Washington, Pa. 1983.

FUNK -- Fazel, R. Gray
Some descendants of Jacob Funk (-1746) Strasburg, Virginia.
Petersburg. 1954.

FUNKHOUSER -- Bly, Daniel W.
Early Funkhouser pioneers and the descendants of Jacob Funkhouser, Jr.
Harrisonburg. 1974.

FUNKHOUSER -- Funkhouser, Jacob
A historical sketch of the Funkhouser family. Harrisonburg: Rockingham
Register Press, 1902.

FUNKHOUSER -- Zeutenhorst, Charlotte
Eight generations of Funkhouser from Isaac and Catherine (Boyer) of
Shenandoah and Augusta Counties of Virginia. Second edition with
insertions from 3d ed. to bring up-to-date as of March, 1975.
Tumwater, Wash. 1973.

FUSON -- Ferguson, Sylvia C. Fuson
The Virginia-Ohio Fusons: a genealogical history of the Virginia-Ohio
branch of the Fuson family in America. Oxford, Ohio: The Oxford
Press, 1939.

FUSON -- Ferguson, Sylvia Celicia Fuson
     The Virginia-Ohio Fusons: a genealogical (sic) history of the Virginia-
     Ohio branch of the Fuson family in America. Evansville, Ind. 1979.

GADD -- Gadd, Joseph Hayden
     Gadd genealogy. Princeton, W. Va. 1939

GAINES -- Furner, Evelyn P. Gain
     Descendants of Adam J, and Susan Fleming Gain, Arnold's Creek,
     Doddridge County, W. Va. Bristol, W. Va. 1980.

GAINES -- Gaines, L. P.
     The Gaines Genealogy. Our line from 1629 to 1918. Calhoun, Ga. 1918.

GAINES -- Gaines, Thomas R.
     Frances Gaines of Albemarle County, Va. and Elbert County, Georgia.
     Anderson, S.C. 1966.

GAMBILL -- Johnson, W. P.
     Gambill of Texas and Virginia. Denton, Tex. 1972.

GAMBLE -- Chrisman, Pattie Hamilton
     Gamble-Montgomery: history and genealogy and connected families.
     Moorefield, W. Va. 1979.

GANDY -- Gandee, Lee R.
     A brief sketch of the Gandee family of Gandeeville, West Virginia. 1949.

GANTHAM -- Bates, Robert L. and Harry H.
     The story of Smithfield Middleway, Jefferson County, West Virginia.
     Endicott, N.Y. 1958.

GARBER -- Garber, S. W.
     Family tree of Jacob Garber of Augusta County, Virginia and his
     descendants. Ottumwa, Iowa. 1919.

GARDNER -- Gardner, Mary Machin
     The Gardners of Virginia. Chicago, Ill. 1923.

GARDNER -- Gardner, Vernon Everett
     Descendants of Mr. and Mrs. Thomas Gardner of Roscommon, Ireland.
     Arlington, 1963.

GARNER -- Ritchie, Ruth and Sudie Rucker Wood
     Garner-Keene families of Northern Neck, Virginia. Charlottesville.
     1952.

GARNETT -- Garnett, James Mercer
Genealogy of the Mercer-Garnett family of Essex County, Virginia.
Supposed to be descended from the Garnetts of Lancashire, England.
Comp. from original records, and from oral and written statements
of members of the family. Richmond: Whittet & Shepperson, 1910.

GARNETT -- Garnett, William Edward and Emma Garnett McCoy
The Garnetts of Albemarle County, Virginia: James Muscoe and Cornelia
Wingfield Garnett, antecedents and descendants. 1963.

GARRETT -- Garrett, Rev. Clyde B. and Miss Mary E. Gaither
The genealogy in part of Stephen and William Garrett of Buckingham,
Virginia, with some historical data of the families. Marshall, Tex.:
Marshall News Messenger Pub. Co., 1926.

GARRETT -- Garrett, Hester Elizabeth
A book of Garrotts, descendants of John and Susanna Garrott of Amelia
County, Virginia including notes on the following--Agee, Bondurant,
Cayce, Faure, Featherstone, Garnett, Jones, and Waggener. Lansing,
Mich. 1980.

GARRETT -- Garrett, Hester Elizabeth
A book of Garretts: supplement number two: includes all known Garretts
not included in supplement number 1. Owensboro, Ky.: McDowell Pub.
1981.

GARRETT -- Gardner, Lester Durand
The Garrett family of Louisa County, Va. Williamsburg. 1932.

GARRISON -- Murphy, Marion Emerson
The ancestry and descendants of Marion Simon Garrison of Morgantown,
West Virginia, and allied families - Ammons, Kendrick, Metz, Murphy,
Tripp. San Diego, Calif. 1973.

GARWOOD -- Baldwin, Homer
Garwood genealogy. Manassas. 1968.

GARY -- Updike, Ethel Speer
Gary family of England to Virginia to South Carolina. Phoenix, Ariz.
1976.

GASTON -- Gee, Mary Gaston
The ancestry and descendants of Amzi Williford Gaston II (1841-1911)
of Spartanburg County, South Carolina. Charlottesville. 1944.

GATEWOOD -- Miller, Adrian Cather
Gaskins, Gatewood, George, Moncure, Oliver, and other related families,
as copied by William O. Moncure of Falls Church, Virginia, from Bible
records in his possession. Washington. 1977.

GATEWOOD -- Uhrbrock, Richard S.
Gatewood family of Essex County, Virginia. Palo Alto, Calif. 1979.

GATLIFF -- Black, Helen J.
Gatliff family, ancestors and descendants of Captain Charles Gatliff of Va. and Ky. Wichita, Kans. 1970.

GAY -- Montgomery, R. H.
Gay families of Augusta and Rockbridge Counties, Va. Cambridge, Mass. 1951.

GAYDEN -- Robertson, Amanda Blalock
The Gaydens and their descendants and allied families. Arlington. 1958.

GEE -- Gee, Wilson
The Gee family of Union County, South Carolina. Charlottesville: Jarman's Incorporated, 1935.

GEE -- Gee, Miss Maud
Ancestry and descendants of Edward C. Gee and his wife, Mary Frances Webb Gee, of Lunenburg Co., Va. This chart copied from the original November 24, 1936, by Wilson Gee. 1935.

GEE -- Fletcher, W. J.
The Gee family; descendants of Charles Gee (d. 1709) and Hannah Gee (d. 1728) of Virginia; with a chapter on the English background. Rutland, Vt.: Tuttle Publishing Co., Inc., 1937.

GEE -- Gee, Samuel Edward
The kin of Dr. Ned Gee, Lunenburg County, Virginia. Arlington. 1975.

GEORGE -- George, Thomas R.
George family record: descendants of Col. George of Virginia. Houston, Tex. 1978.

GIBBONS -- Archer, George W.
Every name index: "Gibbens-Butcher genealogy," by Alvaro F. Gibbens, Gordon B. Gibbens, publisher, Parkersburg, 1894. Arlington. 1982.

GIBBONS -- Gibbens, Alvaro Franklin
Gibbens-Butcher genealogy. Embracing also ... other pioneer families of Virginia who migrated west of the Alleghanies. Parkersburg. 1894.

FILBERT -- Gilbert, Dorthy Louise
The Gilberts of southeastern United States. Falls Church. 1979.

GILBERT -- Price, Mary F.
History of the Gilbert family of Maryland, Virginia, Kentucky, et al. 1948.

GILE -- Harley, Winifred J.
My great-grandmother, Judith Sargent Gile, 1804-1891. Lancaster. 1963.

GILES -- Fisher, Ruth Giles
Giles Walton and Cox families. Bassett: Bassett Printing Co., 1957.

GILES -- Vinton, John Adams
The Giles memorial, genealogical memoirs of the families bearing the names of Giles, Gould, Holmes, Jennison, Leonard, Lindall, Curwen, Marshall, Robinson, Sampson, and Webb. Boston, Mass.: Dutton & Son Printers, 1864.

GILL -- Gill, Thomas Franklin
History of the Gill family. Annandale. 1984.

GILLENWATERS -- Gillenwater, Joseph R.
The Gillenwater family of southwest Virginia. Charlottesville. 1972.

GILLIAM -- Gilliam, Robert Skelton
The Richard Davenport Gilliam (1855-1935) and Irene Jones Gilliam (1864-1926) family. Charlottesville. 1985.

GILLILAND -- Gilliland, Lyle Willis
Willis and Gilliland families of Hanover County, Virginia, Rutherford County, North Carolina, Pendleton County, South Carolina, Brown County, Ohio, Putnam County, Illinois, Douglas County, Oregon. Eugene, Oregon. 1979.

FILMORE -- Gi;;more, William Bruce
A De Vault genealogy, with Gillmore and Hunt supplements. Arlington. 1954.

GLASCOCK -- Glassco, Lawrence A.
The Glas(s)cocks of England and America: Glas(s)cocks of England prior to 1643 and of America after 1643. Alexandria. 1984.

GISH -- Hamaker, J. I.
Matthias Gish of White Oak. Lynchburg. 1940.

GIST -- Gee, Wilson
The Gist family of South Carolina and its Maryland antecedents. Charlosttesville: Jarman's Inc., 1934.

GIVEN -- Morris, Alfred N.
A genealogy of the Given family, with historical sketches, 1570-1942. Huntington, W. Va. 1942.

GIVENS -- Givens, Dorothy Hall
Givens-Hall family history from pre-revolutionary times to 1970; including such as Alexander, Bowman, Black, Chapman, French, Green, Johnston, Phlegar, Ross, Snidow, Stafford, Welker and others. Radford: Commonwealth Press, 1971.

GIVENS -- Givens, Dorothy H.
    More Daniel Givens descendants: supplement I to A Givens-Hall family
    history from pre-revolutionary times to 1970. Radford: Commonwealth
    Print, 1977.

GLASS -- Foote, William Henry
    Genealogy of the Glass family in Virginia, also of the families of
    Vance, Hoge, White. 1948.

GLASSBURN -- David Glassburn, Virginia pioneer, his ten children & related
    families: Carpenter, Persinger, Pottenger, Jacobs, Robinson, and others.
    Los Angeles, Calif.: Ward Ritchie Press, 1964.

FLASSELL -- Hayden, Rev. Horace Edwin
    Virginia genealogies. A genealogy of the Glassell family of Scotland
    and Virginia, also of the families of Ball, Brown, Bryan, Conway, Daniel,
    Ewell, Holladay, Lewis, Littlepage, Moncure, Peyton, Robinson, Scott,
    Taylor, Wallace, and others, of Virginia and Maryland. Wilkes,Barre,
    Pa. 1891.

GLEN -- Miller, Lucile Glenn, and Jeanette May Christopher
    Glenn and kin: descendants of James Glen of Hanover County, Virginia,
    1717-1974. Batesville, Miss. 1975.

GLENGARRY McDONALDS -- Williams, Mrs. Flora McDonald
    The Glengarry McDonalds of Virginia. Louisville: George G. Fetter
    Company, 1911.

GLICK -- Glick, Joseph M. Family Historical Committee
    Across the years; a story of and a stream through the Glick family in
    the Shenandoah Vellye of Virginia. Charlotte, N.C.: Delmar Print
    Co., 1959.

GOCHENOUR -- Evans, Robert Lee
    History of the Descendants of Jacob Gochenour. Boyce: Carr Publishing
    Co., 1977.

GODDARD -- Goddard, Charles Austin
    The Samuel Goddard families. Fayetteville, W. Va. 1935.

GODDIN -- Vaughan, Arnette Goodin
    Genealogy of the Goddin family. Richmond: Lewis Printing Co., 1923.

GOFF -- Barnes, John Philip
    The history and genealogy of the Nathan P. Goff family of Randolph
    County, West Virginia, Delaware County, Indiana, and Madison County,
    Iowa. St. Louis, Mo. 1972.

GOFF -- Goff, Thomas T.
    Ancestors and Descendants of John Goff, Jr. of Amherst County, Virginia.
    Wodland Hill, Calif. 1975.

GOFF -- Lockhart, Roy L.
The Goff family. Parkersburg, W. Va. 1974.

GOFORTH -- Goforth, George T.
The Goforth genealogy. Annandale. 1971.

GOOCH -- Sweeney, Mary A.
Gooch families of Virginia. 1948.

GOOD -- Goode, G. Brown
Virginia cousins: a study of the ancestry and posterity of John Goode
of Whitby, a Virginia colonist of the seventeenth century, with notes
upon related families, a key to Southern genealogy and a history of
the English surname Gode, Goad, Goode or Good from 1148 to 1887.
Richmond: J. W. Randolph & English, 1887.

GOOD -- Hulvey, June Good
History of the William Good family. Bridgewater: Beacon Press, 1976.

GOOD -- Winfield, Marshall
Pioneer families of Franklin County, Virginia. Berryville: Chesapeake
Book Co., 1964.

GOODBAR -- Clark, Carmen E.
Goodbars I found, 1774-1978: descendants of Joseph (1) and William (2)
of Rockbridge. Lexington. 1980.

GOODE -- Goode, G. Brown
Virginia cousins. Bridgewater: C. J. Carrier Co., 1963.

GOODE -- Virginia Cousins -- Goode, G. Brown
A Study of the Ancestry and Posterity of John Goode of Whitby.
Richmond. MDCCCXXXXVII.

GOODFELLOW -- Parker, Lois Goodfellow
Goodfellow; a family history of the Ira Goodfellow family. Arlington.
1974.

GOODWIN -- Goodwin, John S.
Christmas questions for the Goodwins of Virginia. Chicago, Ill. 1896.

GOODWIN -- Godwin, John S.
Goodwin Families in America. Supplement William and Mary College
Quarterly, October, 1899. Williamsburg.

GOODWIN -- Genealogical chart of the Goodwin and Hiter families. Pulaski. 1948.

GORDON -- Gordon, Alexander
Some colonial families of Virginia. Baltimore. 1939.

GORDON -- Gordon, Armistead C.
Gordons in Virginia, with notes on Gordons of Scotland and Ireland.
Hackensack, N.J. 1918.

GORDON -- Gordon, Armistead C.
Colonel James Gordon of Lancaster (1717-1768). Read at the presentation
by his descendants to the county of Lancaster, Virginia, of a portrait
of Col. James Gordon, July 21, 1913. Staunton. 1913.

GORDON -- Hodges, Frances Beal Smith
Gordons of Spotsylvania County, Virginia, with notes on Gordons of
Scotland. Wichita Falls, Tex.: Wichita Multigraphing Company, 1934.

GORDON -- Jones, Christine
Col. James Gordon, merchant of Lancaster County, Virginia. Lancaster:
Mary Ball Washington Museum and Library, 1983.

GOSE -- Gose, George
Pioneers of the Virginia Bluegrass (and their descendants). Radford:
Commonwealth Print, 1968.

GOTTWALD -- Robert, Joseph C.
Gottwald family history: the first century of the Gottwalds and
Freyfogles in Richmond, Virginia, 1822-1922. Richmond. 1984.

GOULDMAN -- Yates, Helen Kay
Thomas Gouldman of Essex County, Va., and some of his descendants.
Mechanicsville. 1972.

GRADY -- Grady, H. Gamble
The John Grady I descendants of Virginia, West Virginia; genealogical
record. Laguna Hills, Calif. 1974.

GRAFFENRIED -- The De Graffenried family scrap book, 1191-1956, seven
hundred and sixty five years. Charlottesville: University of Virginia
Press, 1958.

GRAHAM -- Barr, Lockwood
... Graham family of Virginia and Kentucky; descendants of Christopher
Graham born in Scotland or Ireland, who settled first in Pennsylvania;
and then migrated to Virginia with his family before 1740. Pelham Manor,
N.Y. 1941.

GRANBERY -- Granbery, Julian Hastings
John Granbery, Virginia. New York, N.Y. 1953.

GRANT -- Heller, Dick D.
Grant family of Fauquier County, Va., Fleming Co., Ky., Rush, Wabash,
and Jasper Counties, Ind. in the 18th, 19th, and 20th century. Decatur,
Ind. 1974.

GRANT -- Lockwood, Patricia W.
   The Grant, Emory, Martin, LaHay family, 1725-1911. Burlington, W. Va.
   1984.

GRAVATT -- Fox, Sallie Gwathmey Gravatt
   The Gravatt family of the Rappahannock Valley in Virginia, 1740-1946.
   Richmond. 1946.

GRAVES -- The Graves family of Virginia, being a transcript of an unpublished
   manuscript now in Grosvenor Library, Buffalo, New York. With index
   and supplements.

GRAVES -- Graves, Charles Marshall
   The Graves family of Eastern Virginia, 1608-1936. 1936.

GRAVES -- Graves, Kenneth Vance
   Robert Graves of Anson County, N.C. and Chesterfield County, S.C.:
   ancestors and descendants (ca. 1580-1979): a branch of the descendants
   of Capt. Thomas Graves, 1608 immigrant to Jamestown, Va. Baltimore:
   Gateway Press, 1980.

GRAVES -- Graves, Louise
   Graves: twelve generations, some descendants and kin: Captain Thomas
   Graves, progenitor, ancient planter in Colony of Virginia, 1608 to and
   including Henry Lee Graves, Dallas, Texas, 1977. Dallas, Tex. 1977.

GRAY -- Goodnight, Gertrude Hamilton
   An Old Dominion genealogical line. 1938.

GRAYSON CO. -- Nuckolls, Benjamin Floyd
   Pioneer Settler of Grayson County, Virginia. Bristol, Tenn.: The King
   Printing Co., 1914.

GREEN -- Bellis, Genevieve Hoehn
   Our ancestors: Greens, Wathens, Byrnes, Hoehns, and others. Arlington.
   1975.

GREEN -- Dade, Thomas Green
   The Green family of Virginia and Kentucky. 1969.

GREEN -- Green, Sylvester
   Greens from Westmoreland County, Virginia: with sketches and index of
   interrelated families, especially Spilman, Hudson, Barham, Owen, Chaplin,
   Perkins, Short, Reese, and Howell. Greenville, N.C. 1975.

GREEN -- Lewis, A. A.
   The Green family of Culpeper County, Virginia ... 1939-1940.
   Fredericksburg. 1940.

GREENLEE -- Greenlee, Ralph S.
Genealogy of the Greenlee families in America, Scotland, Ireland and England ... Also genealogical data on the McDowells of Virginia and Kentucky. Chicago, Ill. 1908.

GREENLEE -- Greenlee, William Clarkson
The descendants of Edward Greenlee of West Virginia. Winter Park, Fla.

GREENWOOD -- Greenwood, Frederick
Greenwood genealogies, 1154-1914; the ancestry and descendants of Thomas Greenwood, of Newton, Massachusetts; Nathaniel and Samuel Greenwood, of Boston, Massachusetts; John Greenwood, of Virginia, and many later arrivals in America. Also the early history of the Greenwoods in England, and the arms they used. New York, N.Y.: The Lyons Genealogical Company, 1914.

GREEVER -- Greever, John
History and genealogy of the Greever/Griever/Greaver family of Virginia. Clremeont, Calif. 1978.

GREGG -- Ewers, Dorothy W.
Some Gregg records. Records of birth, marriages and deaths, etc. of the members of Fairfax Monthly Meeting at Waterford, Loudoun County, Va., 1740-1880. Crete, Ill. 1963.

GREGG -- Gilchrist, Cleo Gregg Johnson
William Grigg I, immigrant to the Virginia Colony: 340 years of his descendants, 1640-1980. Boise, Idaho. 1980.

GREGG -- Kendall, Hazel M. M.
This book records the descendants of Wm. Gregg the Friend immigrant to Delaware, 1682 from which nucleus disseminated nests of Greggs to Pa., Va., and N.C. Anderson, Ind. 1944.

GREGORIE -- Wilsom, Carrie Price
Gregorie family of Middlesex County, Virginia, and Charleston, S.C. 1925.

GREGORY -- The maternal ancestors and kindred of Margaret Jane Crocker. Published in the Virginia society quarterly. Portsmouth: W. A. Fiske's Printery, 1914.

GRESHAM -- Jones, W. Macfarlane
Gresham family from Edward Gresham, England, 1312-1400, to Thomas Gresham, Virginia, 1923. Richmond: Brown-Neill Printing Co., 1923.

GRIFFITH-MERIWETHER -- Griffith, W. R.
The Record of Nicholas Meriwether of Wales and descendants in Virginia and Maryland. St. Louis. 1899.

GRIMES -- Gottschalk, Katherine Cox
Grimes family of Virginia. 1947.

GRIMMETT -- Price, David L.
   The Grimmetts of Virginia of the Revolutionary War era and their
   descendants. Brentwood, Tenn. 1980.

GRISSOM -- Grissom-Price family of Virginia and Ohio.

GRUBB -- Wanger, Geo. F. P.
   The Grubb families of America; Christian Grubb of Va. Pottstown, Pa.
   1913.

GUNNELL -- Richards, Indi Anna Leona
   Information pertaining to some members of the Gunnell family of Virginia.
   Middletown, Conn. 1962.

GURLEY -- Simmons, Julia Clare
   The Gurley-Simmons families as related to the Spotswood-Moore-West-
   Dadndridge families of Virginia. Houston, Tex. 1968.

GUTHRIE -- Dunn, Harriet H.
   Records of the Guthrie family of Pennsylvania, Connecticut, and Virginia,
   with ancestry of those who have intermarried with the family. Chicago,
   Ill. 1898.

GUTHRIE -- Guthrie, Joseph A.
   Early Virginia Guthries and their Kentucky descendants. Kansas City,
   Mo. 1946.

GUTHRIE -- Guthrie, Laurence R.
   American Guthrie and allied families; lineal representations of the
   colonial Guthries of Pennsylvania, Connecticut, Maryland, Delaware,
   Virginia, North and South Carolina, some post-revolutionary emigrants
   and of some allied families. Chambersburg, Pa.: Kerr Printing Company,
   1933.

GUTHRIE -- Guthrie, Laurence Rawlin
   American Guthrie and allied families: Lineal representations of the
   colonial Guthries of Pennsylvania, Connecticut, Maryland, Delaware,
   Virginia, North and South Carolina, some post-revolutionary emigrants,
   and of some allied families. Baltimore: Gateway Press, 1985.

GUYNES -- Sands, John Alexander
   Guynes. Alexandria: John A. Sands, 1976.

GWIN -- Gwin, Jessa B.
   History of the Gwin family; (Gwin, Gwinn, Gwyn, Gwynn, Guin, Wynn,
   Wynne). Fairfax. 1961.

GWINN -- Feigley, Dorothea Gwinn
   Gwinn; family history of Gwinn and allied lines, 1725-1959. Oakton.
   1959.

GWYN -- Gwin, Jesse Blaine
    History of the Gwin family (Gwin, Gwinn, Gwyn, Gwynn, Gwynne, Guin,
    Gwuinn, Wynn, Wynne). Fairfax. 1961.

HACKLEY -- Hackley, Woodford B.
    Notes on the descendants of John Hackley of Old Rappahannock and Essex
    Counties, Virginia, including sidelights and a suggestion as to John's
    English ancestry. 1968.

HADEN -- Haden, Dorothy K.
    John Haden of Virginia, his parents, and some of his descendants,
    compiled from family records of descendants and other reliable
    sources. Chicago, Ill.: Adams Press, 1968.

HADLEY -- Headlee, A. J. W.
    The Headlee family: five brothers and two uncles, John Headlee,
    Ephraim Headlee, Elisha Headlee, Joshua M. Headlee, Thomas Headlee,
    Major Francis Headley, Joseph Headley. Morgantown, W. Va. 1980.

HAILE -- Green, Dorothy C.
    Haile, Ferguson, Chestnut, Owens, Howard, Wills, tombstones & records -
    Virginia, South Carolina, Georgia. 1958.

HAINES -- Haines, John Wesley
    Richard Haines and his descendants. Boyce. 1961.

HAIRSTON -- Hairston, Elizabeth Seawell
    The Hairstons and Penns and their relations. Roanoke: Walters Printing
    & Manufacturing Co., 1940.

HAISELUP -- Descendants of Elijah Haiselup and Eleanor Eberhardt of state
    sic Virginia, Ohio and Bartholomew County, Indiana. 1978.

HALBERT -- Waddell, Florence and Kenneth
    Joel Halbert and his descendants, being a historical and genealogical
    account of Joel Halbert, immigrant to Essex County, Virginia, about
    1700-1710 A.D. and his many descendants now scattered throughout all
    America. Washington. 1947.

HALE -- Crowe, Maude
    Descendants from first families of Virginia and Maryland: a family
    history and genealogy covering 350 years, 1620-1970. Fordsville,
    Ky. 1978.

HALE -- Hale, Nathaniel Claiborne
    Roots in Virginia; an account of Captain Thomas Hale, Virginia
    frontiersman, his descendants and related families. With genealogies
    and sketches of the families of Hale, Saunders, Lucke, Claiborne,
    Lacy, Tobin and contributing ancestral lines. Philadelphia, Pa. 1948.

HALE -- Rich, Anna Gleaves
Hale Family Chart. Wytheville.

HALE -- Whitley, Edythe Rucker
Lineage of Mrs. E. P. McKellar through the Hale family of Virginia
and Tennessee. Nashville, Tenn. 1945.

HALEY -- Haley, Alex
Roots. Garden City, N.Y.: Doubleday, 1976.

HALEY -- Haley, Eva F.
Haley and related families. Radford: Commonwealth Press, 1979.

HALIFAX -- Carrington, Mrs. Wirt Johnson
A History of Halifax County, Virginia. Richmond: Appeals Press,
Inc., 1924.

HALL -- Greene, Anne J.
The Hall family of Virginia. 1950.

HALL -- Hartley, Elizabeth J. H.
Descendants of Moses Hall, John Doudna and Benjamin Hall (Quaker fams.
of Belmont County, Ohio, from Va., and N.C.). Denver, Colo. 1958.

HALL -- Marvin F.
History of the Hall - Ayers - Holland family: Virginia, North Carolina,
Georgia, Tennessee, Texas. Scarsdale, N.Y. 1976.

HALL -- Parrish, Verle Hamilton
Who's who in my Hall family (of Virginia, North Carolina and Kentucky).
Farmington, Utah. 1982.

HALL -- Williams, Tasker H.
Genealogy of Thomas Hall, his children and grandchildren. With added
notes, pictures and documents on the Halls, Regers, and other early
settlers of Volga, Barbour County, West Virginia. Parsons, W. Va.:
McClain Print Co., 1967.

HALTERMAN -- Grady, H. Gamble
Ancestors and descendants of Christian Halterman of Hardy County,
Virginia, now West Virginia, genealogical record. Laguna Hills, Calif.
1973.

HALTERMAN -- Wertz, Mary A.
History of the Halterman (Holdiman, Holeman, Haldiman) Ross, Cullers,
O'Flaherty fams. of the Shenandoah Valley, Va. Leesburg. 1973.

HAMAKER -- Hamaker, John Irvin
Our immigrant ancestor, Adam Hamaker, and his family. Lynchburg. 1954.

HAMILTON -- Baskervill, Patrick Hamilton
The Hamiltons of Burnside, North Carolina, and their ancestors and
descendants. Richmond: W. E. Jones' Sons, Inc., 1916.

HAMILTON -- Diehl, George West
The saga of Hamilton's school house. Lexington. 1956.

HAMILTON -- Donnelly, Mary Louise
Imprints, 1608-1980: Hamilton, allied families. Burke. 1980.

HAMILTON -- Genealogical tables of the descendants of John Hamilton of "Locust
Hill," Lexington, Virginia, born 1789 - died 1825. 1933.

HAMLETT -- Baldridge, Blanche Hamlett
My Virginia kin; comprising the Hamlett, Witt, Giles, Wills, Eubank-
Fortune, Mullenix, Lynchard, Talbot and Hight families ... Loving
family. Strawberry Point, Iowa: Press-Journal Pub. Co., 1958.

HAMM -- Whitley, Edythe Rucker
Ham, Hamm, Farneyhough, Farneyhow, Warren, Lucas, Thrift and some
related families of Virginia. 1967.

HAMMER -- Boggs, Else Byrd
The Hammers and allied families; with their family circles centering
in Pendleton County, West Virginia. Harrisonburg: Joseph K. Ruebush
Co., 1950.

HAMMOND -- Hammond, Fiske E.
Hammond genealogy ... descended from Peter Hamman. Roanoke. 1919.

HAMNER -- Hamner, Jerome H.
The descendants of James and Sarah Hamner of Mecklenburg County,
Virginia. Little Rock, Ark. 1974.

HAMNER -- Hooker, Ruth N.
The Hamner family of Albemarle County, Virginia and Tennessee. Memphis,
Tenn. 1949.

HAMPDEN-SYDNEY -- Morrison, A. J.
College of Hampden-Sydney. Dictionary of Biography, 1776-1825.
Hampden-Sydney.

HAMPSHIRE -- Maxwell, Hu and H. L. Swisher
History of Hampshire County, W. Va. Morgantown, W. Va.: A. B.
Boughner, 1897.

HAMPTON -- Hampton family of Virginia, North and South Carolina & Kentucky.

HAMPTON -- Meynard, Virginia Gurley
The venturers: the Hampton, Harrison, and Earle families of Virginia, South Carolina and Texas. Easley, S.C.: Southern Historical Press, 1981.

HAMPTON -- Robarts, William Hugh
Two southern families; place of the Hamptons and the Lees in history. The men on horseback. 1893.

HANCOCK -- Bloore, Helen L.
A genealogical record of the descendants of Hancock, Cofer, Jones, Massie families of Virginia and Kentucky. Glendale, Calif. 1962.

HANCOCK -- Hancock, Clifton Dillon
Hancock family history: some descendants of John Hancock & Frances Farrar. Annandale. 1981.

HANCOCK -- Hancock, Richard Ramsey and Walter
Some descendants of John Hancock (1733-1802) of Goochland, Fluvanna and Patrick counties, Virginia. Woodbury, Tenn. 1938.

HANCOCK -- Hancock, Richard R.
John Hancock of Virginia, and his descendants. Chattanooga, Tenn. 1957.

HANCOCK -- Marshall, Thomas Edward
Some descendants of Anthony Hancock and son Martin Hancock of Red House, Virginia. Radford. 1984.

HANDCOCK -- St. Amand, Jeanette C.
William Handcock of Virginia and Craven County, North Carolina. Wilmington, N.C. 1960.

HANES -- Foster, Edith
John Hanes (died Tyler County, Va., 1815) and some of his descendants ... Elburn, Ill. 1963.

HANKS -- Baber, Adin (with a number of Hanks descendants)
The Hanks family of Virginia and westward; a genealogical record from the early 1600's, including charts of families in Arkansas, the Carolinas, Georgia, Illinois, Indiana, Iowa, Kentucky, Missouri, Oklahoma, Ohio, Pennsylvania, and Texas. Kansas, Ill. 1865.

HANSARD -- Hansard, Sam L.
Descendants of John Hansard of Amherst County, Virginia, 1766-1976. Knoxville, Tenn. 1977.

HANSFORD -- Hansford, Thelma Ironmonger
Hansford and kinsmen, 1642-1957; a family history. Seaford. 1958.

HANSFORD -- Torrence, Clayton
An account of the descent of the Hansford family from John Hansford, of York County, Va., to his grandson William Hansford, of Spotsylvania and Culpeper Counties, Va., with notes on the Sallis and Foliott connections. Richmond. 1949.

HANSON -- Hanson, Raymond A.
These Irishmen called Hanson, 1750-1976; an accounting of the descendants of John Hanson of early colonial Virginia. Bloomington, Minn. 1976.

HARBOR -- Williams, Louis J.
The Harbours in America(Harber, Harbor, Harbur, Harbour, Arbour): with brief sketches of some early Virginia related families--Arrowsmith, Dalton, Fuson, Hall, Houchins, Pedigo, Pilson, Reynolds, Ross, Spurlock, Turman, Witt. Lubbock, Tex. 1982.

HARDAWAY -- Carlisle, Maxine Fallers and Denzil Lark Carlisle
The descendants of John Clack Hardaway and Mary Hardaway Harwell of Virginia, Chambliss and Sarah Carlisle of North Carolina. San Francisco. 1958.

HARDAWAY -- Hubert, Sarah Donelson
Thomas Hardaway of Chesterfield County, Virginia, and his descendants. Richmond: Whittet & Shepperson, 1906.

HARDIN -- Jones, Clement R.
The Hardin family; early genealogy and historical notes including family traditions and miscellaneous incidents and stories concerning the family. Morgantown, W. Va. 193-.

HARDIN -- Wulfeck, Dorothy Ford
Hardin and Garding of Virginia and Kentucky. Naugatuck, Conn. 1963.

HARDING -- Waring, Lucy L.
Hardings of Northumberland County, Virginia and their related families; mini-history, homes and churches. Wicomico Church. 1971.

HARDY -- Hardy, Stella P.
Colonial Families of the Southern States of America. New York, N.Y. 1911.

HARGRAVE -- Hargrave, Harry S.
A brief history of the Quakers in England and Virginia and the Hargrave family, 1634-1939 ... Los Angeles, Calif.: William J. Dankers Company, 1939.

HARGRAVE -- Hargrave, Helen M.
Hargrave forebears: a genealogy and history of some descendants of Richard Hargrave, Sr. of Lower Norfolk County, Va., 1634-1968 with notes on the English family background of Richard and on other Hargrave family lines in America. Walnut Creek, Calif. 1968.

HARLESS -- Pritchard, Jacob Le Roy
Lineage of Philip Harless, 1716-1772, and his wife, Anna Margaretta
(Preisch) Harless, 1718-1784; an immigrant family from the Rhine
Palatinate to Virginia 1738. San Jose, Calif. 1949.

HARLESS -- Pritchard, J. L.
Harless genealogy, John Philip and Anna Margaretha (Preiss) Harless;
pioneers in western Virginia and some of their descendants. Cupertino,
Calif. 1962.

HARLOE -- Harloe, Dr. Charles Bruce
Harloe-Kelso genealogy of the descendants of John William Harloe and
James Kelso, from the beginning of their lineages in this country to
the present time, with a number of allied families and many historical
facts. Winchester: Pifer Printing Co., 1943.

HARLOW -- Harlow, Michael G.
The Harlow family in Virginia. Louisa. 197-.

HARLOW -- King, Martha Eheart
Harlow-Harlowe. Manassas. 1980.

HARMAN -- Harman, John Newton, Jr.
Harman genealogy (Southern Branch), with Biographical Sketches, 1700-1924.
Richmond: W. C. Hill Printing Co., 1925.

HARMAN -- Harman, John William
Harman-Harmon Genealogy and Biography, with Historical Notes, 19 B.C.
to 1928 A.D. Parsons, W. Va. 1928.

HARMON -- Harmon album. Harman, W. Va. 1965.

HARMON -- The remarks, on Harmon history, of Artemas C. Harmon, read at the
Harmon reunion held at Harman, West Virginia, on August 27th, 1927. 1927.

HARPER -- Boland, Micajah
Sarah Harper and her descendants, the Terrys. London Bridge: Dietz
Press, 1958.

HARPER -- Grant, Howard B.
Henry Harper of Randolph County, Virginia. Philippi, W. Va. 1934.

HARPER -- O'Beirne, Frank
The Harpers of Virginia, West Virginia, and Mississippi. Arlington. 1982.

HARPER -- Walter, Alice G.
Harper family of St. Brides Parish, Norfolk County, Va., 1756-1801.
Virginia Beach. 1964.

HARPINE -- Harpine, Jacob William
Philip Harpine and Catherine and their descendants. Staunton: McClure
Printing Co., 1952.

HARRACH -- Preston L.
   The discovery of County Harrach's masterpiece, the ruby vases. Leesburg.
   1928.

HARRINGTON -- Bagley, David Harrington
   The ancestry of Marie Louise Harrington and her Bagley descendants.
   Vienna. 1983.

HARRINGTON -- Harrington, James Robert
   A family tree. Arlington. 1975.

HARRIS -- Harris family of Virginia from 1611-1914. Data gathered and
   printed for Thomas Henry Harris of Fredericksburg, Va. 1914.

HARRIS -- A chart of some of the descendants of Captain Thomas Harris of
   Henrico County, who came to Virginia in 1611, with an appendix of
   Illustrative documents. Richmond: W. E. Jones, Printers, 1893.

HARRSION -- The Harrison family. Arlington: American Genealogical Research
   Institute, 1972.

HARRISON -- Benjamin Harrison of Berkeley, Walter Cocke of Surry; family
   recorss (sic) I. Tappahannock. 1962.

HARRISON -- Bundick, Katherine Epps
   Harrison family genealogy, 1673-1976. South Hill. 1977.

HARRISON -- Harrison, Mrs. Kate Estess Du Val
   Family tree of the Harrisons of James River. 1910.

HARRISON -- Harrison, Kate Du Val
   Randolphs of Virginia. 1928.

HARRISON -- Harrison, Henry Tazewell
   A brief history of the first Harrisons of Virginia, descendants of
   Cuthbert Harrison, esq. of Ancaster, England, from A.D. 16600 to
   A.D. 1915. Washington: National Capital Press, 1915.

HARRISON -- Harrison, J. Houston
   ... Settlers by the long grey trail, some pioneers to old Augusta
   County, Virginia, and their descendants, of the family of Harrison
   and allied lines. Dayton: Joseph K. Ruebush Company, 1935.

HARRISON -- Warner, Pauline Pearce
   Benjamin Harrison of Berkeley; Walter Cocke of Surry; family records.
   Tappahannock. 1962.

HARRISON -- Williams, Frank L.
   John Garrison of 96 District, South Carolina and Botetourt County,
   Virginia, between 1771 and 1808. Hot Springs, Ark. 1970.

HART -- Frame, Katherine Hart
The Harts of Randolph: or, Mostly descendants of Edward and Daniel Hart, sons of John Hart the Signer, with some allied families. Parsons, W. Va.: McClain Print, 1976.

HART -- McIver, Helen H.
Hart family of Virginia. 1938.

HARTMAN -- Shank, Merna B.
The Hartman history; descendants of Samuel Hartman. Harrisonburg: Park View Press, 1959.

HARVEY -- Creecy, John Harvie
The Harvie family of Virginia. Richmond. 1949.

HARVEY -- Shelburne, Robert Craig
The Harvey family of Montgomery County, Virginia. 1935.

HARVIE -- Harvie, L. E. and J.s., and Mrs. Carter W. Wormeley. Richmond.

HARWOOD -- Atkins, Susan W., William Rogers Herod, and Maud Harrington Darrach
Hereward record and papers, 1620-1940; 329 years of history and genealogy. The first record of the part played by the Harwood group of Virginia in the winning of the West for America, compiled from English and American historical sources, government records, state histories and records, county histories and records, court records from ten states, diaries and private papers. Greenfield, Ind.: WM. Mitchell Printing Co., 1940.

HATHAWAY -- McComb, Virginia M.
Hathaway and Lawson families of Virginia. Chambersburg, Pa, 1950.

HATCHER -- Ackerly, Mary D.
"Our kin"; the genealogies of some of the early families who made history in the founding and development of Bedford County, Va. Lynchburg. 1930.

HATCHETT -- Prince Edward County, Virginia. A short narrative of the life of John Hatchett ... Farmville.

HAUGHT -- Clark, Jean Marshall
The Indian Creek community and the Haught family. Grantsville, W. Va.: Grantsville Print. Co., 1983.

HAWES -- Ryland, Elizabeth Hawes
Hawes of Caroline County, Virginia. 1947.

HAWKINS -- Fedorchak, Catherine F.
Hawkins family: material on Rev. Wm. Hawkins ... Joshua Hawkins, of Marion County, W. Va. ... also misc. Hawkins material from Maryland sources. Gary, Ind. 1959.

HAWKINS -- Wulfeck, Dorothy Ford
Hawkins of Virginia, the Carolinas, and Kentucky; court records, queries, brief lineage, genealogical notes. Naugatuck, Conn. 1962.

HAWORTH -- Haworth, James R.
George Haworth and some of his descendants with some memoranda concerning several families connected with the Haworths by marriage. Huntington, W. Va. 1965.

HAYDEN -- Hayden, Horace E.
Virginia Genealogies, etc. Wilkes-Barre, Pa. 1891.

HAYES -- Hathaway, Bernice F.
Hayes-Maddock-Stubbs and allied lines; many of the ancestors and descendants of Bailey Hayes and Mary Stubbs, married ... 1802. Early Pennsylvania, Virginia, Maryland, North Carolina, Georgia and Ohio lines. Denver. 1969.

HAYES -- Repass, Mary Eva Berry
The Hayes family of Lawrence County, Kentucky: descendants of Bazeal Hayes. Fredericksburg. 1978.

HAYMOND -- Haymond, Henry
The Haymond family. Clarksburg, W. Va. 1903.

HAYNE -- Campbell, Julia Anna Francis Courtenay
The Hayne family of South Carolina and some relatives in these lines: Martin, Davidge, Barnwell, Courtenay, Beattie, Adams, Hazelhurst, Black, Hasell, Davis, Foster, Houston, McIver, Woodward, Baldwin, Brevard, Trapier, Motte, Shubrick, Perry, Swinton (and) Splatt. Charlottesville. 1956.

HAYNES -- Carrier, Armetha Haines
Samuel Haines of Hampshire County, Virginia, and his descendants. Annandale. 1982.

HAYNIE -- Rossman, Loyce Haynie
A Haynie genealogy: their 1650 Virginia roots, 1839 Texas trunk, nine limbs, many branches, twigs and some leaves. Fredericksburg. 1963.

HAZEN -- Hazen, James K.
Genealogy of the Hazen family: eight American generations. Richmond: Whittet & Shepperson, 1892.

HEADLEE -- Headlee, Alvah John Washington
The Headlee family. Morgantown, W. Va. 1980.

HEADLEE -- Headlee, W. W.
Headlee and allied family records. Added to and arranged in this workbook by Alvah J. W. Headlee. Morgantown, W. Va. 1973.

HEATWOLE -- Heatwole, E. A.
A History of the Heatwole Family. Dale Enterprise, Va. 1882.

HEATWOLE -- Heatwole, Ralph F.
Enos and Clara (Shank) Heatwole family. Dayton, Va. 1973.

HEAVENER -- Bodell, Dorothy H.
The Heavener family of Montgomery County, Virginia, 1797-1982.
Blacksburg. 1983.

HECK -- Heck, Arch Oliver
Descendants of Daniel David Heck, a settler in the lower part of the
Shenandoah River Valley near the Virginia Natural Bridge during the
latter part of 1700's. Columbus, Ohio. 1970.

HECKERT -- Heckert, C. W.
The German-American diary: notes of related historical interest,
including translated excerpts from the Wiederholdt diary, American
Revolutionary War. Buckhannon, W. Va. 1980.

HEDDERICH -- Hedrick, Ralph W.
Moses Hedrick: his ancestors and descendants, 1750-1973. Parkersburg,
W. Va. 1973.

HEIN -- Stapleton, Harriet L.
Hein family history. Conrad Hein and descendants. Arlington. 1970.

HELMICK -- Helmick, Kyle
The Helmick family history. Buckhannon, W. Va. 1984.

HELMS -- Helms, Samuel King
The Helm family of Virginia. Baltimore: Gateway Press, 1985.

HENCKEL -- New Market, Virginia, imprints, 1806-1876. A check-list, edited
by Lester J. Cappon and Ira V. Brown, with the co-operation of the
Historical records survey, Service division, Work Projects Administration ..
ed. Lester Jesse Cappon. Charlottesville: Alderman library, 1942.

HENCKEL -- Barker, Burt Brown
Henckel family records. New Market: Heckel Press, 1958.

HENCKEL -- Kellogg, Joseph M.
Kellogg notebook on West Virginia families: The Henckel family. Lawrence,
Kans. 1958.

HENDERSON -- Henderson research - Virginia, Georgia, Ky., Tenn.

HENDERSON -- Brodie, Louise Henderson
Henderson, Nicholls, Clapton & Jackson families of Va., & Ga. 1971.

HENDERSON -- Miller, Joseph Lyon
Ancestry and descendants of Lieut. John Henderson, of Greenbrier County,
Virginia, 1650-1900. Richmond: Whittet & Shepperson, 1902.

HENDERSON -- Roberts, H. D.
   Henderson family research; (Virginia, Kentucky, Tennessee, Georgia,
   Indiana, etc.). Organge, Calif. 1967.

HENDERSON -- Tribble, Anna Laura Henderson
   The family tree of Henderson. Blacksburg. 1983.

HENKEL -- Henkel, Elon O.
   Henckel family news letter; a semiannual supplement to the Henckel
   family records. New Market. 1928-1930.

HENKEL -- Stapleton, A.
   Henkel. Henkel memorial, historical, genealogical and biographical,
   etc. New Market. 1910-1919.

HENNEN -- Hennen, Dorothy T.
   Hennen's Choice; a compilation of the descendants of Matthew Hennen
   (1752-1839). Parsons, W. Va.: McClain Print, 1970-72.

HENRICO -- Brock, R. A.
   The Vestry Book of Henrico Parish. Annals of Henrico Co., etc. by
   Rt. Rev. L. M. Burton. Richmond: Williams Printing Co., 1904.

HENRY -- My Henry family (Pennsylvania, Virginia, Tennessee, Alabama,
   Mississippi, and incidentally, Oklahoma. New Market, Ala.: Southern
   Geneal. Services, 1973.

HENRY (Hanover) -- Henry, William Wirt
   Patrick Henry-Life, Correspondence and Speeches. New York, N.Y.: Charles
   Scribner's Sons, 1891.

HERBERT -- Walter, Alice Granberry
   Herbert in England & Virginia, 1399-1900s. Virginia Beach. 1977.

HEREFORD -- Countess, Mary Bivins Geron
   Hereford family of Virginia and Alabama. Huntsville, Ala. 1961.

HEREFORD -- Pfeifer, Esher Hereford
   The Hereford family of Virginia. 1929.

HERNDON -- Herndon, John Goodwin
   The Herndon family of Virginia. Philadelphia, Pa.: Engineering Pub.
   Co., 1952.

HERNDON -- Froom, Grace Yager
   A collection of facts and recollections of the descent line and the
   relationships among some descendants of--William Henderson of England
   and New Kent Co., Va. ... Indianapolis, Ind. 1983.

HERNDON -- Shields, Ruth Herndon
   The descendants of William and Sarah (Poe) Herndon of Caroline County,
   Va. and Chatham County, N.C. Chapel Hill, N.C. 1956.

HERRMAN -- Heck, Earl L. W.
    Augustine Herrman: beginner of the Virginia tobacco trade, merchant
    of New Amsterdam and the first lord of Bohemia Manor in Maryland.
    Englewood, Ohio. 1941.

HERSHBERGER -- Hershberger, George W.
    Brief history of the Herschberger family in Page County, Va.
    Winchester. 1932.

HICKMAN -- Hickman, Clarence N.
    Genealogy of the Hickman families of Virginia, Kentucky, Indiana,
    and Texas. Jackson Heights, N.Y. 1967.

HICKMAN -- Hilton, Hope A.
    Edwin and Elender Webber Chiles Hickman; some progenitors and descen-
    dants, early pioneers of Virginia, North Carolina, Kentucky, Missouri,
    and Utah. Salt Lakt City, Utah. 1967.

HIERONYMUS -- The Hieronymus story, 1985/the Hieronymus Family in America,
    HIFIA. Baltimore: Gateway Press, 1985.

HIESTAND -- Moore, Barbara J. H.
    Hiestand family, in memory of my dad, Herschel Hiestand ... Alexandria.
    1969.

HIESTAND -- Trimble, David B.
    Hiestand family of Page County, Virginia. San Antonio, Tex. 1974.

HIGDON -- Coone, Lucille Barco
    Colonial Higdons, and some of their descendants. Manassas: L. B.
    Coone, 1976.

HIGGINBOTHAM -- Lutz, Anna L.
    Five generations of the Higginbotham family, Kanawha, Putnam, and
    Mason Counties, West Virginia. Charleston, W. Va. 1981.

HIGGINSONS -- Higginsons of England and America, Part I, English Ancestry of
    N.E. and Va. Families. Eben Putnam. 1903.

HIGHLAND -- Highland, Scotland G.
    The Highland Patton, Maxwell, Earle, Morris genealogies. Clarksburg,
    W. Va. 1926.

HIGHLAND -- Highland, S. G.
    Record of the colonial forebears, descendants, kinsmen and childhood
    friends ... of the late Lucinda Earle Patton Highland, West Milford,
    W. Va. Clarsburg, W. Va. 1929.

HIGHLAND -- Highland, Scotland G.
    Highland genealogy. Clarksburg, W. Va. 1936.

HIGHLAND CO. -- Morton, Oren F., B.L.
A History of Highland County, Va. Monterey, Va.

HIGHLEY -- Wagnen, F. L. Van
James Highley of Franklin County, Va. and Grant County, Ind., a record of his descendants. Buffalo, N.Y. 1952.

HIGHT -- Creasy, Mary Hight
History of the John Hight family of Nelson County, Virginia: notes on the related families of George Washington Stratton, James Loving, John Preston Campbell, Thomas Jones. 1979.

HILL -- Courtney, Mrs. Giles C., nee Elizabeth S. Hill
The Hill family of Virginia. 1905.

HILL -- Hill, Stuary H.
The Hill family of Bertie, Martin and Halifax Counties, North Carolina. Also Bryan, Whitmel, Blount, Norfleet, Pugh, Hall, Stuart, Weldon, Spruill, Long, Williams, Smith, Jacocks and other allied families of North Carolina and Virginia. New York, N.Y. 1922-36.

HILL -- Furman, Thomas deS.
Descendants of Henry Hill of Nansemond Co., Virginia. 1949.

HILL -- Young, Dvid G.
Genealogy of the Hill family, Kentucky and Virginia. Pub. by F. H. Kuhn, 1969.

HILDRETH -- Heldreth, Larry
The Heldreth family. Dry Fork. 1978.

HILLDRUP -- Pullen, William E.
A Virginia genealogy: from Jamestown, Yorktown, and Appomattox, to the Argonne, the beaches of Normandy and Iwo Jims, in the annals of the Hilldrups, Guerrants, and their allied Virginia families. Hollywood, Fla. 1978.

HILLMAN -- Counts, Belva Marshall
Unto the hills, some Hilmans and others: a partial genealogy of the southwest Virginia families of Carrico, Edwards, Hillman, Newberry, Stallard, Wells and other allied families. Radford: Commonwealth Press, 1979.

HILLESTAD -- Gardner, Vernon E.
Descendants of Mr. and Mrs. Kristoffer Hillestad. Arlington. 1963.

HINDS -- Hines & allied families of Virginia & Kentucky. 1911.

HINES -- Hines, Benjamin McFarland
Hines and allied families: some descendants of William Hines of Sussex
County, Virginia (ca. 1690-1760) and a record of their principal allied
families, Watson (Virginia, Mississippi); Shackelford (Virginia, South
Carolina, Georgia); Nisbet (North Carolina, Georgia); and Kennon
(Virginia). 1981.

HINES -- Lanier, Clara Hines
Descendants of Joab D. Hines of Lauderdale County, Alabama. Luray. 1974.

HISTORY OF AUGUSTA CHURCH, ETC. -- Deventer, Rev. J. W.
Staunton. 1900.

HOBBS -- Chapman, George E.
Hobbs family history. New Cumberland, W. Va. 1954.

HODGES -- Hodge, Robert Allen
Hodge family in America, 1831-1955. Charlottesville. 1955.

HODGES -- McNaught, Virginia Eliza Hodge
Hodge-Berry-Fairfax families. 1934.

HODNETT -- Pendergrast, Robert Allison
John Hodnett of Colonial Virginia. Atlanta, Ga. 1976.

HOFF -- Lemons, Betty Hoff
Genesis Hoff & Hooffs of Virginia, 1730-1980. Vienna. 1980.

HOFFMAN -- Gottschalk, Katherine Cox
The Hoffman family of Virginia. 1930.

HOGE -- Life and Labors of Moses D. Hoge, D.D., LL.D. Richmond. 1899.

HOGE -- Tyler, James Hoge
The Family of Hoge. A Genealogy compiled by James Hoge Tyler. Edited
and published by James Fulton Hoge. Richmond. 1927.

HOGG -- Ironmonger, Elizabeth Hogg
Hogg family of York and Gloucester Counties, Va. Seaford. 1968.

HOLLAND -- Holand, Irma Ragan
The Hollands from Virginia to North Carolina. 197-.

HOLLAND -- Holland, Kirk Davis
Holland; a history of the Virginia Holland families from 1620 to 1963.
Salado, Tex.: Reproduced by the Anson Jones Press, 1963.

HOLLIDAY -- Holliday, Omar
Some Holidays of Virginia, Georgia, Missouri and California with families
allied by marriage of Omar Holliday and Rosalie Willet Holliday. Palos
Verdes Estates, Calif. 1939.

HOLLOWAY -- Hopkins, Garland E.
Colonial cousins; being the history, genealogy, heraldry, homes and traditions of the family of Holloway and related families, originating in the original shire of Charles river, now York County, Va. Norfolk. 1940.

HOLSINGER -- Holsinger, Paul G.
Descendants of David Holsinger of Virginia. Martinsburg, Pa. 1969.

HOLSTEIN -- Holstein, Hettie Pauley
The Holstein family of southern West Virginia (Holston-Holstein-Holestin). Danville, W. Va. 1982.

HOLSTEIN -- Holstein, P. E.
Descendants of Peter Holstine. Charleston, W. Va.

HOLT -- Early, Margaret Abigail Holt
Holt-Bennett family history. Clarksburg, W. Va. 1974.

HOLT -- Tatum, V. Holt (from notes provided by Maudie Holt Black & others)
The Holt family in Europe and America, 1248-1971; a brief account of the genealogy, history, and armory in England and Germany in Europe: also in the States of Massachusetts, Connecticut, Virginia, North Carolina, Tennessee, Mississippi and Utah in America. Cincinnati, Ohio. 1971.

HOLTZCLAW -- Holtzclaw, B. C.
The genealogy of the Holtzclaw family, 1540-1935. Richmond: Old Dominion Press, Inc., 1936.

HOOE -- Hayden, Horace E.
Hooe-Barnes of Virginia and Maryland. Washington. 1931.

HOPKINS -- Bruhn, Reva Hopkins
Hopkins forever: James Hopkins, revolutionary soldier, Virginia, North Carolina, Kentucky, Tennessee, Illinois, and Missouri. Visalia, Calif. 1984.

HOPKINS -- Hopkins, Walter Lee
Hopkins of Virginia and related families. Richmond: J. W. Ferguson & Sons, Printers, 1931.

HOPKINS -- Hopkins, Walter Lee
Hopkins of Virginia and related families. Harrisonburg: C.J. Carrier Co., 1980.

HORD -- Hord, Rev. Arnold Harris
Thomas Hord, gentleman; born in England, 1701, died in Virginia, 1766; a supplement to the Genealogy of the Hord Family. Philadelphia, Pa.

HORD -- Hord, Rev. Arnold Harris
   The Hord Family of Virginia. A Supplement to the Genealogy of the
   Hord Family. Philadelphia, Pa.: Ferris & Leach, 1915.

HORD -- Hord, Rev. Arnold Harris
   English ancestry of the Hord family of Virginia, with supplementary
   data. 1940.

HORNBECK -- Sayre, Ralph H., Mrs.
   Warnaar Hornbeck descendants (New York to California). Parsons, W.
   Va.: McClain Print., 1977.

HORNISH -- Hornish family records; some of the descendants of Martin B.
   Hornish and Helena Rupert of Point Pleasant (now West) Virginia
   (ca. 1824) Centreville, Wayne County, Indiana (ca. 1829 to 1856) and
   Tazewell and Peoria Counties, Illinois (1856-   ). Whiting, Ind.
   1951.

HORNSBY -- Bible record of the Hornsby family of Virginia.

HORSLEY -- Osborne, Kathryn Mitcham
   Descendants of Mary Cabell Horsley. Roanoke. 1978.

HOSKINS -- Warner, Charles W. Hoskins
   Hoskins of Virginia and related families. Tappahannock. 1971.

HOSTETTER -- Reynolds, Agnes Virginia Hostetter
   George William Hostetter, ancestors and descendants, Rockbridge County,
   Virginia. Aexandria. 1983.

HOTTEL -- Huddle, Rev. W. D., Rev., B.S. (completed by his wife, Lulu May Huddle
   History of the descendants of John Hottel (immigrant from Switzerland to
   America) and an authentic genealogical family register of ten generations
   from the first of the name in America, 1732, to the present time, 1929,
   with numerous brief biographical sketches, collected and compiled from
   many indisputable sources: court and church records, old and late family
   records and tombstones of the many states in the Union ... Strasburg:
   Shenandoah Publishing House, Inc., 1930.

HOUGH -- Hough, Orville Louis
   Hough in Loudoun County, Virginia, 1744-1850; an unfinished history.
   Denver. 1974.

HOUNSHELL -- Canfield, C. R.
   Hounsell family of Southwest Virginia. Frankfurt, Germany. 1973.

HOUSE -- Loeb, Helen House
   Source records of the House, Houze, Howse, Jenkins and Clift families
   of Maryland, Virginia, and North Carolina. 1980.

HOUSTON -- Campbell, Leslie L.
   The Houston family of Virginia. Lexington. 1956.

HOVATTER -- Grant, Howard B.
   Christopher Hovatter; copyright ... Philippi, W. Va. 1936.

HOWARD -- Arnaudo, David
   Howard and Belknap family histories. Alexandria. 1983.

HOWARD -- Howard, Walter L.
   Ten generations of Virginia Howards. Davis, Calif. 1949.

HOWE -- Howe, Daniel Dunbar
   Listen to the mockingbird; the life and times of a pioneer Virginia
   family. Boyce: Carr Pub. Co., 1961.

HOWELL -- Genealogy of the southern line of the family of Howell, from the
   original progenitor of the line in America, John Howell, Virginia
   colonist. Atlanta. 1930.

HOXTON -- Reid, Legh W.
   English ancestry of the Hoxtons of Maryland and Virginia. Richmond. 1952.

HUBBARD -- Hubbard, Robert Merrill
   Genealogy of the Hubbard and associated families of northern Indiana.
   Charlottesville. 1970.

HUDDLESTON -- Huddleston, Lawrence M.
   The Huddlestons, my kin. Parsons, W. Va.: McClain Print Co., 1974.

HUDDLESTON -- Loving, Charissa S.
   The Huddleston Family. Deepwater, W. Va. 1924.

HUDGINS -- Callender, Estelle V.
   The Hudgins family of Virginia and their kin. Rosslyn: Monitor
   Newspaper Co., 1912.

HUDSON -- Hudson, Malcolm H.
   Hudson marriages in Virginia: a research for genealogists. Longview,
   Tex. 1980.

HUGER -- Descendants of John Huger of South Carolina, son of the emigrant,
   Daniel Huger. Charleston, W. Va. 1911.

HUGHES -- Edmunds, Mary Burnley Wilson
   Ancestry of Janie Blackwell Hughes, 1879-1968. Lynchburg. 1969.

HUGHES, ETC. -- Horton, Lucy Henderson
   Family History, including Hughes, Dalton, Martin, Henderson, all
   originally of Virginia, and many Kindred Branches. Franklin, Tenn.
   1922.

HUGHES -- Hughes, Lydia Annie and Richard Hughes Sullivan
   Hughes family of Kentucky and Virginia. Columbia, S.C. 1920.

HUGHES -- Manley, Ida Hughes
Peter Hughes, his descendants and related families (also Hues and Hughs.
Alexandria. 1969.

HUGUENOT -- The Huguenot. Published by the Huguenot Society Foundation of
Manakin in the Colony of Virginia (pedigrees of Reamy, Cabaniss, Pasteut,
Witt, Michaux, Marye, Maupin, etc.).

HUGUENOT EMIGRATION -- Brocks, R. A.
Documents, chiefly Unpublished, Relating to the Huguenot Emigration to
Virginia. With an Appendix of Genealogies, etc. Richmond: Virginia
His. Society, MDCCCLXXXVI.

HULBERT -- Deans, Arline Mary Hulbert
Hulbert family. Alexandria. 1976.

HULVEY -- Hulvey, Velma June Good
Hulvey clan historical ties: a history of Conrad Hulvey of Virginia with
his sons Conrad Hulvey, George Hulver, and John Hulva: there is mention
of other Hulvey and connected families. Bridgewater. 1984.

HUME -- Donaldson, O. Clyde
A Hume chronicle: Andrew Hume of Fauquier County, Virginia, his Scottish
heritage and American descendants. Hopkins, Minn. 1982.

HUME -- Hume, Edgar Erskine
A colonial Scottish Jacobite family; the establishment in Virginia of a
branch of the Humes of Wedderburn; illustrated by letters and other
contemporary documents. Richmond: Old Dominion Press, 1931.

HUME -- Statement of Francis Charles Hume of Galveston, Texas. Bound with
Pamphlets of Va. Genealogy, Va. His. Society. Galveston, Tex.: F. L.
Finck & Co., Stationers and Printers.

HUMPHREY -- Abee, Blanche Humphrey
Colonists of Carolina in the lineage of Hon. W. D. Humphrey. Richmond:
William Byrd Press, Inc., 1938.

HUMPHREY -- Holcomb, Brent
Ancestors and descendants of Charles Humphries (d. 1837) of Union District,
South Carolina, 1677-1874: including records from Virginia, North Carolina,
South Carolina, Mississippi, and other states. Columbia, S.C. 1985.

HUMPHREY -- Humphries, John D.
Descendants of Charles Humphries of Virginia, Nathaniel Pope of Virginia,
Reuben Brock I of Ireland and Aaron Parker of Virginia. Atlanta, Ga. 1938.

HUMSTON -- Humston, Ezra Sams and Edward Albert Humston
The Humston family, a genealogy of the descendants of Edward Humston of Stafford County, Virginia, 1667, together with accounts of the allied families of Humstone, Humpstone & Humpston in the United States. Manhattan, Kans. 1943.

HUNSBERGER -- Huntsberry, Thomas Vincent
Maryland and Virginia Hundsberger, Hunsberger, Hunsberry, Huntzberry, Huntsberry, 1760 to 1981. Baltimore. 1981.

HUNT -- Hunt, John G.
The descendants of Thomas Hunt, Sr. Arlington. 1936.

HUNTER -- Ball, Mary A. H.
Records of Hunter of Hunterston, Abbot's Hill and Park, Ayreshire, and Ayrehill, Fairfax Co., Va. Washington.

HUNTER -- Bull, Mary Alice Hunter
Record of Hunter of Hunterston, Ayrshire, Scotland ... record of Hunter of Abbotshill and Park, County Ayr, Scotland, descendants of Hunter of Hunterston ... record of Hunter of Ayrhill, Fairfax County, Virginia descendants from Hunter of Abbotshill and Park County Ayr, Scotland ... Washington: Gibson Bros., 1902.

HUNTER -- Chilton, Harriett A.
Hundred Hunter cousins: grandchildren of Benjamin Hunter, Senior (1770-1845) of Appomattox County, Virginia. Falls Church. 1976.

HUNTER -- Culbertson, Sidney Methiot
The Hunter family of Virginia and connections, embracing portions of families of Alexander, Pearson, Chapman, Travers, Tyler, West, Gray, Smith, and Safford of Virginia and Maclay, Colhoun and Culbertson of Pennsylvania. Denver, Colo. 1934.

HUNTER -- Hardie, Catherine M. C.
Hunter scrap-book. Hunter family. The Rambler writes of the Virginia Hunters. Washington. 1919-23.

HUNTER -- Hunter, Isabel Sewall
Hunter ancestry. Richard Sewall Hunter, his ancestry. Rosslyn. 1942.

HUNTER -- Hunter, Isabel Sewall
Hunter ancestry. Gilbert Thurston Hunter. Arlington. 1944.

HUNTER -- Hunter, Mary Kate
The Hunters of Duns, Berwick County, Scotland to Fredericksburg, Virginia. Palestine, Tex. 1940.

HUNTER -- Hunter, Walter M.
The Hunters of Medford County, Virginia; notes and documents on the family
of James Hunter, regulator leader of N.C. including forebears in
Pennsylvania, Virginia, North Carolina, Louisiana and Texas. Cottonport,
La. 1973.

HUNTER -- James, Jessamine B.
Hunter and Alford families of Virginia and Kentucky. Tucson, Ariz. 1954.

HUNTER FAMILY REGISTER -- Descendants of Samuel Hunter of Augusta Co., Va.
Dubuque, Iowa. 1895.

HUNTINGTON -- Huntington, Richard Thomas
The Huntington family in America. Hartford, Conn. 1915.

HURT -- Battey, George Magruder
The Hurt "land empire" in early Virginia; an imperfect but partly
scientific analysis. Kimball. 1947.

HURT -- Battey, George Magruder
Hurt-Shorter genealogy. Kimball. 1948.

HUSSEY -- Turnbull, Thomas
(Descendants of) John Hussey, of Dorking, England. Casanova. 1942.

HUTCHINS -- Crider, Mrs. Gussie Waymire & Edward C. Crider
Four generations of the family of Strangeman Hutchins and his wife,
Elizabeth Cox, as known January 10, 1935. An old Virginia family along
the James River. Kokomo, Ind. 1935.

HUTCHINS -- Crider, Edward C.
Descendants of Strangeman Hutchins of the James River in Virginia.
Kokomo, Ind. 1950.

HUTCHINS -- Hudgins, Edgar H.
Hudgins, Virginia to Texas. Houston, Tex. 1983.

HUTCHINS -- Low, Miss Mary Elizabeth
Hutchings, Powell, Moore, Thweatt, Critchlow, Sutherland, Cattles,
Edenton, etc. Nashville, Tenn. 1940.

HUTCHINS -- Townsend, Rita Hineman
Hutchins-Hutchens, descendants of Strangeman Hutchins, born 1707, of the
James River in Virginia and Surry (Yadkin) County, North Carolina.
Baltimore: Gateway Press, 1979.

HUTCHINSON -- Hutcheson, Herbert F., Jr.
The Hutcheson family of Mecklenburg, Virginia. Boydton. 1968.

HUTCHINSON -- Dickinson, Helen E. H.
  Some descendants of Joseph Hutchinson of Loudoun County, Virginia, a
  soldier of the American Revolution. Huntington, W. Va. 1976.

HUTCHISON -- Dickinson, Helen Elsie Hutchison
  Some descendants of Joseph Hutchison of Loudoun County, Virginia.
  Redondo Beach, Calif. 1970.

HYER -- Swisher, Robert Edward
  The Hyers of West Virginia: an account of the Hyre or Hyer families,
  descended from Liener the immigrant, who settled as pioneers in Grant,
  Upshur, Jackson, and Braxton Counties, West Virginia. Richmond. 1977.

HYRE -- Swisher, Robert Edward
  The Hyres of West Virginia. Richmond: Whittet & Shepperson, 1977.

IRBY -- Turner, W. R.
  Notes concerning the Irby family. Blackstone: Nottoway Publishing Co.,
  1930.

IRONMONGER -- Ironmonger, Elizabeth Hogg
  Ironmonger and connections, 1624-1924. Seaford. 1956.

IRONMONGER -- Ironmonger, Elizabeth Hogg
  Ironmonger and connections updated: Iremonger-Ironmonger. Seaford. 1972.

IRVIN -- Morris, Margaret Logan
  The Irvins, Doaks, Logans and McCampbells of Virginia and Kentucky.
  Corydon, Ind. 1916.

IRVINS, DOAKS, ETC. -- Morris, Margaret Logan
  The Irvins, Doaks, Logans, and McCampbells of Virginia and Kentucky.
  Indianapolis, Ind.: C. E. Pauley & Co., 1916.

ISHAM -- Longden, Rev. Henry Isham
  Some notes on Sir Euseby Isham, of Pytchley in the county of Northampton,
  with special reference to his Virginia descendants. London: Mitchell and
  Hughes, 1898.

IVES -- Ivy, Robert Adams
  The Ivy family of Virginia, Georgia, and Mississippi. Columbus, Miss.
  1984.

IBEY -- Jones, W. Mac
  Notes on the Ivey Family. Etbrick: A. E. Ivey, 1929.

JACKSON -- Arnold, Thomas Jackson
Early Life and Letters of General Thomas J. Jackson, "Stonewall" Jackson.
New York, N.Y.: Fleming H. Revell Co., 1916.

JACKSON -- Cook, Roy Bird
The family and early life of Stonewall Jackson. Richmond: Old Dominion
Press, Inc., 1924.

JACKSON -- Cook, Roy Bird
The family and early life of Stonewall Jackson. Charleston, W. Va.:
Charleston Print Co., 1948.

JACKSON -- Doughman, M. P.
Some of the descendants of Edward William Jackson, born New Jersey, 1730,
and died, Virginia, 1807. Lebanon, Ohio. 1966.

JACKSON -- Gerlach, Mary Ruth Jackson
Isaac Jackson, Virginia, 1797, Bullitt County, Kentucky, 1822 and
descendants. Louisville, Ky. 1985.

JACKSON -- Porter, Kenneth Wiggins
The Jacksons and the Lees; two generations of Massachusetts merchants,
1765-1844. Cambridge, Mass.: Harvard University Press, 1937.

JACKSON -- Stonewall Jackson. Sketch of the life of Stonewall Jackson written
by Mrs. Emil Shaffer, nee Miss Anna Jackson Preston, and presented to the
Senate on May 10, 1928, by Hon. Cole L. Bleade, senator from South
Carolina ... Washington: U. S. Govt. Print. Off., 1936.

JACKSON -- Shoop, Michael I.
The genealogies of the Jackson, Junkin & Morrison families. Lexington:
Garland Gray Memorial Research Center, Stonewall Jackson House, Historic
Lexington Foundation, 1981.

JACKSON -- The Virginia Jackson. The Scot-Irish family which produced
"Stonewall."

JACOBI -- Beach, Louis A.
The family history of Mary Ann Stierstedter and Philip Jacobi, Sr.
Alexandria. 1976.

JAMES -- The Court record following (of) Fauquier Co., Va., concerns the
James family. 1818.

JAMES -- Ironmonger, Elizabeth Hogg
Thomas James (clerk of Kingston Parish 1783-1796) ancestry and descendants,
1653-1961. Crozet. 1961.

JARRETT -- Patterson, Richard E.
West Saxony, 452--America, 1982: 1,529 years of family history. Virginia
Beach. 1982.

JAQUELIN -- du Bellet, Louise Pecquet
   Some prominent Virginia families. Lynchburg: J. P. Bell Company,
   Inc., 1907.

JEFFERS -- Hagan, Erma Jeffers
   The descendants of John H. Jeffers of Gallia County, Ohio and related
   families, 1844-1975. Parsons, W. Va.: McClain Print, 1976.

JEFFERS -- Jeffers, Joseph C.
   Simon Jeffers of Salem, Mass. and some of his descendants. Charleston,
   W. Va. 1975.

JEFFERSON -- Davis, Betty Elise
   Monticello scrapbook; little stories of the children and grand-children
   of Thomas Jefferson. New York, N.Y.: M. S. Mill Co., Inc., 1941.

JEFFERSON -- Jefferson, Thomas
   Thomas Jefferson and his unknown brother, Randolph. Charlottesville,
   Univ. of Va., 1942.

JEFFERSON -- Shackleford, George Green
   Collected papers to commemorate fifty years of the Monticello Association
   of the descendants of Thomas Jefferson. Monticello Association. 1965.

JEFFERY -- Hanks, Dale E.
   Genealogical record of the descendants of James Jeffery, England, 1700-
   America, 1976. Richmond. 1976.

JEFFRIES -- Andrew, Louise Jeffreys
   Marmaduke Norfleet Jeffreys, his ancestors and descendants. Springfield.
   1983.

JENKINS -- Bowen, Nettie Jenkins
   The Jenkins family of Virginia and North Carolina and three allied
   families: Yarboro, Crask and Cook. Raleigh, N.C. 1966.

JENKINS -- Johnson, Maude Horne
   Aaron Jenkins of Frederick County, Virginia and his descendants/comp. by
   Maude Horne Johnson and Ralph Walter Johnson. Loa Angeles, Calif. 1963.

JENNINGS -- Clinton, Thomas G.
   Jennings' estate; to the heirs of John Jennings who left Whitehaven,
   England and arrived in Fredericksburg, Va. 1754. Washington: Kirkwood
   and McGill, 1852.

JENNINGS -- Jennings family convention. Charlottesville. May 15, 1850.
   Charlottesville. 1850.

JENNINGS -- White, Lillie Pauline
   Jennings, Davidson and allied families, a genealogical list and history
   of the descendants of the immigrants, John Jennings, Southampton, N.Y.,
   and John Davidson, Augusta Co., Va. Seattle, Wash.: Sherman Printing &
   Binding Co., 1944.

JERNIGAN -- Worley, Lillian J.
   Jernigan reunion; a gathering of some descendants of Thomas Jernigan,
   immigrant 1635 of Nansemond County, Virginia ... Clinton, N.C. 1971.

JETT -- Jett, Jeter Lee
   The Jett family of Virginia. Kilmarnock. 1970.

JETT -- Jett, Jeter Lee
   The Jett and allied families: a genealogical reference book of Jett and
   allied families. Baltimore: Gateway Press, 1977.

JOHNSON -- Johnson, C. S.
   Virginia ancestors. 1963.

JOHNSON -- Johnson, Eddis
   The Johnsons and Johnstons of Carrowaugh in the Isle of Wight County,
   Virginia. Martinsville, Ind. 1979.

JOHNSON -- Johnson, Katherine Baker
   The family of the Reverend William Johnson of Virginia and Knox County,
   Tennessee. 1945.

JOHNSON -- Johnson, Lorand V.
   We are looking for you. "The descendants of William and John Johnson" -
   Colonial freinds of Virginia. A series of charts ... Boston, Mass. 1935.

JOHNSON -- Johnson, Lorand V.
   The descendants of William and John Johnson, colonial Friends of Virginia.
   Cleveland, Ohio. 1940.

JOHNSON -- Johnson, Loran V.
   The descendants of William and John Johnson, colonial friends of Virginia.
   Shaker Heights, Ohio. 1942.

JOHNSON -- Johnson, Lorand V.
   Selected references relating to the ancestry of William and John Johnston,
   colonial Friends (Quakers) of Virginia; an account of the connections of
   the family of Johnston of Caskieben, and of that ilk, of the Garioch,
   Aberdeenshire, Scotland. Shaker Heights, Ohio. 1972.

JOHNSON -- Knobe, Damaris
   The ancestry of Grafton Johnson, with its four branches: the Johnson,
   the Holman, the Keen, the Morris; the history and genealogy of paternal
   progenitors, as confined to the United States, of the second Grafton
   Johnson of Greenwood, Indiana, great-great-grandson of the first Isaac
   Johnson, who reverts to the middle of the eighteenth century in Virginia.
   Indianapolis, Ind.: Hollenbeck Press, 1924.

JOHNSON -- Layman, Laura T.
   Scottish ancestry of Dempsey Johnson of Colonial Virginia and his
   descendants, 1326-1948.

JOHNSON -- Reynolds, Katherine
   Some descendants of Gideon Johnson, Sr. of Virginia and North Carolina.
   1966.

JOHNSON -- Williams, Marguerite White
Jeffrey Johnson and Margaret of Fauquier County, Virginia. 1970.

JOHNSTON -- Johnston, C. K.
William Johnston of Isle of Wight, Virginia and his descendants, 1648-1964.
West Hartford, Conn. 1965.

JOHNSTON -- Johnston, Everett D.
Esau Johnston family. Tappahannock. 1980.

JOHNSTON -- Johnston, Elbert Felton
Johnston of Caroline County, Virginia; some of the descendants of William
and Ann Chew Johnston (1697-1778). Wolfe City, Tex.: Henington Pub. Co.,
1964.

JOHNSTON -- Johnstone, Jeffrey Marwill
Genealogy of the Johnstone family of Utica, New York, and Hampton, Virginia.
Rochester, N.Y. 1978.

JOHNSTON'S OLD VA. CLERKS -- Johnston, Frederick
Memorials of Old Virginia Clerks, etc. Lynchburg: J. P. Bell Co. 1888.

JOINER -- Joyner, U. P.
Joyner of Southampton; a study of Thos. Joyner of Isle of Wight Co., Va.
and his descendants. Orange. 1975.

JOLLIFF -- Jolliff, Oliver P.
Family record and genealogy of the Jolliff family from the year 1760 to
1878, inclusive. Morganton, W. Va. 1878.

JOLLIFFE -- Jolliffe, William
Historical, Genealogical and Biographical Account of the Jolliffe Family
of Virginia, 1652 to 1693. Philadelphia, Pa.: J. B. Lippincott
Company, 1893.

JONES -- Ewing, Evelyn Jones
Joseph Jones of Gates County, North Carolina: ancestors and descendants,
1635-1985. Emporia. 1985.

JONES -- Fothergill, Augusta B.
Peter Jones and Richard Jones genealogies. Richmond: Old Dominion
Press, Inc., 1924.

JONES -- Jones, C. R.
Jones family; genealogy, historical notes, family traditions and anecdotes.
Morgantown, W. Va.

JONES -- Jones, Lewis H.
Major Thomas Jones of Bathurst, Va.

JONES -- Jones, L. H.
Captain Roger Jones, of London and Virginia. Some of his antecedents
and descendants. With appreciative notice of other families, viz:
Bathurst, Belfield, Browning, Carter, Catesby, Cocke, Graham, Fauntleroy,
Hickman, Hoskins, Latane, Lewis, Meriwether, Skelton, Walker, Waring,
Woodford, and others. Albany, N.Y.: J. Munsell's Sons, 1891.

JONES -- Jones, Judge L. H.
Captain Roger Jones of London and Virginia, etc. Albany, N.Y. 1891.
Repub. with additions, 1907.

JONES (BRUNSWICK) -- Jones, Walter B.
John Burgwin Carolinian * * * John Jones Virginian, etc. Montgomery,
Ala. 1913.

JONES -- Stickney, Alpheus B.
Lucy and Oliver, some West Virginia genealogy: Pierpoint, Smell, Jones,
Fetty. Pittsburg, Pa. 1953.

JOHN WISE -- Wise, J. C.
Col. John Wise of England and Virginia, 1617-1695, His Ancestors and
Descendants.

JORDAN -- Anderson, Stanley J.
The Jordan family. Cleveland, W. Va. 1978.

JORDAN -- Zoellner, L. R.
Jordan family of Virginia and North Carolina. Los Angeles, Calif. 1945.

JUNKINS -- Junkin, Francis T. A.
Genealogical chart showing the descent from several lines and some
interesting family connections of the Virginia families of Alexander,
Anderson, Aylett, Bruce, Dandridge, Fontaine, Henry, Junkin, Moore,
Poindexter, Spotswood, West &c. 1908.

JUNKINS -- Robinson, Richard D.
Repassing at my side ... a story of the Junkins. Balcksburg. 1975.

KAISER -- Rose, Mildred Gail Kiser
Kiser, family and descendants of John Mulkey Kiser of Dumps Creek,
Russell County (southwest Virginia). Hubbard, Ore. 1980.

KASPER -- Prichard, A. M.
Some of Lewis P. Kasper's kin. Staunton: Campfield Printing Co., 1946.

KAY -- Freeman, Kent Kay
The four children of James Kay of Essex County, Va., and some of their
descendants. Tacoma, Wash. 1978.

KEIM AND ALLIED FAMILIES -- Keim, DeB. Randolph
A Bi-Centennial Commemoration. Harrisburg, Pa.: Publishing Co., 1898.

KEINADT -- A historical sketch of Michael Keinadt and Margaret Diller his
wife. Staunton: Campfield Printing Co., 1941.

KEISTER -- Keister, Elmo Earl
Strasburg, Virginia, and the Keister family. Strasburg. 1972.

KEITH -- Somerville, Keith Frazier
Family tree of the descendants of Rev. Keith of Va. Cleveland, Miss.
1947.

KEITH -- Somerville, Keith Frazer
Additional information about the children and descendants of Rev. James
Keith of Virginia and his wife, Mary Isham Randolph. 1949.

KELLEY -- Moore, Elizabeth Saylor
The Kelley family of Virginia. Knoxville, Tenn. 1973.

KELLEY -- Pendergrass, Anita Ball
That the next generation may know: the Kelly's of Virginia and Kentucky.
Keokee. 1973.

KELLY -- Allison, Elizabeth Kelly
Early Southwest Virginia families. Auburn, Ala. 1960.

KELLY -- Cook, Roy Bird
Lon H. Kelly, 1871-1938. Charleston, W. Va. 1939.

KELSO -- Kelso, Hugh
The Kelso family of Virginia's Eastern Shore: their origins and chronicles.
1983.

KEMPER -- Kemper, Willis Miller and Harry Linn Wright
Genealogy of the Kemper family in the Unites States, descendants of John
Kemper of Virginia; with a short historical sketch of his family and of
the German reformed colony at Germanna and Germantown, Va. Chicago,
Ill.: G. K. Hazlitt & Co., 1899.

KENDALL -- Davis, Will
Genealogical chart of Elias Kendall and Isabel Snodgrass, his wife.
Sutton, W. Va. 1939.

KENDALL -- Kendall, John S.
Notes on the Kendall family of Virginia, West Virginia, Kentucky, and
Texas. With references to allied families. New York, N.Y. 1939.

KENDALL -- Kendall, John Smith
A collection of notes, letters, and genealogical tables of the Kendall family of Virginia, Maryland and Kentucky. Berkeley, Calif. 1945.

KENDALL -- Kendall, Norman Festus
History and genealogy, Kendalls, Cunninghams, Snodgrasses. Grafton, W. Va.: Grafton Sentinel Pub. Co., 1942.

KENDALL -- Walker, Anne Kendrick
The storied Kendalls; with historical and genealogical records of Scottish and allied families. Richmond: Dietz Press, 1947.

KENNEDY -- Cannady, Clark Frieda Elizabeth
A history of the Cannaday family of Virginia. St. Petersburg, Fla.: Hazlett Print., 1983.

KENNEDY -- Kennedy, Mary Selden
Seldens of Virginia and Allied Families. New York, N.Y.: Frank Allabon Genealogical Co., 1911.

KENNER -- Cleveland, Paul Wood
Kenner; a compilation of family letters and data pertaining to the Kenner and related families, their early life in Virginia and subsequent years after migration to Ohio. Erie, Pa. 1966.

KENNERLY -- Atkinson, S. D.
Kennerlys of Virginia. 1928.

KENNEY -- Keeney, Roscoe C.
2,597 Keeney relatives: a genealogical record of Keeney origins in America, with special attention to those who came into West Virginia. Parsons, W. Va.: McClain Print, 1978.

KEY -- Key, Marcus M.
The family of John Key, Sr., of Virginia and allied families of Virginia and Georgia. 1950.

KIBLER -- Ping, Donald Harper
Some Kiblers from the Shenandoah Valley, including the descendants of Adam and Barbara Pence Kibler, 1764-1975. Warren, Ind. 1975.

KIDD -- Pierepont, Alice V.
Reuben Vaughan Kidd, soldier of the Confederacy. Petersburg. 1947.

KILBY, ETC. -- Kilby, C. M.
Genealogy of Kilby, Tynes, etc. Lynchburg. 1924.

KILBY -- Kilby, Clinton M.
Genealogy; Kilby, Tynes, Riddick, Smith, Glazebrook, etc. Lynchburg. 1942.

KILGORE -- Addington, Hugh Milburn
Charles Kilgore of King's mountain, a new history of the Kilgore family.
Nickelsville: Service Printery, 1935.

KILHAM -- Kilham, Austin D.
Notes on the descendants of Austin and Alice Kilham and related families.
Charlottesville: Bailey Printing, 1970.

KILNER -- Kilner, Charles Frances Thomas
Descendants of Thomas Kilner believed to be a brother of James Kilner.
Arlington. 1949.

KIMBALL -- Goddard, Charles Austin
Kimball ancestry of my mother Eureka Kimball Goddard. Fayetteville,
W. Va. 1937.

KIMBLE -- Alt, H. A.
Genealogies of the Kimble and Alt families from the time of the first
settler in Hardy County, Va. to the fifth generation following, and
other miscellaneous matters. Petersburg, W. Va. 1937.

KINCAID -- Kincaid, Clyde Edward
Kincaid: the family of John Kincaid, Sr. (1710-1811) and Kincaids of the
Carolinas and Virginia with expanded research in Burke and Cladwell
Counties, North Carolina. Asheville, N.C. 1983.

KINDLEY -- Wimberly, Bessie Jewel Mayes
The William Kindley family genealogy: his nine sons and their descendants.
Arlington. 1967.

KING -- Wilson, Reba S.
Lees and Kings of Virginia and North Carolina, 1636-1976. Ridgely, Tenn.
1975.

KING -- Yoder, Isabelle K.
Centennial memoir: the life story and genealogy of Abraham and Mattie King.
Harrisonburg. 1949.

KINNEY -- McIlhany, Hugh Milton, Jr.
Some Virginia families; being genealogies of the Kinney, Stribling, Trout,
McIlhany, Milton, Rogers, Tate, Snickers, Taylor, McCormick and other
families of Virginia. Staunton: Stoneburner & Prufer Printers, 1903.

KINSOLVING -- Gilbert, Arthur A.
Kinsolving (Kingsolver) family of Washington County, Virginia. Chicago,
Ill. 1936.

KINSOLVING -- Kinsolving, Wythe Leigh
Early history of Virginia and Maryland and seven centuries of lines ...
Studies in pre-American and early American colonial times. Halifax. 1935.

KIRK -- Barekman, June B.
   Kirk of Virginia. Chicago, Ill. 1972.

KIRK -- Fields, Bettye-Lou
   Kirks of Grayson County, Virginia. Mouth of Wilson. 1980.

KIRKPATRICK -- Kirkpatrick, Martin Glen
   John and Priscilla Kirkpatrick of Prince William County, Va., and their
   descendants; records. Skyland, N.C. 1959.

KITH AND KIN -- Sampson, Mrs. John Russell
   Kith and Kin. The William Byrd Press, Inc., 1922.

KNIGHT -- Harlander, Anna Knight
   Knight family history: descendants of Richard Knight, of Virginia,
   17--1760-61. Charlottesville. 1984.

KNISKERN -- Some of the descendants of Johann Peter Kniskern of Schoharie
   County, New York, born circa 1685, died November 11, 1759. Petersburg:
   Plummer Print Co., 1960.

KNOTT -- Amato, Irene E.
   William and Eleanor Nutt of Virginia and Carolina: their descendants and
   allied families. Carson City, Nev. 1977.

KNOX -- Dix, Emily Woolsey
   Reminiscences of the Knox and Soutter families of Virginia. New York,
   N.Y.: De Vinne Press, 1895.

KNOX -- Goodman, Hattie S.
   The Knox family; a genealogical and biographical sketch of the descendants
   of John Knox of Rowan County, North Carolina, and other Knoxes.
   Richmond: Whittet & Shepperson, 1905.

KOINER -- History and Genealogy. An Historical Sketch of Michael Klenadt and
   Margaret Diller, his wife. Prepared by a Committee, etc. Staunton:
   Stoneburner & Prufer, Publishers, 1893.

KOOGLER -- Whitney, Virginia Koogler
   The Koogler family of Virginia and allied families of Austin, Good, Hahn,
   Heatwole, Hemp, Knicely, Martin, Rhodes, Showalter, Snead, Taylor and
   Witmer. Aztec, N. W. 1968.

KOONTZ -- Koontz, Lowell L.
   History of the descendants of John Koontz. Parsons, W. Va.: McClain
   Print Co., 1979.

LACKOR -- Middleton, Mary McCall
The Lackor family (Lackore - Lacore - La Core - Lucore). Strasburg:
Shenandoah Pub. House, 1970.

LACY -- Chce, Harriet E. N.
The Walter Garner Lacy branch of the Lacy family of colonial Virginia.
Washington. 1925.

LACY -- Lacey, Hubert Wesley
The Thomas Lacy III family of Hanover and Buckingham Counties, Virginia:
with forebears, descendants, and some allied families. Baltimore: Gateway
Press, 1983.

LACY -- Lawler, Hazel
The Stephen Lacy family of Goochland County, Virginia: with forebears,
descendants, and allied families. Fredericksburg. 1981.

LACY -- McColloch, Lacy Porter
Theophilus Lacy of colonial Virginia and his descendants. Kensington,
Md. 1972.

LACY -- Rose, Ben Lacy
Lacy-Burwell anthology, with some material on the Smith family. Richmond.
1981.

LADD FAMILY -- Ladd, Warren
John Ladd of Charles City Co., Va. New Bedford, Mass. 1890.

LAMB -- Lamb, Maud J.
Descendants of Anthony Lamb (in) Virginia, Ohio and Iowa. 1949.

LAMB -- Sanderlin, Ben Garrett
Lamb. Portsmouth. 1960.

LAMONT -- Lamont, Thomas
A brief account of the life at Charlottesville of Thomas William Lamont
and of his family; together with a record of his ancestors, of their
origin in Scotland, and of their first coming to America about 1750.
New York, N.Y. 1915.

LANCASTER -- Lancaster, Robert A., Jr.
Historic Virginia Homes and Churches. Philadelphia and London: J. B.
Lippincott Company, MCMXV.

LANCASTER -- Rogers, Mary N.
Lancaster, from Virginia to Texas. Rosenberg, Tex. 1975.

LANDER -- Lander, David
History of the Lander family of Virginia and Kentucky. Chicago, Ill:
Regan Printing House, 1926.

LANDRUM -- Wiley, Roberta V. Landrum
   Some descendants of Thomas Landrum of Amherst Co., Va. & allied families.
   Parkville, Mo. 1974.

LANGDON -- Williams, Harriet Langdon
   Memory pictures. Parkersburg, W. Va. 1908.

LANGHORNE -- Winn, Alice
   Always a Virginian. Richmond: Westover Pub. Co., 1973.

LANIER -- Sawyer, Mamie Chambers
   The Lanier family of France, England, Virginia, and Fuplin (sic) County,
   N.C.; a genealogy of Stephen Lanier (1760-about 1838) of Duplin County,
   N.C., his ancestors and descendants. Elizabeth City, N.C. 1972.

LANIER -- Thompson, Margaret Drody
   Elizabeth Jane Lanier (Mrs. William Johnson): her ancestors from circa
   1540 and descendants to 1982, including the families of Harold Drody,
   Alexander McIver, John Lanier McIver, William Johnson, Matthew Benjamin
   Floyd & Sidney Lanier, beloved southern poet. Roanoke. 1982.

LANTZ -- Lantz, Jacob W.
   The Lantz family record, being a brief account of the Lantz family in the
   United States of America. Cedar Springs. 1931.

LAREW -- Larew, John J.
   A Larew family history. Waynesboro. 1970.

LA RUE -- Mather, Otis M.
   Six generations of La Rues and allied families: containing sketch of Isaac
   La Rue, senior, who died in Frederick County, Virginia, in 1795, and some
   account of his American ancestors and three generations of his descendants
   and families who were connected by intermarriage, among others, Carman,
   Hodgen, Helm, Buzan, McDonald, Castleman, Walters, Alexander, Medley,
   McMahon, Vertrees, Keith, Wintersmith, Clay, Neill, Grantham, Vanmeter,
   and Enlow; copies of six old wills and other documents; various incidents
   connected with the settlement of the Nolynn Valley in Kentucky; also a
   chapter on the La Rue family and the child of Abraham Lincoln. Hodgenville,
   Ky. 1921.

LA VELLE -- Leavell, Charlotte Henry
   Genealogy of the nine Leavell brothers of Oxford, Mississippi.
   Charlottesville. 1957.

LAWRENCE -- History of the Lawrence family in England, Virginia, and North
   Carolina, with historical sketches and genealogical outlines of the
   Lawrence family in Connecticut, Maryland, Massachusetts, New Jersey, New
   York, and South Carolina. Also including genealogical records of other
   families coverging with the Lawrence family of Virginia-North Carolina:
   Vaughan with Lawrence 1805, Rea with Lawrence 1836, Jordan with Darden
   1825, Darden with Pruden 1844, Pruden with Lawrence 1870, Moorman with
   Lawrence 1901. Bristol. 1964.

LAWSON -- Bulkley, Caroline Kemper
Lawson of Virginia, North Carolina, Georgia. 1932.

LAWSON -- Porter, Bill
William Lawson, a Scottish rebel. Radford: Commonwealth Press, 1983.

LAWSON -- Willis, B. L.
Sketches and genealogy of the Bailey-Craddock-Lawson families of Virginia
and North Carolina. Alexandria. 1974.

LAYNE -- Lane, Ralph Hoover
Descendants of John Layne of Goochland County, Virginia, (1685-1963).
Washington. 1965.

LEA -- Dixon, Elizabeth W.
The Lea family of Virginia, North Carolina and Mississippi. 1958.

LEA -- Lea, Reba Fitzpatrick
The Lea family in Nelson County, Virginia. Lovingston. 1954.

LEA -- Lea, Reba F.
The Lea family in Nelson County, Virginia: their history and genealogy.
Lynchburg. 1946.

LEACH -- Jones, Mrs. E. Camden
Leach family chart of West Virginia. Smithton, W. Va. 1910.

LEADBETTER -- Ledbetter, Roy C.
Ledbetters from Virginia. Dallas. 1964.

LEAGUE -- Willia, Betty
The League family of Virginia and South Carolina. Amarillo, Tex. 1976.

LEAVELL -- Leavell, Charlotte Henry
Genealogy of nine Leavell brothers of Oxford, Mississippi. Charlottesville.
1957.

LEDYARD -- Ivy, Frances Ledyard
The Ledyard family of Connecticut, New York, Alabama, and Mississippi and
allied families, including the Heards of Virginia, Georgia, and Mississippi.
Columbus, MS.: Columbus, MS. Lowndes County Dept. of Archives and History,
1979.

LEE -- Alexander, Frederick Warren
Stratford Hall and the Lees connected with its history; biographical,
genealogical and historical, comp. Oak Grove. 1912.

LEE -- Bettis, Emma L.
Lee family of Shropshire, England, 1100 a.d. to 1961 in America, called
the Lee family of Virginia. Montgomery, Ala. 1961.

LEE -- Lee, Cassius F.
A record of the descendants of Col. Richard Lee, of Virginia. Boston.
1872.

LEE -- Cousins, Virginia
Lees of Virginia.

LEE -- The descendants of General Robert E. Lee, from King Robert the Bruce, of Scotland. A paper read before the Southern historical association, of Louisville, Ky., March 29, 1881. By Wm. Winston Fontaine. 1881.

LEE -- Genealogy of the Lee family of Virginia and Maryland. An original drawing. 1886.

LEE -- Hendrick, Burton J.
The Lees of Virginia; biography of a family. New York, N. Y.: Halcyon House, 1937.

LEE -- King, George Harrison Sanford
The family tree of Caroline Jackson Lee (1864-1947). Fredericksburg. 1954.

LEE -- Lea, J. Henry
Lee of Virginia. Boston. 1892.

LEE -- Lee of Virginia. Genealogical notes proving the error of the previously accepted pedigree. Communicated by J. Henry Lea, Cedarhurst, Fairhaven, Mass. Boston. 1890.

LEE -- Lee, Edmund Jennings
Lee of Virginia, 1642-1892; biographical and genealogical sketches of the descendants of Colonel Richard Lee, with brief notices of the related families. Philadelphia, Pa. 1895.

LEE -- Lee, Edmund Jennings
Lee of Virginia, 1642-1892; biographical and genealogical sketches of the descendants of Colonel Richard Lee. Baltimore: Genealogical Pub. Co., 1974.

LEE -- Lee, Edmund Jennings
Lee of Virginia, 1642-1892: biographical and genealogical sketches of the descendants of Colonel Richard Lee: with brief notices of the related families of Allerton, Armistead, Ashton, Aylett, Bedinger, Beverley, Bland, Bolling, Carroll, Carter, Chambers, Corbin, Custis, Digges, Fairfax, Fitzhugh, Gardner, Grymes, Hanson, Page, Randolph, Shepherd, Shippin, Tabb, Taylor, Turberville, Washington, and others. Baltimore, Md.: Genealogical Pub. Co., 1983.

LEE -- Lee, Rev. Frederick George
Genalogy of the family of Lee of Chester, Bucks, and Oxon, shewing the lineal descent of the late Robert E. Lee of Virginia, America, from Sir John Lee, knot. With arms, notes, etc. London: Mitchell and Hughes, 1884.

- 116 -

LEE -- Lee, Ronald C.
The Lee family of Middlesex, Va. 1970.

LEE -- The Lees of Virginia. Descendants of Richard Lee and Anna Constable,
who came to Jamestown in 1639. Arlington. 1967.

LEE -- Mead, Edward C.
Genealogical history of the Lee family of Virginia and Maryland, from
A.D. 1300 to A.D. 1866. New York, N.Y. 1868.

LEE -- Mead, Edward C.
Genealogical history of the Lee family of Virginia and Maryland from
A.D. 1300 to A.D. 1866, with notes and illustrations. New York, N.Y.:
University Publishing Co., 1871.

LEE -- Old Stratford and the Lees who lived there. Charlottesville: Society
of the Lees of Virginia, 1925.

LEE -- Orr, Lucinda Lee
Journal of a young lady of Virginia: Lucinda Lee, 1787. c1976.

LEE -- Rose, Ben Lacy
Report of research on the Lea family in Virginia & North Carolina before
1800. Richmond. 1984.

LEE -- Rucker, Elizabeth Hoyle
Genealogy of William Lee I of England and of Virginia and his descendants,
900-1945. Miami, Fla.: Franklin Press, Inc., 1945.

LEE -- Seaman, Catherine H. C.
The Lees of 17th century York County, Virginia: a case study of family,
kinship, and land tenure in the 17th century. Sweet Briar: Sweet Briar
College Print. Press, 1985.

LEE -- Wilson, Reba Shropshire
The Lees and Kings of Virginia and North Carolina. Ridgely, Tenn.: Wilson
and Glover Pub. Co., 1975.

LEE -- Wayland, John W.
Robert E. Lee and his family. Staunton. 1951.

LEFTWICH -- Hopkins, Walter Lee
Leftwich-Turner familes of Virginia and their connections. Richmond: J. W.
Ferguson & Sons, 1931.

LEHEW -- LeHue, J. H. and Edith Foster
Peter Lehew of Front Royal, Virginia, and some of his descendants. Elburn,
Ill. 1967.

LEHMAN -- Lehman, James O.
The Willis and Sarean Amstutz Lehman family calendar. Harrisonburg. 1981.

LEMEN -- Lemen, Frank B.
History of the Lemen family of Illinois, Virginia and elsewhere, with
gallery of portraits, biographical sketches and genealogical tables,
1650-1898. Collinsville, Ill. 1898.

LEMLEY -- Headlee, Alvah J. W.
George Lemley and his wife Catherine Yoho and their descendants for two centuries. Morgantown, W. Va. 1975.

LEMMEX -- Morey, Ellen Lemmex
Biographical notes of the Lemmex family. 1954.

LEWIS -- Anderson, Sarah Travers Lewis Scott
Lewises, Meriwethers and their kin; Lewises and Meriwethers with their tracings through the families whose records are herein contained. Richmond: Dietz Press, 1938.

LEWIS -- Family record of Lawrence Lewis (Washington's nephew), and Nellie Park Custis (Washington's adopted daughter). Transcribed from Martha Washington's Bible, which was sold by order of H. L. D. Lewis, administrator to the estate of Mrs. Lorenzo Lewis. Philadelphia, Pa. 1890.

LEWIS -- Lewis, Andrew Aldridge
Descendants of William Lewis, emigrated from Wales and settled in Northumberland County, Virginia, married Elizabeth Markham. Fredericksburg, 194-.

LEWIS -- Lewis, Enoch J.
Research and recollections on 'the Lewis family.' Culpeper. 1943.

LEWIS -- Lewis, G. R.
Brief history of the Lewis family on the Eastern Shore of Maryland and Virginia. Washington. 1971.

LEWIS (Augusta) -- Lewis, L. L.
A Brief Narrative. Richmond. 1915.

LEWIS -- Moses, Grace McLean
The Welsh lineage of John Lewis (1592-1657), emigrant to Gloucester, Va. McLean. 1983.

LEWIS -- Nelson, Alice Jean
Virginia lineages, letters & memories: Lewises of Portici on Bull Run with related families from twenty counties. Sarasota, Fla. 1984.

LEWIS -- Van Meter, Benjamin F.
Genealogies and sketches of some old families who have taken prominent part in the development of Virginia and Kentucky especially, and later of many other states of this Union. Louisville: J. P. Morton & Co., 1901.

LEWIS -- Williams, Clarence Russell
The Lewis-Gwathmey family of Richmond, Virginia. 1947

LEWTER -- West, Belle Lewter
Luter-Lewter family of England, Virginia, North Carolina, and States
south and west. Durham, N.C. 1974.

LICHTENSTEIN -- Lichtenstein, Gaston
The Virginia Lichtenstein Family. Richmond: H. T. Ezekiel, Printer,
1912.

LILLARD -- Lillard, Jacques Ephraim
Lillard; a family of colonial Virginia, 1415 to 1928; including authentic
revolutionary service references, early marriage records, wills, deeds,
legal documents, original family letters of early American Lillards, etc.
Richmond: Williams Print Co., 1928.

LILLARD -- Lillard, Gerald F.
A compilation of the known descendants of Thomas and Rhoda Patterson
Lillard. Arlington. 1950.

LILLY -- Lilly, David H.
Genealogy of Guy Erastus Lilly and Clara Susan Neely Lilly. Hinton,
W. Va. 1982.

LINCOLN, Abraham, 1809-1865--Family -- Semones, Hattie
Duel with destiny. Radford: Commonwealth Press, 1976.

LINCOLN -- Wayland, John W.
The Lincolns in Virginia. Staunton: McClure Print. Co., 1946.

LINDAMOOD -- Harpine, J. William
Lindamood family history. Harrisburg. 1965.

LINDSAY -- Brien, Lindsay B. M.
Clan Lindsay; Lindsay families of Virginia, North Carolina, South Carolina.

LINDSAY -- Jones, Gordon C.
The Albemarle Lindseys and their descendants, 1585-1979. Chesapeake. 1979.

LINDSAY -- Lindsay, Margaret Isabella
The Lindsays of America: a genealogical narrative and family record:
beginning with the family of the earliest settler in the mother state,
Virginia, and including an appendix of all the Lindsays of America.
Baltimore: Gateway Press, 1979.

LINDSAY -- Sparacio, Ruth Trickey and Sam
Pamunkey neighbors of Orange County, Virginia: transcriptions from the
original files of county courts in Virginia, Kentucky, and Missouri of
wills, deeds, order books & marriages as well as some family lines:
Lindsay, Mills, Mountague, Stevens and related families and neighbors.
Baltimore: Gateway Press, 1985.

LINDSAY -- Wood, Forest Patrick
The Lindsay-Lindsey family of Pa., Va., Ky., & Ind. Seattle, Wash.
1966.

LINNEY -- Linney, James Erle
Genealogy of the Linney family in England, Virginia, Maryland ... and
possibly other states. Harrodsburg, Ky.: Harrodsburg Herald, 1974.

LIPSCOMB -- Helmer, Dorothy Garr
Lipscomb, 300 years in America, 1679-1979: English background and some
descendants of Ambrose II, William, and John, the three sons of our
immigrant ancestor Ambrose Lipscomb I whose first record in Virginia was
in 1679. Indianapolis. 1979.

LITTLE -- Lytle, Leonard
The descendants of John Little of Botetourt and Rockbridge Counties,
Virginia. Detroit. 1960.

LITTLE -- Warrell, Mary Margaret Freese
How our little family grew. Wheeling, W. Va. 1964.

LITTLETON -- Robins, Robert P.
A tentative pedigree of the Littleton family of Virginia. Boston. 1887.

LIVERS -- Donnelly, Mary Louise
Arnold Livers family in America (Lyvers, Lievers). Burke. 1977.

LOCKE -- Brown, Dorothy L. W.
George and Sarah (Niett) Locke family of Virginia; a genealogy of many
of their descendants. La Grange, Ill. 1961.

LOCKE -- Hayes, Donald P.
Locke genealogy: supplement: including the families of Capt. John Locke
of Portsmouth and Hampton, New Hampshire, William Locke of Woburn, Mass.,
and George Locke of Virginia. Ann Arbor, Mich. 1979.

LOCKETT -- Blankenburg, Katherine Dixon Carter
Thomas Lockett of Virginia; genealogical memoir. San Diego, Calif. 1940.

LOGAN -- Logan, George William
A record of the Logan family of Charleston, South Carolina. Richmond.
1875. New edition with preface, biographical additions and tables, by
Lily Logan Morrill. Cincinnati. 1923.

LOGUE -- Buchanan, Jane Gray
John Logue of North Carolina: history and hypothesis: Logue and related
families of Delaware, Maryland, Pennsylvania, Virginia, and Tennessee.
Oak Ridge, Tenn. 1980.

LOMAX -- Lomax, Joseph
   Genalogical and Historical Sketches of the Lomax Family. Grand Rapids,
   Mich.: The Rookus Printing House, 1894.

LOMAX -- Genealogy of the Virginia family of Lomax ... by one of the seventh
   generation in the direct line; with references to the Lunsford, Micou,
   Roy, Caronim, Eltonhead, Tayloe, Plater, Addison, Tasker, Burford,
   Wilkinson, Griffin, Gwynn, Lindsay, Payne, Presley, Thornton, Savage,
   Wellford, Randolph, Isham, Yates, and other prominent families of Virginia
   and Maryland. Chicago, Ill.: Rand, McNally & Co., 1913.

LOVE -- Connally, Mary Virginia
   A partial history of the families of Joseph Love of Augusta County,
   Virginia. Atlanta, Ga. 1902.

LOVE -- Love, Mary Elizabeth
   History and genealogy of the families related to Henry Hicks Love.
   Lunenburg County, Va.: Lunenburg, 1972.

LOWE -- McDuffie, Eva Loe
   The Lowe-Loe-Low family in Virginia, North Carolina, Mississippi,
   Tennessee, Kentucky and Missouri. 1955.

LOWER SHENANDOAH -- Norris, J. E.
   History of the Lower Shenandoah Valley (Counties of Frederick, Berkeley,
   Jefferson and Clarke, etc.). Chicago, Ill.: A Warner & Co., Publishers,
   1890.

LUCK -- Sims, Mary Inglis
   Luck, genealogical research findings and notes on the family & neighbors
   of Francis Luck of Virginia. Sacramento, Calif, 1979.

LUDWIG -- Davis (Ludwig) Lilliam Virginia
   Solomon Ludwig family: a short sketch of the ancestry of Solomon Ludwig
   and the records of his lineage. Front Royal. 1973.

LUMPKIN -- Battey, George Magruder, III
   Wilson Lumpkin, governor of Georgia, and his Virginia ancestry, with
   notes on in-laws of the Lumpkin family in Halifax County, Virginia,
   including Hendricks, Hurts, Smiths. Washington. 1944.

LUMPKIN LORE -- Cody, L. L.
   Lumpkin Lore. Macon, Ga. 1928.

LUMPKIN -- Lumpkin, Ben Gray and Martha Neville Lumpkin
   The Lumpkin family of Virginia, Georgia and Mississippi. Clarksville,
   Tenn. 1973.

LUMPKIN -- Lumpkin, Martha Neville
   Minor, Scales, Cottrell, and Gray families of Virginia, North Carolina,
   and Mississippi. Clarksville, Tenn. 1974.

LYLE -- Lyle, Daniel
   Daniel Lyle, immigrant; one of the Lyle family who emigrated from Ireland
   to America and settled in the valley of Virginia in 1740. Peck, Idaho.
   1946.

LYLE -- Lyle, Oscar K.
   Lyle family, the ancestry and posterity of Matthew, John, Daniel and
   Samuel Lyle, pioneer settlers in Virginia. New York, N.Y.: Lecouver
   Press Company, 1912.

LYNCHBUEG -SKETCHES AND RECOLLECTIONS OF LYNCHBURG, VIRGINIA -- By the
   oldest inhabitant. Richmond. 1858.

MABRY -- Shea, Patricia A.
   The Maybury family. Alexandria. 1979.

MACBRYDE -- Dixon, Ben F.
   ... A McBride chronology, with a perspective view of the findings, a
   series of notices on "McBride" from the public records of early Virginia
   and Kentucky, chronologically arranged with an interpretation of their
   evidence. Washington. 1941.

MACBRYDE -- Love, Robert Abner
   The story of James McBride of Whitehall, Illinois; a report of a
   genealogical search undertaken for Carol Joyce McBride. Arlington.
   1949.

MACKENZIE -- Mackenzie, George N.
   Colonial Families of the United States of America, etc. 7 vols. New
   York and Boston. 1907.

MACLIN -- Bond, Octavia Zollicoffer
   The family chronicle and kinship book of Maclin, Clack, Cocke, Carter,
   Taylor, Cross, Gordon, and other related American lineages. Nashville,
   Tenn.: McDaniel Printing Co., 1928.

MACON -- Macon, Alethea Jane
   Gideon Macon of Virginia and some of his descendants. Macon, Ga. 1956.

MADAN -- Harney, Alice Lucille
   The Madden's and the Harney's. McLean. 1978.

MADDY -- Maddy, Olive
   Us Maddys; an account of the family in England and the descendants of
   William Maddy of Fairfax County, Virginia, and James Maddy of Fairfax and
   Orange Counties, emigrants. Oskaloosa, Ia. 1952.

MADISON -- Clarke, Allen C.
Life and Letters of Dolly Madison, Etc. Washington: W. F. Roberts
Company, 1914.

MAGGARD -- Gottschalk, Katherine Cox
The Maggard Family of Virginia. 1931.

MAGILL -- Graham, J. R.
Sketches, biographical and genealogical of the Magill family of
Winchester. Winchester. 1908.

MAGILL -- Magill, Robert M.
Magill Family Record. Richmond. 1907.

MAGNA CHARTA BARONS -- Browning, C. H.
The Magna Charta Barons and their American Descendants, etc.
Philadelphia, Pa. 1898.

MAGRUDER -- Magruder, Caleb Clarke
Nathan Magruder of "Knave's dispute." Reprinted from Year book of
America clan Gregor society. Charlottesville. 1915.

MAGRUDER -- Magruder, Caleb Clarke, Jr.
Nathaniel Magruder of "Dunblane." Richmond: Appeals Press, Inc., 1917.

MAGRUDER -- Magruder, Caleb Clarke
Descendants of Isaac Magruder, revolutionary soldier. Charlottesville.
1929.

MAHONE -- Blake, Nelson Morehouse, Ph.D.
William Mahone of Virginia, soldier and political insurgent. Richmond:
Garrett & Massie, 1925.

MAJOR -- Cabell, James Branch
The Majors and their marriages, with collateral accounts of the allied
families of Aston, Ballard, Christian, Dancy, Hartwell, Hubard, Macon,
Marable, Mason, Patteson, Piersey, Seawell, Stephens, Waddill, and
others. Richmond: W. C. Hill Printing Co., 1915.

MAJOR -- Downing, George C.
The Major genealogy of Franklin County, Ky. Descendants of John Major.
Roanoke. 1958.

MALLARD -- Fairbank, Eula Mae Priscilla Sturdivant
History of the Mallard family; an account of their ancestors and descendants,
with the allied families of Sturdivant, McWatty, Fairbank, and Poe; also
Holland, Rees, McGhee, and Crawford. Richmond. 1960.

MALLORY -- Moyer, Julia M.
  John Mallory, Virginia soldier, 1777-1782. Paris, Tex. 1939.

MALLORY -- Mallory, Henry R.
  Genealogy of the Mallorys of Virginia. Hartford, Conn. 1955.

MANAHAN -- Manahan, John E.
  Manahan family (1750-1950) and allied families of Cassell, Ogg, Frizzell
  and others. Radford. 1952.

MANN -- Mann, George S.
  Mann memorial. A record of the Mann family in America. Genealogy of the
  descendants of Richard Mann, of Scituate, Mass. Preceded by English family
  records, and an account of Wentham, Rehoboth, Boston, Lexington, Virginia,
  and other branches of the Manns who settled in this country. Boston: D.
  Clapp & Son, 1884.

MAPP -- Eichelberger, Pierce
  The Mapp family on the Eastern Shore of Virginia. Quinby. 1972.

MARSHALL -- Beveridge, Albert J.
  The Life of John Marshall. Boston and New York: Houghton-Mifflin Co.,
  1916.

MARSHALL -- Turner, Alienne W.
  John Marshall, Sr.; genealogy and history of some of the descendants of
  John Marshall, Sr. of Brunswick County, Va., 1732-1956. Henderson,
  N.C. 1956.

MARTIN -- Brinkley, Beatrice Martin
  Records of Martin-Crawford-Rodes-Dishman families in Virginia, Kentucky
  and Texas. 1972.

MARTIN -- Gallaway, Irene Dabney
  The Martin family, descendants of Thomas Martin of Goochland Co., Virginia.
  Fayetteville, Ark. 1906.

MARTIN -- Martin, Claude O.
  Martin records of the families of Peter Martin of Prussia, Va. & Ky.;
  Sarah Redding Martin of Eng., Va., Ky. and John Martin of Va. & Ky.
  & Sarah Jeffries Martin of Va., Ky., and Ind. Madera, Calif. 196-.

MARTIN -- Martin, John
  Valentine Martin of Cumberland County, Virginia. Saint Joseph, Mo. 1960.

MARTIN -- Nash, Ralph G.
  Martin. Springfield. 1980.

MARTIN -- Polk, Cynthia Martin
  Some old colonial families of Virginia. Memphis, Tenn.: Paul & Douglass
  Co., 1915.

MARTIN -- Watson, Estelle Clark
   Some Martin, Jeffries, and Wayman families and connections of Virginia,
   Maryland, Kentucky, and Indiana. Skokie, Ill. 1965.

MARYE -- Eberhart, Edith Whitcraft
   The Maryes of Virginia, 1730-1985. Baltimore: Gateway Press, 1985.

MASON -- Copeland, Pamela C. and Richard K. MacMaster
   The five George Masons: patriots and planters of Virginia and Maryland.
   Charlottesville: University Press of Virginia, 1975.

MASON -- Dobyns, Kenneth W.
   The family of John Baxter Mason (1811-83) of Campbell County, Va. Arlington.
   1980.

MASON -- Genealogy of George Mason of Gunston Hall, 1725-1792, author of the
   Virginia Declaration of rights. Lorton. 1970.

MASON -- Ingersoll, R. E.
   Some of the descendants of George Mason of Gunston Hall, Mary Thomson
   Mason, Thomson Mason of Rasberry Plain. 1951.

MASON -- The Mason Family. Arlington: American Genealogical Research
   Institute, 1972.

MASON -- By his daughter
   The Public Life and Diplomatic Correspondence of James Mason, Etc.
   Roanoke: The Stone Printing and Manufacturing Co., 1903.

MASON -- Mason, Mary Eliza
   Genealogy and history; the family of Hugh Mason, William Mason, and
   allied families. Parkersburg, W. Va. 1930.

MASON -- Rowland, Kate Mason
   Life of George Mason. New York, N.Y.: G. P. Putnam's Sons, 1892.

MASSIE -- Kelsey, Mavis Parrott
   The family of John Massie, 1743-1830, Revolutionary patriot of Louisa
   County, Virginia. Houston, Tex. 1979.

MASSIE -- Massies of Virginia. Descendants from the Massies (Mascy-Masse-
   Massey) of Cheshire England.

MATHENY -- Metheny, William B.
   Matheny-Metheny family of Virginia. Volume I (1941-1949). Philadelphia,
   Pa. 1949.

MATHENY -- Metheny, W. Blake
   Genealogical notes concerning the Matheny-Metheny family of Virginia. 1955.

MATHEWS -- Montgomery, Anne D.
   The Mathews family of Virginia and allied families. San Francisco, Calif.
   1968.

MATHIAS -- Griffiths, George R.
The Mathias family of Hardy County, Virginia and West Virginia: a
pioneer mountain family. Chicago, Ill.: Adams Press, 1977.

MATTHEWS -- Matthews, William Kennon
Luke Matthews of Brunswick County, Virginia, 1739-1788, and his
descendants. Kobe, Japan. 1937.

MAUCK -- Brubaker, Mary S.
Mauck-Brubaker families of the Page Valley of Virginia. 1980.

MAUCK -- Davis, Lillian Virginia Ludwig
Frederick George Mauck family. Strasburg. 1969.

MAUCK -- Wolph, William Richard
The descendants of Peter Mauck, 1708-1980. Arlington. 1980.

MAUPIN -- Maupin, Florence Mary
Notes on the Maupin family. Portsmouth. 1981.

MAUZY -- Mauzy, Richard
Genealogical record of the descendants of Henry Mauzy, a Huguenot
refugee, the ancestor of the Mauzys of Virginia and other states, from
1685 to 1910, and of the descendants of Jacob Kisling from 1760 to 1910.
Harrisonburg. 1911.

MAXEY -- Clark, Edythe Maxey
The Maxeys of Virginia. Baltimore: Gateway Press, 1980.

MAXWELL -- Houston, Florence Wilson, Laura Cowan Blaine & Ella Dunn Mellette
Maxwell history and genealogy, including the allied families of Alexander,
Allen, Bachiler, Batterton, Beveridge, Blain, Brewster, Brown, Callender,
Campbell, Carey, Clark, Cowan, Fox, Dinwiddie, Dunn, Eylar, Garreston,
Gentry, Guthrie, Houston, Howard, Howe, Hughes, Hussey, Irvine, Johnson,
Kimes, McCullough, Moore, Pemberton, Rosenmuller, Smith, Stapp, Teter,
Tilford, Uzzell, Vawter, Ver Planck, Walker, Wiley, Wilson. Also
baptismal record of the Rev. John Craig, D.D., of Augusta County, Virginia,
1740-1749, containing one thousand four hundred and seventy four names.
Indianapolis, Ind. 1916.

MAXWELL -- Norman, Annie, Helen Maxwell Longino, and Annie Low Maxwell
Thomas Maxwell of Virginia and Georgia and his descendants. Macon, Ga.:
J. W. Burke Co., 1956.

MAY -- Coke, Ben H.
John May, Jr. of Virginia: his descendants and their land: with an
account of some early descendant families including Cocke, Coke, Joplin,
Love, Percefull, Tompkins. Baltimore: Gateway Press, 1975.

MAY -- Mays, Rayford Glynn
  Mays and Pullen pioneers: Tideland Virginia to Tennessee and North
  Alabama: across four centuries. Franklin, N.C. 1983.

MAY -- Swango, Maxine Virginia May
  Our family tree, May--Spurlock. St. Albans, W. Va. 1979.

MAY -- Woodruff, Audrey L. W.
  Descendants of John May, Sr. and Sarah Jane (Phillips) May, 1760-1967 of
  Virginia, Tenn., Kentucky ... and allied families of Hanson, Wall, Rook
  (and) Mundell. Kansas City. 1967.

MAYO -- Battey, George Magruder, III
  Mayos of Virginia and kinsmen, Smiths of Virginia and others of the
  connections. Washington. 1940.

McALLISTER -- McAllister, J. M. and Laura B. Tandy
  Genealogies of the Lewis and Kindred Families. Columbus, Mo. 1906.

McALLISTER -- McAllister, Rev. D. S.
  Genealogical record of the descendants of Col. Alexander McAllister, of
  Cumberland County, N.C.; also of Mary and Isabella McAllister.
  Richmond: Whittet & Shepperson, 1900.

McALLISTER -- McAllister, J. Gray
  Family records, comp. for the descendants of Abraham Addams McAllister
  and his wife Julia Ellen (Stratton) McAllister, of Covington, Virginia,
  containing a sketch of A. A. McAllister, prepared and published by the
  conspiracy and co-operation of his sons, and related data, which will
  answer some of the questions our grandchildren are sure to ask. Easton,
  Pa.: Chemical Pub. Co., 1912.

McBRIDE -- Dixon, Benjamin F.
  McBride family of Virginia and Kentucky, and the Rout family of Kentucky.
  Washington. 1971.

McCANN -- Kellogg, Joseph M.
  Kellogg notebooks on West Virginia families: The McCann family. Lawrence,
  Kans. 1958.

McCANN -- McKann, George Cundiff, Jr.
  Pictorial supplement to the history of the Mackans, MacKans, McKans &
  McKanns, an early Virginia family. Evanston, Ill. 1978.

McCANN -- McCann, Robert Lee
  Family of Eliza R. McCann M. Ltyle Griffing. Evanston, Ill. and Hopewell,
  Va.

McCARTY -- O'Brien, Michael J.
  The McCartys of Old Virginia. New York, N.Y. 1907.

McCARTY -- McCarty, Clara S.
   McCartys of Virginia; with emphasis on the first four generations in the
   colony. Richmond: Dietz Press, 1972.

McCARY -- McCary, Ben C.
   McCary and several allied families. Richmond: Tidewater Press, 1972.

McCLANAHAN -- The McClanahans. Roanoke: Stone Printing and Manufacturing
   Co., 1894.

McCLAREN -- Greenway, Carol Forrest
   Alexander McClaren with excursis sic on related families of Va., N.C.,
   S.C., and Tenn. 1977.

McCLURE -- Clemens, William M.
   McClure Family Records. New York, N.Y.: William M. Clemens, Publisher,
   1914.

McCLURE -- McClure, J. A.
   The McClure Family. Petersburg. 1914.

McCLURE -- McCluer, Leon
   Following McCluer: life in Mississippi in the teens, with a line each of
   LaRue, Parrill, Moore, Cox genealogy. Verona: McClure Print Co., 1974.

McCOACH -- Licklider, Louise Carpenter
   A genealogy of the descendants as known on 1 September 1979 of James
   McCoach: immigrant in 1846, Donegal County, Ireland to Tyler County,
   West Virginia. Arlington, Mass. 1979.

McCONNELL -- Addington, Hugh M. and Mattie E.
   McConnell marriage genealogy; ancestors, descendants, marriages of an
   illustrious family of Virginia. Nichelsville: Service Printer, 1929.

McCONNELL -- McConnell, John Preston
   Who am I? A brief sketch of the McConnell and related families in southwest Virginia. East Radford. 1929.

McCORMICK -- Genealogical tables of the descendants of Robert McCormick of
   "Walnut Grove." Rockbridge County, Virginia, born 1780 - died 1846.
   Strasburg: Shenandoah Pub. House, 1934.

McCUE -- McCue, John N.
   The McCues of the Old Dominion. Mexico, Mo. 1912.

McCULLOUGH -- McCullough, Rose Chambers G.
   Yesterday when it was past. Richmond: William Byrd Press, 1957.

McDONALD -- Williams, Mrs. Flora McDonald
The Glengarry McDonalds of Virginia. Louisville: George C. Fetter
Company, 1911.

McDOWELL -- Perdue, Lemuel Ford
A brief history of Ephraim and Joseph McDowell of Virginia and North
Carolina. Houston. 1912.

McGAVOCK -- Gray, Rev. Robert
The McGavock Family. A Genealogical History of James McGavock and his
Descendants from 1760 to 1903. Richmond. 1903.

McGLASSON -- Dye, B. R. E.
McGlasson family in Virginia and Boone County, Ky. Hebron, Ky. 1972.

McGUIRE -- Stanard, William G.
The McGuire family in Virginia, with notices of its Irish ancestry and
some connected Virginia families. Richmond: Old Dominion Press, 1926.

McILHANY -- McIlhany, H. M., Jr.
Some Virginia Families. Staunton. 1903.

McINTIRE -- McIntire, Robert Harry
Ancestry of Robert Harry McIntire and Helen Annette McIntire, his wife.
Norfolk. 1950.

McINTOSH I, AND II -- McIntosh, Charles Fleming
Brief Abstracts of Lower Norfolk County and Norfolk County Wills. The
Colonial Dames of America in the State of Virginia, 1914-1922.

McINTYRE -- Taylor, June R. McIntire
Charles McIntire of Colonial Virginia: with related Bailey, Collyer,
Dick, Dow, Enyart, Evans, Hite, Line, Mounts, Pfeiffer, Salisbury,
Sheldon, Stewart, Turner, Wilson. Sarasota, Fla. 1981.

McIVER -- McIver, Helen M.
Genealogy of the McIver family of North Carolina. Richmond: Whittet &
Shepperson, 1943.

McKEE -- Green, Woodford McKee
Supplement to McKees of Virginia and Kentucky by George W. McKee. 1975.

McKEE -- McKee, George Wilson
The McKees of Virginia and Kentucky. Pittsburg.

McKINNE -- Wood, Lillian F.
Michael Mackquiny of Virginia. 1946.

McMILLAN -- McMillan, Forrest Dale
   The McMillan family of Preston and Monongalia Counties, West Virginia;
   a genealogy. Richmond. 1974.

McNEEL -- Edgar, Betsy Jordan
   The McNeel family record; descendants of pioneer John McNeel and Martha
   Davis of Pocahontas County, West Virginia, 1765-1967. Parson, W. Va.:
   McClain Print Co., 1967.

McNEIL -- Rose, Ben Lacy
   Thomas McNeil of Caswell County, North Carolina: his forebears &
   descendants. Richmond. 1984.

McNEW -- Baer, Frank L.
   The McNew family of Washington Co., Va. 1964.

McROBERTS -- Mills, Harry Willard
   McRoberts family; some notes on: McRoberts' in Pennsylvania, Virginia
   and Kentucky; McRoberts family of Lincoln County, Ky. A family history
   miniature. Washington. 1943.

McWHORTER -- McWhorter, Minnie S.
   History of the Henry McWhorter family of New Jersey and West Virginia.
   Charleston: Charleston Print., 1948.

MEAD -- Baskervill, P. Hamilton
   Andrew Meade of Ireland and Virginia; his ancestors, and some of his
   descendants and their connections, including sketches of the following
   families: Meade, Everard, Hardaway, Segar, Pettus, and Overton ...
   chiefly from letters, papers, and other material furnished by Mrs. Elise
   Meade Skelton Baskervill and from other sources. Richmond: Old Dominion
   Press, 1921.

MEAD -- Prichard, A. M.
   Mead relations; Mead, Brown, Powell, Keyser, Kelly, Trumbo, Austin, Toler,
   Prichard. Virginia, Kentucky. Staunton. 1933.

MEADE -- Baskervill, P. Hamilton
   Andrew Meade of Ireland and Virginia, Etc. Richmond: Old Dominion
   Press, 1921.

MEADE, I, II -- Meade, Bishop
   Old Churches, Ministers and Families of Virginia. (2 vols.) Philadelphia:
   J. B. Lippincott Company, 1889.

MEADE -- Peet, Henry J.
   Chaumiere papers, containing matters of interest to the descendants of
   David Meade, of Nansemond County, Va., who died in the year 1757.
   Chicago. 1883.

MEADOR -- Meador, Daniel Burton
    Genealogical record of some of the Meador family who are descendants of
    Thomas Meador of Virginia. North Newton, Kans.: Mennonite Press, 1968.

MEADOR -- Meador, Edward Kirby
    The Meadors of Virginia. A play in three acts. Boston: Meador Pub.
    Co., 1941.

MEADOR -- Meador, Victor P.
    Our Meador families in Colonial America: as found in the records of Isle
    of Wight, Lancaster, (Old) Rappahannock, Richmond, Essex and Caroline
    Counties, Virginia. Independence, Mo. 1983.

MEADOR -- Nunnally, Perkins
    Descendants of Jonas and Frances Meador of Essex, Caroline and Cumberland
    Counties, Va. Pine Bluff, Ark. 1968.

MEADOWS -- Breeden, Shirley Seal
    The descendants of Francis Meadows of Orange & Rockingham Counties, Va.
    Elkton. 1978.

MEANS -- Means, Daniel Orville
    The Means family of America, supplement to section II, Chapter IV.
    Parsons, W. Va.: McClain Print., 1979.

MEARS -- Morse, Theoda Mears
    Mears families of Virginia and Georgia. 1962.

MEEM -- John G. Meem, Lynchburg, Virginia. Lynchburg. 1869.

MEMORIES OF LIFE IN AND OUT OF THE ARMY IN VIRGINIA -- Blackford.
    Compiled by Susan Leigh Blackford from original and contemporaneous
    correspondence and diaries. Lynchburg. 1894.

MENEFEE -- Genealogy of the John Menefee and Mary James family in America,
    or; The descendants of John Menefee, who died in September or October
    1765 in Culpeper Co., Va. 1971.

MERCER-GARNETT FAMILY -- Garnett, James Mercer
    Genealogy of the Mercer-Garnett Family of Essex Co., Va., Etc.
    Richmond: Whittet & Shepperson, 1910.

MEREDITH -- Meredith, Joseph N.
    The Merediths and Selveys of Virginia and West Virginia. Parsons,
    W. Va.: McClain Print., 1982.

MIDDLESEX PARISH REGISTER -- The parish register of Christ Church, Middlesex
    County, from 1653 to 1812. Richmond. 1897.

MILLER -- Custer, Milo
The Reverend Alexander Miller of Virginia and some of his descendants. Bloomington, Ill. 1910.

MILLER -- Gallaher, D. C.
Genealogical notes of the Miller, Quarrier, Shrewsbury, Dickinson, Dickenson families. Charleston, W. Va. 1917.

MILLER -- Glick, Joseph P.
3-generation genealogy of Rev. Joseph Miller (1787-1851) of Beaver Creek Church, Rockingham County, Va. Waynesboro. 1966.

MILLER -- Johnson, Patricia Givens
Elder Jacob Miller (1735-1815), a founder of the Brethren Churches and Dunkard settlements in Franklin County, Virginia (1775), Ohio (1800), and Indiana (1810), and some of his descendants. 1977.

MILLER -- Miller, J. Carson
Jacob Miller of 1748, his descendants and connections. Moores Store. 1936.

MILLER -- The Miller family. Arlington: American Genealogical Research Institute, 1972.

MILLER -- Nesbitt, Virginia Bell
Some of the ancestors and descendants of Samuel Brady Miller, 1834-1905, and Jane Pollock Miller, 1836-1910. Alexandria. 1977.

MILLER -- Smith, Elizabeth V. M.
Descendants of Samuel Miller, John Detrick, John and Mary Snell of Rockingham County, Va., 1777-1943. Kingston, Pa. 1943.

MILLS -- Taylor, Eva Mills Lee
Andrew Mills and his descendants, with genealogies of related families. Strasburg: Shenandoah Pub. House, 1944.

MILLS -- Mills family magazine: genealogical records of Mills and allied families. Arlington. 1949.

MILLS -- The Mills family. Arlington: American Genealogical Research Institute, 1972.

MINOR -- Minor, John B.
The Minor family of Virginia. Lynchburg: J. P. Bell Co., 1923.

MIMS -- Whitley, Edythe
One branch of the Mims family of Virginia. 1965.

MITCHELL -- Allen, Estill Franklin
Cousins: handbook and family history of Mitchell, Allen, Gilleland, and
relatedfamilies from Virginia into Georgia, North Carolina, Kentucky,
Tennessee, Missouri, Mississippi, Illinois, Iowa, Arkansas, Louisiana,
Oklahoma, New Jersey, Texas, California, Florida, and Idaho, mid 1700's
to 1980. Brownwood, Tex.: Howard Payne University, 1981.

MITCHELL -- Fowke, Gerard
Mitchell, Smith, Fowke of Maryland, Virginia, Kentucky. 1924.

MITCHELL -- Kelloff, Joseph M.
Kellogg notebooks on West Virginia families: The Mitchell family.
Lawrence, Kans. 1958.

MOAK -- Moak, Lennox Lee
The Moak and related families of South Carolina and Mississippi,
1740-1960; with notes as to members of the family in Tennessee and
Illinois and also notes as to other Moak families in New York,
Pennsylvania, Maryland and Virginia. Fort Washington, Pa. 1960.

MONCURE -- Duncan, Marion Moncure, Adrian Cather Miller and Peyton Sagendorf
          Moncure
House of Moncure genealogy ... including European & colonial ancestral
background. Alexandria. 1967.

MONGER -- Monger, Billie Jo
The Mongers, a family of old Virginia. Elkton. 1980.

MONONGAHELA -- Butcher, Bernard L.
Genealogy and personal history of the Upper Monongahela Valley, West
Virginia, under the editorial supervision of Bernard L. Butcher. New
York: Lewis Historical Publishing Co., 1912.

MONROE -- Lewis, Edward S.
Ancestry of James Monroe, President of the United States. Williamsburg.
1923.

MONROE -- Morgan, George
Life of James Monroe. Boston: Small, Maynard and Company, 1921.

MONTAGUE -- Montague, George Wm.
History and genealogy of the Montague family of America, descended from
Richard Montague of Hadley, Mass., and Peter Montague of Lancaster Co.,
Va., with genealogical notes of other families by name of Montague. Rev.
and ed. by William L. Montague. Amherst, Mass. 1886.

MONTAGUE -- Montague, George William
History and genealogy of Peter Montague of Nansemond and Lancaster
Counties, Virginia, and his Descendants. Amherst, Mass.: Press of
Carpenter & Morehouse, 1894.

MONTGOMERY -- Montgomery, Walter R.
    The family history of Walter Raymond Montgomery and Elsie Louise Mock.
    Virginia Beach: Farmers Press, 1975.

MONTGOMERY -- Wingfield, Marshall
    Pioneer families of Franklin County, Virginia. Berryville: Chesapeake
    Book Co., 1964.

MONTROSS -- Taylor, John Wilson and Eva Mills Lee Taylor
    Montross: family history; Pierre Montras and his descendants, a record
    of 300 years of the Montras, Montross, Montrose, Montress family in the
    United States and Canada. Staunton. 1958.

MOODY -- Park, Clara Lorene Cammack
    Francis Moody (1769-1821): his ancestors, descendants, and related
    families, and all Moodys in the early records of Chesterfield County,
    Virginia. Baltimore: Gateway Press, 1984.

MOORE -- Hall, David Moore
    Six Centuries of the Moores of Fawley and their Descendants, Etc.
    Richmond: C. E. Flanhart, Printers, 1904.

MOORE -- Moor, Steven Richard
    The Moore Huffman family: with subsequent related materials of the
    history of the Moore (More), Williard (Viellard), Huffman (Hoffman),
    and Lail (Lagle) branches and their arrival and settlement in the areas
    of Pennsylvania, Maryland, Virginia, and North Carolina. Jamestown, N.C.
    1978.

MOORE -- Moore, George Lunceford
    A history of the descendants of Shildes Moore, in America. Belleville,
    Ill.: Risdon Alexander Moore, 1891.

MOORE -- Schoene, Charles E.
    The Moores of Virginia and Kentucky. Belleair Bluffs, Fla. 1974.

MOORE -- Sheffield, Sarah Sherrod
    Some data regarding the Moore, Billups, and Sherrod families of Va.,
    Ga., Ala., & Mississippi. 1911.

MOREHEAD -- Morehead, J. M., III
    The Morehead Family of North Carolina and Virginia. New York. 1921.

MORGAN -- Haymond, Henry
Historical reference to Pricketts' fort and its defenders, with incidents
of border warefare in the Monongahela Valley and ceremonies at unveiling
of monument marking site of Prickett's fort, erected in 1774; including
brief sketches of Major William Haymond and the ancestors of the Morgan
and Prickett families. Clarksburg, W. Va. 191-.

MORGAN -- Jones, Lizzie E. Boice and Martha Armstrong Watson
Ancestry and descendants of Catherine Weas of West Virginia. Des Moines,
Iowa. 1920.

MORGAN -- Morgan, Clarita H.
Reverend Edward Morgan, 1751-1844; pioneer local preacher of the Methodist
Episcopal Church in Southwest Virginia. Ordained by Bishop Francis
Asbury, 1801. Radford. 1973.

MORGAN -- Morgan, French
A history & genealogy of the family of Col. Morgan Morgan, the first white
settler of the State of West Virginia. Washington. 1950.

MORGAN -- Sims, Annie Noble
Francis Morgan, an early Virginia burgess, and some of his descendants.
Savannah, Ga.: Braid & Hutton, Inc., 1920.

MORRIS -- Beeler, Flora M. D.
Morris and Jarretts of West Virginia, descendants and connecting families.
Knoxville, Tenn. 1974.

MORRIS -- Morris, Roy G.
Morris and Morriss genealogy and related families of Charles Morris,
Revolutionary War Service, Virginia, 1712-1972. 1972.

MORRIS -- Highland, Scotland G.
Descendants of the Rev. Isaac Morris ... An historical and genealogical
narrative. Clarsburg, W. Va. 1928.

MORRIS -- Morris, W. R.
Folklore of early settlers of America and their ancestral lineage. Fancy
Gap. 1958.

MORRISON -- Morrison, Granville Price
History of a branch of the Morrison family whose progenitor emigrated to
America, and located in Virginia in colonial days. Also a sketch of the
New Hampshire and Pennsylvania Morrisons settling in those states at an
earlier date. Charleston, W. Va.: Jarrett Print Co., 1928.

MORRISON -- Morison, Leonard A.
  The history of the Morison or Morrison family with most of the "Traditions
  of the Morrisons" (clan Mac Gillemhuire), hereditary judges of Lewis, by
  Capt. F.W.L. Thomas, of Scotland, and a record of the descendants of the
  hereditary judges to 1880. A complete history of the Morison settlers of
  Londonderry, N.H., of 1719, and their descendants, with genealogical
  sketches. Also, of the Brentwood, Nottingham, and Sanbornton, N.H.
  Morisons, and branches of the Morisons who settled in Delaware, Pennsylvania,
  Virginia, and Nova Scotia, and descendants of the Morisons of Preston
  Grange, Scotland, and other families. Boston. 1880.

MORRISON -- Morrison, Sarah
  The Morrison family. Richmond. 1980.

MORTON -- Katz, Gertrude Morton Price
  Several old letters concerning the Mortons of Virginia and allied families.
  1970.

MORTON -- Johnson, Beulah Jeannette
  Genealogy of John Morton, Henrico County, Virginia. Oklahoma City, Okla.
  1939.

MORTON -- McKenney, Ruby Griffin
  Genealogical records of John Morton and his descendants of Pennsylvania,
  Virginia, North Carolina, Georgia & Florida. 1961.

MORTONS AND THEIR KIN -- Morton, Daniel, M.D., F.A.C.S.
  A genealogy and a source book. Volume One, "The Mortons"; Volume Two,
  "The Morton Kin." A collection of genealogical material from original
  sources relating to the Morton family of Virginia and especially to
  John Morton and his descendants, together with a great amount of data
  concerning families kin to the Mortons. St. Joseph, Mo. 1920.

MORTON -- Morton, Duval, M. D.
  Morton Data. St. Joseph, Mo. 1901.

MORTON -- Swiger, Elizabeth Davis
  History and family record of the Morton family of Webster County, West
  Virginia: the continuing story. Grafton, W. Va.: Mountain Heritage
  Genealogy Society, 1984.

MOSELEY -- Moseley, George Carrington, M.A.
  Genealogy of Moseley family of Bedford County, Va. Richmond. 1912.

MOSLEY -- Moseley, R. L.
  Epitome of the history of the Moseley family: ancestry and descendants
  of Lt. Robert Moseley of Virginia and Kentucky. Winter Park, Fla.:
  College Press, 1979.

MOSLEY -- Moseley, Thomas Byred
  A Moseley genealogy: England, Holland, Virginia, the Carolinas, Georgia,
  Alabama, Mississippi, Louisiana, Texas, to the West Coast. Baltimore:
  Gateway Press, 1985.

MOSELEY -- Roberts, Jeane F.
Tables of genealogy of descendants of Virginia Moseleys. Washington.
1961.

MOSS -- Wulfeck, Dorothy Ford
Moss of Virginia. Naugatuck, Conn. 1961.

MOTTLEY -- Mottley, Bessie M.
Dr. Robert Cobbs Mottley, John Lewis Mottley. Richmond. 1964.

MOYER -- Moyer, Julia M.
The Mallory family of Virginia. Paris, Tex. 1939.

MUNSEY -- Carter, John Denton
The Munsey ancestors of Rhoda Munsey Weems Carter (1814-1800) of Russell
County, Virginia, and Newton County, Missouri. Biloxi, Miss. 1969.

MUNGER -- Monger, Billie Jo
The Mongers, a family of old Virginia. Elkton. 1980.

MURPHY -- Archer, George W.
Every name index: History of Rev. William Murphy and his descendants,
1798-1918, by Alice Murphy Strugess. Arlington. 1982.

MURDOCH -- Leslie, J. D.
Genealogy of the Murdoch family. Dallas, Tex. Lynchburg, Va. 1934.

MURROW -- Mirrow, Charles Harland
The Murrow family of Virginia, Kentucky, Indiana, Iowa, and Kansas.
Descendants of James Murrow ... A partial genealogy, compiled from
1910 to 1940. Des Moines, Iowa. 1940.

MURPHY -- Murohy, Marion Emerson
Early Murphys - Murpheys in Pittsylvania County, Virginia, Robertson and
Carroll Counties, Tennessee. San Diego, Calif. 1975.

MUSSETTER -- Hodge, Lois L. R.
Descendants of John and Christopher Mussetter, sons of Christian Mussetter.
Fredericksburg. 1968.

MUSSETTER -- Hodge, Lois R.
Mussetters and related families, 1769-1975. Fredericksburg. 1976.

MUSE -- West, Mary Hope
The Muse family of Virginia. 1939.

MUSICK -- Musick, G. C.
Genealogy of the Musick family and some kindred lines. Meadow Bridge,
W. Va. 1964.

MUSTOE -- Grant, Howard B.
Chambers Mustoe; copyright. Philippi, W. Va. 1936.

MYERS -- Shahan, Jeanette L.
Myers, Plum, Burns and allied families. Parsons, W. Va.: McClain Print,
1980.

NAFF -- Boitnott, John W.
    Naff and related families. Bridgewater. 1979.

NANCE -- Nance, Davidson
    History and genealogy of the Nances; but more particularly of the
    descendants of John and Jane Nance, of Mecklenburg County, Virginia.
    Marshville, N.C. 1930.

NANCE -- Nance, Geo. W.
    The Nance memorial; a history of the Nance family in general, but more
    particularly of Clement Nance, of Pittsylvania County, Virginia, and
    descendants, containing historical and biographical records with family
    lineage. Bloomington, Ill.: J. E. Burke & Co., 1904.

NANCE -- Nance, Robert B.
    Nance records. Radford College, Radford. 1957.

NASH -- Nash, Claude W.
    Some Nashes of Virginia, 100 years of an American family, 1774-1974.
    Bristol. 1975.

NASH -- Nash, Ralph G.
    Nash, a family genealogy. Springfield. 1982.

NAUGLE -- Baer, Mabel Van Dyke
    Naugle family of Pennsylvania, Virginia and Indiana. 1972.

NAY -- Nay, Ernest Omar
    Genealogy of the Nay family, a record of the descendants of Jacob Nay
    of Virginia, from 1723 to 1949, with supplement. Terre Haute, Ind.
    1949.

NEAL -- Neal, Carl B.
    The Beaver Pond Neals of Virginia. Olympia, Wash. 1965.

NEALL, Harry L.
    Genealogy of the American family of Neall; it being a branch of the
    Bedfordshire, Eng. family of Neale ... ca. 1630 ... who settled at
    Accomack, Va. and Salem, Mass. ... DeSabla, Calif. 1924.

NEELY -- Jones, Mrs. E. Camden
    Neely family chart of West Virginia. Smithton, W. Va. 1910.

NEESE -- Neese, Edward Holt
    The ancestors and descendants of William Thomas Neese and Barbara Ellen
    Holt. Alexandria. 1983.

NEFF -- From the Alps to the Appalachians; a brief history including some of
    the Neff family of Switzerland, Germany, Pennsylvania, Virginia, and
    statistics on the descendants of Michael H. Neff, 1833-1922, of the
    Shenandoah Valley of Virginia. Arlington. 1967.

NEIKIRK -- Neikirk, Floyd Edwin
Ohio descendants of seventeenth century ancestors in Plymouth and
Providence Plantations, Massachusetts Bay and Connecticut Colonies,
New York, Pennsylvania, Virginia, Maryland, New Jersey, 1620-1960.
Clyde, Ohio. 1960.

NELSON -- Gibson, Olive Nelson
Descendants of John Nelson, Sr.: Mary Toby Stafford County, Virginia,
1740-1959, with related families. Redlands, Calif. 1961.

NELSON -- Nelson, John F.
Journal of proceedings, the Daniel and Sarah Nelson family reunion.
Clarksburg, W. Va. 1960.

NESTOR -- Nester, Carl K.
Descendants of Jacob Nester, 1761-1844. Wolf Summit, W. Va. 1982.

NEVILLE -- Osborne, Nina S.
The Neville family of Maryland and Virginia; from John Neville, 1635
to Robert William White, 1928, and including families of Harris,
Sullivan and Sutton.

NEW -- Allgood, Ann Wall
The family of New: genealogy of descendants of Richard New, immigrant
to Virginia in 1637 ... Natchez, Miss. 1981.

NEWBERRY -- Newberry, John A.
History and genealogy of the Newberry family, 1066-1943. Huntington,
W. Va. 1943.

NEWBY -- Walker, Elizabeth Parcher
Descendants of Joshua and Ann Newby of West Virginia, 1833-1904.
Manchester, Conn. 1981.

NEWMAN -- Johnson, Virginia Bondurant
Harriet Lucretia and Charles Jacob Newman: their family. Charleston,
W. Va. 1972.

NICHOLS -- Bartlett, Robert F.
Historical and genealogical sketch of the Nichols-Thomas family in Ohio,
with partial ancestry and collateral relatives in Virginia. Mt.
Gilead, Ohio. 1909.

NICHOLS -- Rogers, George J.
Genealogy of the Nichol family, 1764-1829. Wheeling, W. Va. 1922.

NICHOLSON -- Nicholson, John Bradford
A summary of the genealogy of the Nicholson and Stowers families of the
South, with their principal branches.

NIMMO -- Walter, Alice Granbery
Nimmo of Princess Anne County, Virginia, 1700-1970: and their migrations.
Virginia Beach. 1980.

NIXON --Nixon, Justin Wroe
The story of the Robert P. Nixon family of Boothsville, West Virginia.
1961.

NOCK -- Nottingham, Stratton
Ascendant of Annie Russell Gruver. Onancock. 1968.

NOEL -- Weeks, Jennie Noel
Emigrant Cornelius Noel from Holland to Virginia and his descendants in
America. Salt Lake City. 1977.

NORFLEET -- Norfleet, Fillmore
Nansemond County, Virginia. 1962.

NORFORD -- Marshall, Florence Norford and Grace Norford Barr
Norford family history 1742-1965; memoirs from England - United States.
Charlottesville: Michie Co., 196-.

NORMAN -- Norman, Jane Teel
Thomas Norman of Virginia. Sterling Park. 1976.

NORMAN -- Norman, William E.
Norman genealogy: ancestors and descendants of George Norman I, and
Martha Melhuish Norman, Somerset, England, with descendant and
collateral families of America. Norfolk. 1976.

NORRIS -- Davis, Harry Alexander
The Norris family of Maryland and Virginia; genealogy of Thomas Norris,
1361-1930. Washington. 1941.

NORTHCUTT -- Miller, Elizabeth Ellis
John Northcutt of Prince William County, Virginia, 1740. 1958.

NOTTINGHAM -- Nottingham, William Prosser
Some of the ancestry of the Rev. Luther Nottingham (1817-1867) of
Northampton County, Virginia. Indianapolis, Ind. 1980.

NOWLIN -- Nowlin, James Edmund
The Nowlin-Stone genealogy; a record of the descendants of James Nowlin,
who came to Pittsylvania County, Virginia, from Ireland about 1700; of
Bryan Word Nowlin, grandson of James Nowlin, who was born in Pittsylvania
County, Virginia, about 1740; of Michael Nowlin; and of the earlier
Nowlins (Nowlans) of Ireland; and also a record of the descendants of
George Stone; and of James Hoskin Stone, who was born in Pittsylvania
County, Virginia, in 1778; and also a record of the descendants of
Edwin Fitzgerald. Salt Lake City, Utah. 1916.

NUCKOLLS -- Nuckolls, Bertha
The first Virginia Nuckolls and kindred. Boston, Mass. 1960.

NUGEN -- Nugen, James R.
The history and genealogy of the Nugen family of West Virginia.
Sacramento, Calif. 1969.

NUNLEY -- Shortal, Joseph Adams
Nunnally genealogy. Hampton. 1978.

O'BANNON -- De Huff, Elizabeth Willis
The family of Thomas O'Bannon of Fauquier County, Virginia, and
Barnewell County, South Carolina. Augusta, Ga. 1969.

OBERHOLTZER -- Turn, Helen Overholser
Samuel Overholtzer of Virginia and some of his descendants. Belton,
Tex.: Centex Press, 1981.

O'DEVELIN -- Develin, Joseph C.
Story of an Irish sept. the O'Develins fo Tyrone. Lynchburg. 1937.

OGBURN -- Ogburn, Rubyn Reynolds
As I was told. Richmond: Dietz Press, 1958.

OLD KING WILLIAM -- Clarke, Peyton Neale
Old King William Homes and Families, etc. Louisville: J. P. Morton,
1897.

OMOHUNDRO -- The Omohundro genealogical record; the Omohundros and allied
families in America: blood lines traced from the first Omohundro in
Westmoreland County, Virginia, 1670, through his descendants in three
great branches and allied families down to 1950. Staunton: McClure
Print, 1951.

ONTHANK -- Onthank, Arthur H.
Supplement to The Onthank family, Martinsville, 1959. Fairfax. 1962.

OSBORNE -- Sell, Rose O.
Osborne, Lohr, Budd and Keenan families, Monroe County, W. Va.
Charleston-Kanawha, W. Va. 1914.

OSBORNE -- Sutton, Rita K.
Early Osbornes and Alleys; with notes on allied families. Hist. Soc.
of Southwest Va. 1973.

OTEY -- Carpenter, Arthur Bledsoe
John Otey of New Kent County, Virginia: descendants and related families.
Richmond. 1966.

OVERTON -- Anderson, W. P.
   The early descendants of Wm. Overton & Elizabeth Waters of Virginia,
   and allied families. Cincinnati. 1938.

OVERWHARTON -- Overwharton Parish, 1720 to 1760. Old Stafford County.
   Washington: The Sexton Printing Co., 1899.

OWEN -- Barr, Lockwood
   Owens-Grubbs and allied families of Virginia and Kentucky. New York.
   1940.

OYER -- Oyer, Darrell
   Descendants of Christian Oyer and Katherine Zehr. Alexandria. 1982.

PACA -- Paca, Wabda R.
   Paca, signer, friend of Washington and Lafayette: the Paca family.
   Santa Monica, Calif. 1963.

PACE -- Pace, John
   The trek of the Paces through Henry County and the heritage they left
   behind. Bassett. 1978.

PAGE -- Family chart of the Page family of Virginia. Richmond.

PAGE -- Genealogy of the Page family in Virginia. Also a condensed account
   of the Nelson, Pendleton and Randolph families, with reference to the
   Byrd, Carter, Cary, Duke, Gilmer, Harrison, Rives, Thornton, Wellford,
   Washington, and other distinguished families in Virginia. New York,
   N.Y.: Jenkins & Thomas, 1883.

PAGE -- Page, Richard Channing Moore
   Genealogy of the Page family in Virginia. Also a condensed account of
   the Nelson, Walker, Pendleton, and Randolph families, with reference to
   the Bland, Burwell, Byrd, Carter, Cary, Duke, Gilmer, Harrison, Rives,
   Thornton, Welford, Washington, and other distinguished families in
   Virginia. New York, N.Y.: Publishers' Print Co., 1893.

PAGE -- Page, Richard C. M.
   Genealogy of the Page family in Virginia ... Reprint of 1893 edition.
   Bridgewater. 1965.

PAGET -- Hammon, Stratton O.
   The Paget family of Virginia, Kentucky, and Indiana. 1918.

PAINE -- Payne, Brooke
   The Paynes of Virginia. Richmond: William Byrd Press, 1937.

PAINE -- Payne, E. S.
   Outline of Payne family of Virginia and Kentucky and allied families. 1971.

PALMER -- Johnson, Thomas C.
The life and letters of Benjamin Morgan Palmer (with genealogy).
Richmond. 1906.

PANKEY -- Pankey, George Edward
John Pankey of Manakin Town, Virginia. Ruston, La. 1969.

PANKEY --John Pankey of Manakin Town, Virginia, and his descendants (and)
descendants and connections of his son Stephen Pankey, Sr., of Lucy
Springs, Chesterfield County, Virginia. Ruston, La. 1969.

PANKEY -- Pankey, William Russell
The Pankey family of Virginia, 1635-1968. Richmond. 1968.

PARADISE -- Shepperson, Archibald B.
John Paradise and Lucy Ludwell of London and Williamsburg. Richmond:
Dietz Press, 1942.

PARISH -- Parrish, Agnes B. H.
Parrish family of New Kent County, Virginia and allied families. 1948.

PARK -- Becker, Dorothy Robertson
The Parke family: earliest pioneers of New Jersey with later generations
who pioneered in old Frederick Co., Va., and on into Ohio & Indiana.
Ft. Worth, Tex. 1979.

PARKER -- McSwain, Eleanor Davis
Some ancestors and descendants of Richard Parker, chirurgeon, born in
Cornwall, 1629, died in Virginia, ca. 1680, and many other Parker records.
Macon, Ga. 1980.

PARR -- Family of Parr in Maryland and Virginia.

PARR -- Fleming, Helen Parr
The Parr family. Parsons, W. Va.: McClain Print Co., 1968.

PARR -- Fleming, Helen P.
The Parr family: allied families: Holden, Hutchison, Moore, Jolly,
Franks, Sheets, et al. Parsons, W. Va.: McClain Print., 1969.

PARRISH -- Parrish, Agnes H.
The Parrish family of New Kent County, Virginia. 1953.

PARRISH -- Register, Alvaretta Kenan
One branch of the Parrish family of Bulloch County, Georgia. Norfolk.
1966.

PARSONS -- Benson, Ida R.
Parsons, Stump and Taylor families of Virginia. Mexico, Mo. 1945.

PARSONS -- MacCable, Viriginia P.
   Parsons family history and record. Decatur, Ill. 1913.

PATE -- Pate, John Ben
   The American genealogy of the Pate family from their landing in Virginia,
   1650, to the present time in our line of descent; including a sketch of
   their origin and history in England, back to the fifteenth century, with
   a description of the Pate coat of arms. Amboy, Ga.

PATRICK HENRY -- Henry, William Wirt
   Patrick Henry, Life, Correspondence and Speeches. New York, N.Y.: Charles
   Scribner's Sons, 1891.

PATTERSON -- The Patterson family. Arlington: American Genealogical Research
   Institute, 1973.

PATTERSON -- Smith, Ethel Marion
   An informal history of Virginia-Kentucky Pattersons in Illinois, their
   forebears and their kin including the Lewises of Llangollen. Washington.
   1948.

PATTISON -- Pattison, Hal Cushman
   The descendants of Thomas Pattison of Stillwater, New York. Fairfax.
   1980.

PATTON -- Highland, Scotland G.
   Record of the colonial forebears ... of the late Lucinda Earle Patton
   Highland. West Milford, W. Va. 1929.

PATTON -- Johnson, Patricia Givens
   James Patton and the Appalachian colonists. Verona. 1973.

PAYNE -- Paine, Grace Hillman Benedict
   Ancestors of Thomas Fite Paine, Jr. and Grace Hillman Benedict Paine:
   with sketch of David Campbell, pioneer of "Royal Oak," Virginia:
   (documented biographical notes, illustrations, and index). Nashville,
   Tenn. 1982.

PAYNE -- Payne, Brook
   The Paynes of Virginia. Richmond: William Byrd Press, 1937.

PEARSON -- Smith, Alfred Douglas
   Peerson of Camp Branch, Virginia. Danville. 1970.

PECK -- Peck, Jesse William
   Peck family. Clifton Forge. 1958.

PEDEN -- Peden, Henry C.
   The Pedens of southwest Virginia and southcentral Kentucky, descendants
   of John Peden (1734-1815) and Mary Smith (1734-1806). Edgewood, Md.
   1978.

PEEBLES -- Whitley, Edythe R.
    Peebles family of Virginia, North Carolina, Kentucky, Illinois, Missouri,
    etc. Seattle, Wash.

PEERY -- Perry, Lynn
    A branch of the Peery family tree; ancestors and descendants of James
    Peery who came to Delaware about 1730 ... Strasburg: Shenandoah Pub.
    House, 1931.

PEGRAM -- Simmons, Samuel William
    The Pegrams of Virginia and descendants, 1688-1984. Atlanta, Ga. 1985.

PEIRPOINT -- Stickney, Alpheus Beede
    Lucy & Oliver, some West Virginia genealogy: Peirpoint, Smell, Jones,
    Fetty. Pittsburg. 1953.

PENCE -- Carson, Beatrice
    Pence family genealogy. Fairfax. 1975.

PENCE -- Pence, Kingsley Adolphus
    History of Judge John Pence and Descendants. Born in Shenandoah County,
    Virginia, 1775, etc. Denver. 1912.

PENDERGAST -- Pendergast, Allen
    Pendergast of Virginia and the Carolinas, 1669-1919. Sedona, Ariz. 1977.

PENICK -- Priest, Lyman W.
    The Penick family: descendants of Edward Penick/Penix/Pinix of St.
    Peter's Parish, New Kent County, Virginia. Verona: McClure Print, 1982.

PENN -- Allen, Robert M.
    The ancestry of Joseph Penn of Amherst Co., Virginia. San Jose,
    Calif. 1980.

PENN FAMILY OF VIRGINIA -- A Chronological Record from Christian Penn, 1621,
    Robert, 1621, William, 1635, Francis, 1635, etc. 1915.

PENN -- The Penn family of Virginia; a chronological record. New York,
    N.Y.: W. M. Clemens, 1915.

PENN -- Penn, Mary M.
    The Penn family of Virginia. 1936.

PERCY -- Percy, Truman
    Family record of the Connecticut branch of the Percy family. Norfolk:
    H. C. Percy, 1873.

PERKINS -- Hall, William K.
    The Perkins family of Virginia; descendants of Nicholas Perkins who died
    ca. 1654 in Charles City County. Brideport, Ala. 1953.

PERKINS -- Hall, William Kearney
Descendants of Nicholas Perkins of Virginia. Ann Arbor, Mich. 1958.

PERRY -- Hayes, Mrs. D. G.
Perry family of Virginia and Kentucky. 1970.

PERRY -- The Perry family. Arlington: American Genealogical Research
Institute, 1973.

PERRY -- Perry, Lynn
A branch of the Peery family tree; ancestors and descendants of James
Peery who came to Delaware about 1730. Strasburg: Shenandoah Pub.
House, 1931.

PESCUD -- Ironmonger, Elizabeth Hogg
Three courageous women and their kin; a Pescud family genealogy.
Berryville: Chesapeake Book Co., 1965.

PETERS -- Clark, Bertha Lewis
The Peters family of Monroe County, West Virginia. 1926-1948.

PETTIJOHN -- Chamberlain, Era Jane Pettijohn & Clive Abraham Pettijohn
Something of the Pettijohn (Pettyjohn) family, with particular reference
to the descendants of James Pettyjohn of Hungar's Parish, Northampton
County, Virginia. 1948.

PETTY -- Petty, Gerald M.
Petty, of England & Virginia; Wright of Virginia, Kentucky & Missouri;
Riley of Maryland, Kentucky & Missouri; and related Alexander, Copeland,
Dale, Douglass, Givens, Hubbard, McClung, Owens, Patton, Paxton,
Rowland & Tedford families. Columbus, Ohio. 1973.

PEYTON -- Memoir of John Howe Peyton. Staunton. 1894.

PEYTON -- Peyton Society of Virginia
The Peytons of Virginia, being an account of the ancient and knightly
family of Peyton of Suffolk and especially of those who became planters
in His Majesty's Colony of Virginia. Stafford. 1976.

PEYTON -- Peyton, John Lewis
Memoir of William Madison Peyton, of Roanoke, together with some of his
speeches in the House of delegates of Virginia, and his letters in
reference to secession and the threatened civil war in the United States,
etc. etc. London. 1873.

PEYTON -- Peyton, John Lewis
The adventures of my grandfather/John Lewis Peyton. Charlottesville.
1963.

PEYTON -- Reed, Avery Henry
Genealogy of the Peyton family embracing the lineage of certain 2 immigrant children of that Henry Peyton of "Lincoln's Inn," Amiger, England, middle 1600 immigrants to Virginia; 4 (1) Col. Valentine Peyton, 7 (1) Henry Peyton, adult, and including the lineage of the immigrant Robert Peyton, son of Thomas Peyton, son of Sir Edward Peyton of "Isselham," in England. With appendix of connecting Farish family. Charlottesville. 1963.

PFOST -- Morrison, Okey J.
The slaughter of the Pfost-Greene family of Jackson county, W. Va. A history of the tragedy, with a notice of the early settlers of Jackson County, a sketch of the family and John F. Morgan. Cincinnati. 1868.

PFOST -- Morrison, O. J.
Pfost-Green family of Jackson County, West Virginia. 1897.

PHELPS -- McBride, Nancy S.
Phelps-Marshall kinship. Verona: McClure Press, 1977.

PHELPS -- Roy, Nancy Reba
The Phelps family of Virginia and Kentucky and allied families. La Mesa, Calif. 1960.

PHILLIPS -- Phillips, Robert B.
Phillips and Arthur families of Campbell County, Virginia. Lynchburg. 1975.

PHILPOT -- Philpott, Charles H.
English and American backgrounds of a Philpott family line of Virginia and Maryland U.S.A., a progress report in the form of an annotated bibliography. Durham, N.C. 1970.

PHILPOT -- Smith, Walter Burges
The Philpot family of Maryland and Virginia, preliminary genealogical notes (also Philpot, Phillpot, Phillpott, Philipot, etc.). Washington. 1960.

PHILPOTTS -- Philpott, Jane.
Philpotts in Patrick and Henry Counties, Virginia (1772-1843). Durham, N.C. 1966.

PHIPPS -- Mullins, John C.
The Phipps family of N.C. and Va.: being the history of some of the descendants of Joseph Phipps Senior of Guilford Co., N.C. Clintwood. 1982.

PICKET -- The Picket family. Richmond. 1909.

PIERCE -- The Pierce family. Arlington: American Genealogical Research
     Institute, 1972.

PIERCE -- Bender, Lucy
     Genealogy and history of Pierce and Darby families with collateral
     lineages of Warren, Fiske, Conant, Bemis and others, from Rognwald,
     931 A.D. to the thirty-sixth generation in America. Langley Field.
     1936.

PIERCE -- Pierce, Sarah Betty
     Our family tree. Arlington. 1981.

PIERPONT -- Hedman, Kathyrn Pierpont
     The Pierpoint-Pierpont family of Maryland, Virginia, West Virginia.
     Alexandria. 1973.

PIERPOINT -- Stickney, A.B.
     Lucy and Oliver: some West Virginia genealogy, Pierpoint. Pittsburg.
     1953.

PINKINS -- Johnson, Curtis J.
     How we will know it's us: biography of a black south Louisiana family.
     Newport News. 1985.

PIXLEY -- Pixley, George & Opal Birge
     The Pixley story: historical and biographical sketch from William I
     of Hadley to William Rulison of Centralia; with chronology, memoirs,
     1962 diary, and 1971 letter by Ralph and Pauline Pixley. Norfold.
     1976.

PLANK -- Baylis, Margaret Price
     David Plank family. Front Royal. 1967.

PLAXCO -- Mendenhall, Samuel Brooks
     Plaxco-Robinson. Richmond: Whittet & Shepperson, 1958.

PLEASANT -- Miller, Norma Carter
     Pleasants and allied families: an historical genealogy of the descendants
     of John Pleasants (1644/5-1698) of Henrico County, Virginia, and of
     George Pleasant of York County, Virginia. DeKalb, Ill. 1980.

PLUMB -- Lauritzen, Elizabeth M.
     The Merlin Plumb family. Gloucester. 1975.

PLYMALE -- Plymale, John Fred
     The Plymale family in America. Huntington, W. Va.: Commercial Printing
     & Lithographing Co., 1967.

PLYMALE -- Shingleton, Jewel P.
     The Plymale family in America. Kenova, W. Va. 1979.

POAGE -- Townsend, Catherine Poage
   The Poage family of Kentucky and Virginia. 1939.

POAGE -- Williamson, Andrews Woods
   The descendants of Robert and John Poage. Staunton: McClure Printing
   Co., 1954.

POAGE -- Woodworth, Robert Bell
   The descendants of Robert and John Poage, pioneer settlers in Augusta
   County, Va.; a genealogy based on the manuscript collection of Prof.
   Andrew Woods Williamson, Henry Martyn Williamson, and John Guy Bishop.
   Staunton: McClure Print Co., 1954.

POCAHONTAS -- Pocahontas, alias Matoaka, and her descendants through marriage
   at Jamestown, Virginia, in April, 1614, with John Rolfe, gentleman;
   including the names of Alfriend, Archer, Bentley, Bernard, Bland,
   Bolling, Branch, Cabell, Carlett, Cary, Dandridge, Dixon, Douglas, Duval,
   Eldridge, Ellett, Ferguson, Field, Fleming, Gay, Gordon, Griffin,
   Grayson, Harrison, Hubard, Lewis, Logan, Markham, Meade, McRae, Murray,
   Page, Poythress, Randolph, Robertson, Skipwith, Stanard, Tazewell,
   Walke, West, Whittle, and others. Richmond. 1887.

PODLESAK -- Starrett, Elizabeth Regenstein
   The Podlesak family in America. Berryville. 1982.

POE -- Brannan, Pauline Mae
   The Poe family: a history of the Poe family and collaterals, including
   short stories of collaterals Corley, Hitt, Crim and Spielman, early
   families found in Fauquier, Warren, and Rappahannock Counties, Virginia.
   Bel Air, Md. 1974.

POLK -- Bushman, Katherine Gentry
   Edmund Polk, Junior. Staunton. 1964.

POLK -- Porter, W. L.
   Some descendants from Cap't William Polk of Accomac, Va. Chicago. 1941.

POLING -- Tatterson, Clerissa H.
   History and genealogy of the Poling family. Parsons, W. Va.: McClain
   Print, 1978.

POLLEY -- Cornell, Ruth William
   My family connections. So. Chas., W, Va. 1980-1983.

POPE -- Humphries, John D.
   Georgia descendants of Nathaniel Pope of Virginia, John Humphries of
   South Carolina, and Allen Gay of North Carolina. Atlanta. 1934.

PORTER -- Porter, Mary E.
A family history, William Porter, Jr. of Rockbridge County, Virginia (1740-1804) and five generations of his descendants. El Reno, Okla. 1984.

PORTERFIELD -- Porterfield, Frank Burke
The Porterfields. Roanoke: Southeastern Press, 1947.

POWELL -- Ball, Rosalie Noland
The family tree of Col. Leven Powell's line of the Powells of Virginia. 1938.

POWELL -- de Veau, Katharine Lee
Benjamin and Ambrose Powell of Culpeper County, Virginia; with many descendants of Benjamin. 1041.

POWELL -- Lucas, Silas Emmett
The Powell family of Norfolk and Elizabeth City Counties, Virginia, and their descendants, with notes and data on the collateral families of Bush, Beckwith, Bowles, Cargill, Carter, Clemens, Conner, Creed, Daines, Dendy, Lucas, Maddux, Middleton, Osborn, Smith, Watkins, and Williams. Birmingham, Ala. 1961.

POWELL -- Lucas, Silas E.
The Powell families of Virginia and the South. Vidalia, Ga.: Georgia Genealogical reprints, 1969.

POWELL -- Lucas, S. Emmett
The Powell families of Virginia and the South: being an encyclopedia of the eight (8) major Powell families of Virginia and the South in general. Easley, S.C. 1977, 1969.

POWELL -- Lucas S. Emmett
Index to Powell families of Virginia and the South. Southern Historical Press, 1980.

POWELL -- Manfiedl, James Roger
The Ptolemy Powell family of Spotsylvania County, Virginia. 1971.

POWELL -- Powell, Charles S.
History and genealogy of the Powells in America. St. Petersburg, Fla. 1935.

POWELL -- Powell, family of Va., Conrad, family of Winchester, Va., Fauntleroy, family of Va., Magill, family of Winchester, Va., Holmes, family of Va. Washington. 1928.

POWELL -- Powell, R. C.
  Biographical Sketch of Col. Levin Powell. Alexandria. 1877.

PRATHER -- Tatman, Dudley Austin
  Robert and Marshall, the Prather family in Louisiana, from Wales, England,
  Virginia, Maryland, to the present, 1979, 1981. Opelousas, La. 1982.

PRATT -- Conklin, Mary J. S.
  George Oliver Pratt of Belleville, W. Va. and his descendants. Walnut,
  Ill. 1968.

PRESSON -- Ervin, Mary Lee Martin
  The Presson family of the South, 1690-1974: Nicholas Presson, the Elder,
  of York County, Virginia, and some of his descendants. Oklahoma City,
  Okla.: Hooper Print. Co., 1974.

PRESTON -- Dorman, John Frederick
  The Prestons of Smithfield and Greenfield in Virginia: descendants of
  John and Elizabeth (Patton) Preston through five generations. Louisville,
  Ky. 1982.

PRESTON -- Preston, Thomas L.
  Historical sketches and reminiscences of an octogenarian. Richmond. 1900.

PRESTON -- Williams, L. A. and William Bowker Preston
  The Preston family in Great Britain, New England and Virginia from 1040
  to the Present Times. Salt Lake City. 1900.

PRICE (Culpeper) -- Cox, Rev. John E.
  Thomas Price and his Descendants. A History and Genealogy. Owensville,
  Ind. 1926.

PRICE -- Katz, Gertrude Morton Price
  Two old letters concerning Arjalon Price of Virginia and his family of
  descendants and ancestors of wife, Joyce Barber. 1970.

PRICE -- Price, Rev. Benjamin Luther
  John Price the emigrant, Jamestown colony 1620, with some of his descendants. Alexandria, La. 1910.

PRICE -- Price, Theodore H. and Charlotte P. Price
  The Price family of "Cool Water," Hanover County, Va. Maternal ancestry,
  and descendants in two lines to the year 1906. New York. 1906.

PRICHARD -- Prichard, A. M.
  Descendants of William Prichard. Charleston, W. Va. 1912.

PRILLAMAN -- Rogers, Ellen Stanley
  The Prillaman family; an account of the descendants of Jacob Prillaman,
  Sr. (1721-1796) of Franklin County, Virginia. Hyattsville, Md. 1959.

PRILLAMAN -- Rogers, Ellen S.
The Prillaman family: an account of the descendants of Jacob Prillaman, Sr. (1721-1796) of Franklin County, Virginia. New version. Martinsville. 1976.

PROBST -- Eye, Walter L.
A history of the descendants of John Michael Propst of Pendleton County, Va. (W. Va.). Harrisonburg. 1983.

PROBST -- Propst, Elvin Eston
The Propsts of Pendleton County, Virginia (West Virginia) following the line of Christopher Lewis Propst. Austin, Tex. 1980.

PUCKETT -- Garrett, Hester Elizabeth
Pucketts and their kin of Virginia, Kentucky, and other Southern states. Lansing, Mich. 1960.

PULLEN -- Pullen, William E.
Tide-water to Blue Ridge: Pullen-Walker families of Bedford County, Virginia. Hollywood, Fla. 1977.

PUMPHREY -- Bell, Raymond Martin
Reason Pumphrey, 1736-1812: Maryland-Pennsylvania-West Virginia early Methodist. Washington, Pa. 1984.

PURVIS -- Oliver, Alice Lee Simpson
The Purvis family in Virginia and their kin. 1969.

PURCELL -- Ritchie, Anne R.
Purcell of Virginia with allied families. 1973.

PUTNAM -- Putnam, Thomas Russell
Putnam genealogy (Recording the descendants of Thomas Putnam, the immigrant to Virginia 1647) - Also contains an enumeration of the living descendants of the "Virginia-Carolina-Kentucky" Putnams; also contains brief genealogies of the Harper, Grover, and McGlasson families. Okmulgee, Okla. 1938.

PYRTLE -- Pyrtle, E. Ruth
Early Virginia families. Lincoln, Nebr.: Chaffin Printing Co., 1930.

QUAINTANCE -- Quaintance, Alfred M.
Genealogy of the Quaintance family in Virginia and Kentucky. Englewood, Colo. 1968.

QUANDER -- The Quanders United tricentennial celebration, 1684-1984: June 22, 23 and 24, 1984, Washington, D.C. Washington, D.C.: Quanders United, 1984.

QUARLES -- Quarles, Garland Redd
A history of the ancestors and descendants of William Quarles of St.
Margaret's Parish, Caroline County. Winchester. 1980.

QUARRIER -- Laidley, A. T.
Genealogical Sketch of the Quarrier Family in America. A Genealogical
Sketch and Table of the Quarrier Family of America. Charleston, W. Va.
1890.

QUEEN -- Dyer, Paul E.
John Queen (ca. 1720-1802/1805) of Loudoun County, Virginia and descen-
dants, mainly of Wayne County, West Virginia (early Cabell) and eastern
Kentucky. Louisville, Ky. 1980.

QUILLIN -- MacQuillin, Cluse
The Quillin (Mac Quillin) family. Gate City. 1961.

RACKLEY -- Potter, Eloise F.
Rackley, a southern Colonial family: the descendants of Edward Rackley
of Virginia: with appendixes treating other Rackley family groups living
in the United States prior to 1900. Zebulon, N.C.: Potter Pub. Services,
1984.

RADCLYFFE -- McReynolds, June R.
Our Radclyffe heritage: a history of the Radclyffe family in England
and Virginia. Roanoke. 1975.

RAGSDALE -- Skelton, Caroline Nabors
Godfrey Ragsdale from England to Henrico County, Virginia; one documented
line of descent covering three hundred twenty-seven years in America.
Franklin Springs, Ga. 1969.

RAGSDALE -- Van Leer, Mrs. Blake Ragsdale
Elijah Ragsdale: born Virginia, November 1, 1778 to South Carolina,
died Georgia, May 1, 1858: his antecedents and known descendants. The
Ragsdale family in England and America. Canton, Ga. 1975.

RAMSEY -- Ramsey, Lessel Leslie
The autobiography and family history of Lessel Leslie Ramsey: with a
genealogy of the Ramsey family and the Simpson family. Vienna. 1982.

RAND -- Esker, Katie-Prince Ward
Rand family of Virginia-North Carolina-Alabama. 1047.

RANDOLPH -- Daniels, Jonathan
The Randolphs of Virginia. Garden City, N.Y.: Doubleday, 1972.

RANDOLPH -- Eckenrode, H. J.
The Randophs; the story of a Virginia family. New York, N.Y.: The
Bobbs-Merrill Co., 1946.

RANDOLPH -- Firestone, Eva O. M.
Genealogical notes of Virginia.

RANDOLPH -- Harrison, Kate Du Val
Randolphs of Virginia. 1928.

RANDOLPH -- Krusen, Jessie Ball Thompson
Tuckahoe Plantation. Richmond. 1975.

RANDOLPH -- Selections from the family history of Randolph, Dandridge, Armistead,
Langbourne, Carter and Williams clans in Virginia, 1650 to 1930 A.D. 1930.

RANDOLPH -- Randolph Family of Virginia. Richmond. 1888.

RANDOLPH -- Randolph, Anne Marie Lyman
Randolph Family of Virginia.

RANDOLPH -- Randolph, Blanche
The Randolphs of Prince William County, Virginia. Little Rock, Ark.
1979.

RANDOLPH -- Randolph, John
Randolph family of Virginia. Roanoke. 1810.

RANDOLPH -- Randolph Family of Virginia. Attributed in part to John Randolph
of Roanoke. 1925.

RANDOLPH -- Randolph, Robert Isham
The Randolphs of Virginia, a compilation of the descendants of William
Randolph of Turkey Island, and his wife Mary Isham of Bermuda hundred.
Chicago. 1936.

RANDOLPH -- Randolph, Roberta Lee
The first Randolphs of Virginia. Washington. 1961.

RANDOLPHS -- Randolph, Wassell
William Randolph I of Turkey Island Henrico County, Virginia, and his
immediate descendants. Memphis. 1949.

RANDOLPH -- Randolph, Wassell
Henry Randolph I, 1623-1773 of Henrico County, Virginia, and his descendants. Preceded by short review of the Randolph family in early England
and elsewhere. Memphis. 1952.

RANDOLPH -- Randolph, Wassell
Pedigree of the descendants of Henry Randolph I (1623-1673) of Henrico
County, Virginia. Memphis. 1957.

RANKIN -- Prichard, A. M.
    Rankin relations. Staunton. 1948.

RAPIER -- Donnelly, Mary Louise
    Rapier, Hayden and allied families. Burke. 1978.

RAWALT -- Rawalt, Marguerite
    Descendants of Captain John Rawalt (Rewalt), revolutionary war patriot,
    serving 1775 to 1782. Arlington. 1974.

RAWSON -- Sommerville, Geraldine and Oma H. Mills
    David Rawson: ancestors and descendants, 1636-1974. Parsons, W. Va.:
    McCalin Print. Co., 1974.

RAY -- Froehlich, Dean
    Ray families in Noble County, Indiana, Guernsey County, Ohio, Ohio
    County, Virginia, and Washington County, Pennsylvania. 1982.

RAYBURN -- Jones, Parke and John T. Roberts
    The descendants of Henry Rayburn of Virginia. St. Paul. 1947.

RAYBURN -- Morris, Earle H. (Assos. Ed. John T. Roberts)
    The descendants of Edward Rayburn. Charleston, W. Va. 1950.

READ -- Prichard, A. M.
    Allied families of Read, Corbin, Luttrell, Bywaters. Starting from
    Culpeper County, Virginia, their descendants are now planted in every
    state westward to the Pacific. Staunton. 1930.

READ -- Read, Alice (Mrs. Shelley Rouse)
    The Reads and their relatives; being an account of Colonel Clement and
    Madison Read of Bushy Forest, Lunenburg County, Virginia, their eight
    children, their descendants, and allied families. Cincinnati. 1930.

READING -- Templeman, Eleanor Lee
    Chart showing the ancestry of Eleanor Lee Reading Templeman. Arlington.
    1944.

REARDEN -- Bender, Lucy
    Family Rearden, 1600 - 1936. Langley Field. 1926.

REAVIS -- Hall, Maroe Reavis
    The Reavis family in America since 1700, being the descendants of
    Edward Reavis, immigrant from England, who settled on the James River
    in the Colony of Virginia. Yadkinville, N.C. 1971.

REES -- Reese, Miss Mary E.
    Genealogy of the Reese family in Wales and America, from their arrival
    in America to the present time. Richmond: Whittet & Shepperson, 1903.

REEVE -- Reeves-Graybill, Edward Earl
The greyhound line for XIII generations: descendants of Robert Ryves (legal name, Robert Reve) 1490-1551, Armiger of Dorset: being a supplement to Reliques of the Rives (Ryves)--by James Childs, 1893-198-, Lynchburg, Va., 1929. Alexandria. 198-.

REEVES -- Bacus, Elizabeth R.
Reeves family of Missouri (by way of England, Virginia, Kentucky, Ohio and Indiana.

REEVES -- Ancestral sketches. (A chronicle of the pioneer East Tennessee families: Reeves, Miller, De Vault, and Range of Washington County; Robeson of Sullivan and McMinn Counties; and Easley, Hamilton, Acuff, and Vincent of Sullivan County; and certain of their antecedents in New Jersey, Pennsylvania, Maryland, Virginia, and North Carolina). Lynchburg: J. P. Bell Co., 1951.

REID -- Boden, Sara Lucy Bronson and Nina Beth Goe Cunningham
Reid family history; descendants of John Reid, 1781, Penn. - 1866, Utah and first wife, Jane Haircourt Noel, 1780, Va. - 1836, Ill. Provo, Utah. 1972.

RENDER -- Smith, Pearl O.
Renders and their relatives: Joshua Render of Charles County, Maryland, and Orange County, Virginia, and his descendants, 1720-1985. Arlington. 1985.

RENICK -- Renick, E. I.
The Renick Family of Virginia. 1889.

RENNEKER -- Boaz, Thurmond D.
Renneker family; a record of the descendants of William Jasper Renneker (1854-1924). McLean. 1973.

RENNEKER -- Boaz, T. D.
Garrett Henry Renneker (1830-1877) and his descendants. McLean. 1981.

RENO -- Reno, William L.
The Reno family. Falls Church. 1975.

REPASS -- Hoch, Beverly Repass
Orville Robinson Repass, and the Repass family of Wythe County, Virginia. Darnestown, Md. 1978.

REYNOLDS -- Moffett, Linden B.
Genealogy of the descendants of William, Jr. and Elizabeth Tuggle Reynolds of Montgomery County, Va. Muncie, Ind. 1929.

REYNOLDS -- Reynold, Nancy
Reynolds homestead. Richmond: Robert Kline & Co., 1970.

REYNOLDS -- Reynolds, William Wayne
Reynolds and McGuire ancestors: an account for some of the ancestors of a Virginia family. Raleigh, N.C. 1978.

REYNOLDS -- Tillman, Stephen Frederick
The Rennolds - Reynolds family of England and Virginia, 1530-1948. Washington. 1948.

RHODES -- Culpepper, Ruth Lynn Rodes
My heritage: the ancestors and descendants of Mary Alberta Coiner and Edward Thomas Rodes. Waynesboro. 1982.

RHODES -- Ladson, J. E.
Rhodes story: Rhodes of Virginia, North Carolina, South Carolina, and Georgia. Moultrie, Ga. 1955.

RHODES -- Rhodes, Troas Etta
Some of the early settlers of Pennsylvania, Virginia, Missouri, North Carolina, Indiana, Ohio, Illinois. Palm Desert, Calif. 1977.

RICE -- Taylor, Janie Rice
Thomas Rice of Virginia. 1973.

RICH -- Booher, Emma Rich
Rich Hill, Westmoreland County, Virginia, 1740, to Rich Hill, Noble County, Ohio, 1880. Senecaville, Ohio. 1976.

RICHARDSON -- Roller, Robert Douglas
Richardson-DePriest family. Charleston, W. Va. 1905.

RICKS -- Ricks Family of Virginia and North Carolina.

RICKETTS -- Rocketts, Robert Daniel
Truth and honor: a history of the Ricketts family. Axton. 1981.

RIDDLE -- Hoeman, Andree Sieverin
A partial history of the Riddle-Beavers families of Botetourt County, Virginia, Highland County, Ohio, Decatur and Page Counties, Iowa. Des Moines, Iowa. 1981.

RIDENOUR -- Yarlick, Iva C.
Adam and Magdalene Munch Ridenour and some related families. Arlington. 1973.

RIEGEL -- Kegley, Mary B.
The Riggle family of Wythe County, Virginia. Pulaski. 1978.

RINKER -- Engellant, Beulah Alm
People named Rinker of Maryland and Virginia. Great Falls, Mt. 1981.

RINKER -- Engellant, Beulah Alm
Jacob Rinker and his descendants of Shenandoah County, Virginia. Great Falls, Mt. 1981.

RIONS -- McCann, Wm. R.
Short genealogy of Rions and Ruckers; connecting these families in Kentucky with their Virginia forebears. 1959.

RITCHIE -- Ambler, Charles Henry
Thomas Ritchie; a study in Virginia politics. Richmond. 1913.

RITCHIE -- Lantz, Vergie Ruth Carr
Descendants of Isaac Ritchie of Virginia. Bridgewater. 1983.

RITCHIE -- Ambler, C. H.
Ritchie (Thomas Ritchie). Richmond. 1913.

RIVES -- Childs, James Rives
Reliques of the Rives (Ryves) Family. Lynchburg: J. P. Bell Co., Inc., 1929.

RIVES -- Rives, John Robert Thomas
Green Rives of Dinwiddie County, Virginia, and Lincoln County, Tennessee, and his descendants. Birmingham, Ala. 1958.

RIXEY -- Rixey, Randolph Picton
The Rixey genealogy, with references to the Morehead, Hunton, Gibbs, Hall, Thomas, Jones, Lewis, Chancellor, Pendleton, Smith, and other allied families. Lynchburg. 1933.

ROANE -- Ambler, Charles Henry
Thomas Ritchie; a study in Virginia politics. Richmond. 1913.

ROANE -- Selden, Jefferson Sinclair
Charles Roane the immigrant and his wife Frances Roane: the first of the name in Virginia settled in Gloucester County, Virginia in 1664. Hampton. 1982.

ROBERTSON -- Anderson, William Kyle
Donald Robertson and his wife, Rachel Rogers, of King and Queen County, Virginia, their ancestry and posterity; also a brief account of the ancestry of Commodore Richard Taylor of Orange County, Virginia, and his naval history during the war of the American revolution. Detroit, Mich. 1900.

ROBERTSON -- Ball, Helen A.
Richard David and Eliza Ann Alloway Robertson: their ancestors and descendants, Virginia, Kentucky, Missouri. East Lansing, Mich. 1979.

ROBERTSON -- Dorman, John Frederick
The Robertson family of Culpeper County, Virginia. Richmond. 1964.

ROBERTSON -- Love, Robert A.
Blaze and Hetty Robertson of South Branch, Virginia and their descendants. Arlington. 1950.

ROBERTSON -- Patton, James Samuel
The family of William & Elizabeth Bolling Robertson. Port Royal. 1975.

ROBERTSON -- Patton, James Samuel
The family of William and Elizabeth Bolling Robertson. Caroline County. 1962.

ROBERTSON -- Randolph, Wassell
The Reverend George Robertson (1662-1739) rector of Bristol Parish, Virginia (1693-1739) and his descendants. Memphis. 1955.

ROBERTSON -- Robertson, Amanda Blalock
The ancestry of Benjamin Otis Robertson, Sr. Arlington. 1959.

ROBERTSON -- Robertson, Haywood Lawrence
Colonial roots. Alexandria. 1976.

ROBERTSON -- Robertson, John F.
Descendants of James Robertson of Virginia. Owego, N. Y. 1982.

ROBERTSON -- Robertson, Julian Hart
The family of William and Elizabeth Bolling Robertson of Richmond, Virginia, 1585-1981. Salisbury, N.C. 1981.

ROBERTSON -- Robertson, Wyndham
Pocahontas and her Descendants, etc. Richmond. 1887.

ROBERTSON-TAYLOR -- Anderson, William Kyle
Donald Robertson and Commodore Richard Taylor, of Orange County. Ancestry and Posterity. Detroit. 1900.

ROBINSON -- Boyer, Nathalie Robinson
A Virginia gentleman and his family. Philadelphia. 1939.

ROBINSON -- Reynolds, Katherine
Some descendants of John Robinson of Cumberland County, Virginia. 1973.

ROBINSON -- Robinson, Dale Glenwood
Seventy-five families, our known ancestry. Gloucester. 1981.

ROBINSON -- Robinson, Richard A.
Family record of Lyles Robert and Catherine Worthington Robinson (who resided near Winchester, Va.) and their descendants. Louisville, Ky.: Bewers Print., 1895.

RODEFER -- Power, Carrie Rodeffer
  The Rodeffer family of Rockingham County, Virginia. 1948.

RODES -- Patterson, Shelley Rodes
  A short history and genealogy of the English family Rodes, who reached
  America in the 17th century and first settled in New Kent County, Virginia.
  New York. 1929.

ROEBUCK -- Garner, Sylvia Owen
  The Roebucks of Virginia: a genealogical history of the descendants from
  Robert, George, James, and Benjamin Roebuck (Robuck). Baltimore: Gateway
  Press, 1979.

ROGER JONES -- Jones, L. H.
  Capt. Roger Jones of London and Virginia, etc. Albany, N.Y. 1891.

ROGERS -- Rogers, Ginger Anne
  The Rogers of Reedy Branch, Dinwiddie County, Virginia. McKenney. 1983.

ROGERS -- Rogers, Virgil Madison
  Family history. Falls Church. 1975.

ROHRBACH -- Rorabaugh, James D.
  John R. Rohrbach (Rohrabaugh) 1728-1821: descendants and marriage connections.
  Parsons, W. Va.: McClain Print, 1966.

ROLFE -- Berry, Veronica
  The Rolfe papers: the chronicle of a Norfolk family, 1559-1908. Norwick.
  1979.

ROLFE -- Emberson, Myrtle T.
  Descendants of Pocahontas and the Bentleys of Virginia. Los Angeles. 1931.

ROLFE -- Pocahontas, alias Matoaka, and her descendants through her marriage
  at Jamestown, Virginia, in April, 1614, with John Rolfe, gentleman;
  including the name of Alfriend, Archer, Bentley, Bernard, Bland, Bolling,
  Cabell, Catlett, Cary, Dandride, Dixon, Douglas, Duval, Eldridge, Ellett,
  Ferguson, Field, Fleming, Gay, Gordon, Griffin, Grayson, Harrison, Hubard,
  Lewis, Logan, Markham, Meade, McRae, Murray, Page, Polythress, Randolph,
  Robertson, Skipwith, Stanard, Tazewell, Walke, West, Whittle and others.
  With biographical sketches by Wyndham Robertson and illustrated historical
  notes by R. A. Brock. Richmond. 1887.

ROLFE -- Robertson, Wyndham
  Pocahontas, alias Matoaka and her descendants. Richmond: J. W. Randolph
  & English, 1887.

ROLOFF -- Rohifs, Gleason D.
  A genealogy study. Vienna. 198-.

ROOKS -- Rooks, Russell (assisted by Gerrit J. Rooks)
  The Gerrit Hendrik Rooks family history. Arlington. 1959.

ROOSEN -- Joyner, Peggy S.
Henry Roosen-Rosen. Portsmouth. 1980.

ROSE -- Freese, Eunice Brooks
William Rose of Surry County, Virginia: some of his descendants and related families. 1976.

ROSE -- Rose, Ben L.
Rose-Steel anthology. Richmond. 1982.

ROSE -- Rose, Christine
Abstracts of early Virginia Rose estates, wills, inventories, accounts and administrator's bonds before 1850. San Jose, Calif. 1972.

ROSE -- Rose, Christine
Rev. Robert Rose of Scotland, Essex County, Virginia and Albemarle County, Virginia; the first five generations in America. San Jose, Calif. 1972.

ROSE -- Rose, Christine
Rev. Charles Rose of Scotland & Westmoreland County, Virginia: the first four generations in America. San Jose, Calif. 1976.

ROSE -- Rose, Christine
Ancestors and descendants of Frederick Rose of Sussex County, Virginia, Orange County, North Carolina, and Wayne and Hardin Counties, Tennessee. San Jose, Calif. 1980.

ROSE -- Squires, W. H. T.
The Rose family of colonial Virginia and medievel Scotland. Norfolk. 1942.

ROSE -- Stanard, W. G.
A chart of the ancestors and descendants of Rev. Robert Rose, born at Wester Alves, Scotland, February 12, 1704, came to Virginia in 1725, died June 30, 1751. Richmond. 1895.

ROSENBERGER -- ROSENBERGER, Francis Coleman
A partial list of the descendants of Erasmus Rosenberger who lived in Hanover Township, Lancaster County, Pennsylvania, in the 1750's and settled in Berkeley County, Virginia, now West Virginia, in 1776. Washington. 1951.

ROSEWALL -- Torrence, William C.
Rootes of Rosewall. An account of Major Philip Rootes of "Rosewall." King and Queen County, Virginia, and some of his descendants. Louisville, Ky.: G. G. Fetter Co., 1906.

ROSS -- Heggs, Esther M.
Ross family of Scotland, Virginia, Kentucky, Missouri, Iowa, Texas.

ROSS -- Ross, Howard
    Nancy Adeline Ross (1843-1924): a family history including the early
    development of Gary, West Virginia and the field of coal mining. Superior
    Print Co.

ROTHWELL -- Fischer, Myra Smith
    A Rothwell book, compromising the descendants of Claiborne Rothwell of
    Albemarle County, Virginia, through nine generations, and interesting
    sketches about some of his descendants. Memphis. 1964.

ROUSE -- Lloyd, Emma Rouse
    Rouse family of Virginia and Kentucky.

ROUSE -- Rouse, Nancy E.
    John Rouse of Virginia. 1982.

ROUSH -- Roush, Lester Le Roy
    History of the Roush family in America, from its founding by John Adam
    Rausch in 1736 to the present time. Strasburg. 1928.

ROUSH -- Roush, Lester LeRoy
    The romance of the Roush family association. Parkersburg, W. Va.: Banner
    Print. 1937.

ROUSH -- Roush, Lester L.
    The Roush family in America; history of the Roush family in America.
    Strasburg: Shenandoah Pub., 1963.

ROUSH -- Rouse, Nancy E.
    John Rouse of Virginia and his descendants, 1717-1980. Cincinnati. 1982.

ROWE -- Adkins, Clara Pauline
    Genealogy of the Rowes of Virginia and West Virginia and connecting
    families (1697 to 1977). Fort Gay, Ky. 1977.

ROY -- Roy, Nancy Reba
    The Roy family of Virginia and Kentucky. Fellows, Calif. 1935.

ROY -- Roy, Nancy R.
    Early records of the Roy family of Virginia and Kentucky. La Mesa,
    Calif. 1963.

RUBINCAM -- Rubincam, Milton
    The family of Jacob Revercomb, the first of the race in Virginia.
    Richmond. 1938.

RUCKER -- Wood, Sudie Rucker
    The Rucker family genealogy, with their ancestors, descendants and
    connections, from original records, letters and other material collected
    over a period of theirty years. Richmond: Old Dominion Press, 1932.

RUDDELL -- Smutz, Harold Turk
John Ruddell of the Shenandoah Valley: his children and grandchildren.
Webster Groves, Mo. 1974.

RUDDELL -- Harman, Pauline Ruddle
Ruddle-Riddle genealogy and biography. West Virginia. 1984.

RUDOLPH -- Blum, Willetta B.
The Rudolph family of Virginia. Washington. 1962.

RUEBUSH -- Ruebush, Glenn W.
Mary Ruebush, 1736-1815, and her family in Virginia. Harrisonburg. 1956.

RUFFIN -- Henry, R. B.
Ruffin and Other Genealogies (Beverley, Bland, Bolling, Byrd, de Jarnette,
Meade, Randolph, Ruffin, Shippen, Skipwith, Taylor, Willing, Wormeley).
Printed chart. Va. State Library.

RUNYON -- Runyon, Robert and Amos
Runyon genealogy; a genealogy of the Runyon families who settled early
in Kentucky, North Carolina, Virginia and West Virginia. Brownsville,
Tex. 1955.

RUPPENTHAL -- Allemong, Kathern Ruppenthal
Ruppenthal history. Berkeley Springs, W. Va. 1984.

RUSH -- Ayres, Nellie F.
Genealogy of the Rush family of Virginia. Memphis, Tenn. 1963.

RUSH -- Ayres, Nellie F.
Genealogy of the Rush Family of Virginia and the Terrell genealogy.
Memphis, Tenn. 1946.

RUSS -- Taylor, Dorothy Russ
The Russ family. Alexandria. 1978.

RUSSELL -- The Russell family. Arlington: American Genealogical Research
Institute, 1972.

RUST -- Rust, Ellsworth Marshall
Rust of Virginia; genealogical and biographical sketches of the descendants of William Rust, 1654-1940. Washington. 1940.

SADOWSKI -- Sandusky, A. Clay
... Polish pioneers of Virginia and Kentucky, by Miecislaus Haiman, with
notes on genealogy of the Sadowski family. Chicago. 1937.

SAGE -- The March of the Sages. Research: John Edward (Pat) Gwin-Sage, Marguerite (Sage) Parker (Mrs. Sterling Parker). Editor: Bonnie (Sage) Ball. Associate editor: Sybil Dawson Scofield. Radford. 1967.

SAGENDORF -- Moncure, Peyton Sagendorf and Kathryn Schwartz Callaghan Sagendorf-Safendorph, Segendorf; a genealogy. Vienna. 1972.

SALE -- A scrapbook of Sale kin, Bedford County, Virginia. Bedford. 1969.

SAMPSON -- Sampson, Anne Eliza Woods
Kith and kin, written, at their urgent request, for the children of Mr. and Mrs. John Russell Sampson, by their mother. It includes records of their ancestors bearing the names Baker, Baldwin, Breckinridge, Brown, Bryson, Byrd, Curd, Dudley, Goodman, Horsley, Kennedy, Le Bruen, McClanahan, McDowell, MxKesson, Poage, Reed, Rogers, Thornton, Trice, Sampson, and Woods. Richmond: William Byrd Press, 1922.

SAMPSON -- Sampson, Lilla Briggs
The Sampson Family (Va. Sampsons, pp. 205-222). Baltimore, Md.: Williams and Wilkins Co.

SAMS -- Sams, Crawford F.
The Sams family of Virginia. Atherton, Calif. 1981.

SAMUEL -- Hoffman, Muriel M.
Samuel family story: Virginia, Kentucky, Indiana, Illinois. Anchor, Ill. 1971.

SANDERS -- Sanders, Walter L.
Ancestors and descendants of George William and Roberta (Grayson) Sanders of Virginia. 1972.

SANFORD -- Bendigo, Irma Sanford
Pierce Sanford of Orange County, Virginia. Fort Myers, Fla. 1978.

SANFORD -- Sanford, Walter E.
Sanford, Morris, Faulconer families of Virginia. Alexandria. 1976.

SATER -- Maclay, Isaac Walker
Henry Sater, 1690-1754, the recital of the life and character of an early adventurer to Virginia, and subsequently a settler of the province of Maryland under Lord Baltimore. A representative colonist ... whose strong religious convictions led to the organization of the parent Baptist society of the province. New York. 1897.

SAVAGE -- Burghard, August
America's first family, the Savages of Virginia. Philadelphia: Dorrance, 1974.

SCARBOROUGH -- Donaldson, Evelyn Kinder
Squires and dames of Virginia. Los Angeles, Calif. 1950.

SCHREGARDUES -- Gillespie, Rollin Wilson
Helen Calire Schregardus/Gillespie; her ancestors and relatives. McLean.
1972.

SCHOONOVER -- Lunsford, Ollie Collett
The Van Schoonhoven, Schoonhoven, Schoonover: or mostly descendants of
Benjamin Schoonover of Randol(p)h County, W. Va. Providence, W. Va.
1977.

SCHEITLIN -- Scheitlin, Herbert I.
Genealogy of the Scheitlin families, national and international. Richmond.
1970.

SCLATER -- Wallace, George Selden
The Sclater family in Virginia. Huntington, W. Va. 1938.

SCOGGIN -- Doliante, Joann Sharon Johnson
Genealogical serendipity. Alexandria. 1965.

SCOTT -- Benkelman, Olive P. S.
Importation of James and Rachel Holmes Scott, Aug. 21, 1771. Elk Creek.
1971.

SCOTT -- Cronbaugh, Lois E. W.
Descendants of Joseph and Mary Cain Scott of Virginia and Kentucky. Cedar
Rapids, Iowa. 1976.

SCOTT -- Scott, Corinne
A transcription of Corinne Scott's family reunion notebook. Vienna. 1982.

SCOTT -- Scott, George Wilson
Quotations and excerpts from "McGinness and Scott families..." with
additional supplementary historical and genealogical data of the John P.
Scott branch of the Scott family and their relations with the White, May,
Welch, Reed, Farrar, Cook and Gladden families of Yohogania County,
Virginia. Imperial, Pa. 1953.

SCOTT -- Vercoe, Josephine McCord
A genealogical history of the Scott family; descendants of Alexander Scott
who came to Augusta County, Virginia, ca. 1750; with a history of the
families with which they intermarried. Columbus, Ohio. 1940.

SEAY -- Baer, Mabel Van Dyke
Seay family of Virginia. 1966.

SEAY -- Reese, Margaret C.
Seay-Jennings ancestors. Waynesboro. 1980.

SEAY -- Seay, Burwell Warren
Descendants of Abraham Seay. Palmyra. 1971.

SEAL -- Sprouse, Deborah A.
   The Seale family of old Virginia: a genealogy. 1981.

SEBREE -- Guss, Willa I.
   Sebree studies: lineage of Charles Jenkins Sebree (1854-1913) and collateral
   lines traced to colonial Virginia: conjugate lines including Barnett, Butler,
   Butts, Carter, Gibbs, Hord, Jarrell, Johnson, Sage, Shreves, Thomason, Watts,
   Wilson. Golden, Colo. 1984.

SEIBERT -- Bell, Raymond M.
   The Seibert family: Wolfersweiler, Saar, Tulpehocken, Pennsylvania, Clear
   Springs, Md., Martinsburg, W. Va. Washington, Pa. 1959.

SELDEN -- Kennedy, Mary Selden
   Seldens of Virginia and allied families. New York: Frank Allaben
   Genealogical Co., 1911.

SELDEN -- Selden, Edna Mae
   Selden and kindred of Virginia. Richmond. 1941.

SELDEN -- Selden, Jefferson Sinclair
   Samuel Selden, the immigrant, and his wife Rebecca Yeo Selden: the first
   of the name in Virginia, about 1690, born about 1660, died in Virginia 1720.
   Hampton. 1980.

SELDEN -- Warner, Pauline Pearce
   Some descendants of Thomas Selden, and a facsimile of an ancient Selden
   family tree. Tappahannock. 1967.

SELECMAN -- Cole, Redmond Selecman
   The Selecman family, a history of Henry Selecman and his wife, Margaret
   Harmon, of Occoquan, Virginia, and their descendants, and items dealing
   with families related to them. Tulsa, Okla. 1942.

SHACKELFORD -- George Shackelford and Annette Jeter and their descendants;
   editor-in-chief, Edward Madison Shackelford ... and assistant editor,
   Franklin Shackelford Moseley ... Montgomery, Ala. 1941.

SHACKELFORD -- Shackelford, Robert B.
   The Shackelford family. Charlottesville. 1940.

SHANHOLTZER -- Kerns, Wilmer L.
   Shanholtzer history and allied family roots of Hampshire County, W. Va.
   and Frederick County, Va. Arlington. 1980.

SHANHOLTZER -- Kerns, Wilmer L.
   Shanholtzer history and allied family roots of Hampshire County, W. Va.
   and Frederick County. Va. Parsons, W. Va.: McClain Print., 1980.

SHARP -- Hoff, John D.
   A short history of Julius Sharp of Rockbridge Co., Virginia and some of
   his descendants. Tulsa, Okla. 1972.

SHARP -- Montgomery, Anne Deubery
Sharps of Augusta County, Virginia, Bedford County, Virginia and Three
soldiers of the Revolution came to Kentucky. San Francisco. 1971.

SHARP -- Peters, Genevieve Elizabeth Cummings
Know your relatives: the Sharps, Gibbs, Graves, Efland, Albright, Loy,
Miller, Snodderly, Tillman, and other related families. Arlington.
1953.

SHARPS -- Sharps, Janice Shriver
Jesse and Sarah Sharps (Less) and associate families of Preston, Taylor,
Marion, and Calhoun counties of West Virginia, 1783-1985. Bridgeport,
W. Va. 1985.

SHAW -- Patch, Guthrie Shaw
They took the high road: The Lady Gurtha and the Catamount o' the North,
The Princess Yleria and the Mac-in-Sagart, The puritan woman and the
Scots cavalier, The Virginia girl and Washington's rifleman; romances of
the Shaws of Scotland and America. Richmond. 1946.

SHEDD -- Shedd, Joel P.
The Shedd family of the southern states descended from James Shed of
Loudoun County, Virginia. Arlington. 1981.

SHEFFER -- Loeber, Charles
The Sheffer family, Staunton, Virginia. Staunton. 1942.

SHEFFER -- Loeber, Charles
The Sheffer family of Shenandoah County, Virginia. December 30, 1728 -
December 30, 1944. 1944.

SHEILD -- Vick, Dollie Hughes
Mary Rooksland Sheild; a Va. genealogy, 871-1965. Shelburne, Vt.:
Excelsior Press, 1965.

SHELBURNE -- Shelburne, Robert Craig
The Shelburne family of Montgomery County, Virginia. 1935.

SHELBURNE -- Shelburne, Robert Craig
The monuments erected to the memory of our dead. (The tombstone inscrip-
tion pertaining to the Shelburne and related families, Montgomery County,
Virginia. 1939.

SHELBURNE -- Shelburne, Robert Craig
The Shelburne family. Richmond. 1943.

SHELBURNE -- Shelburne, Robert Craig
The Shelburne family. Christianburg. 1944.

SHELBURNE -- The Shelburne family; the colonial family at Jamestown and Brisland (i.e. Bisland) Parish, James City County, Virginia. 1952.

SHELBURNE -- Shelburne, Robert Craig
The Shelburne family. Roanoke. 1953.

SHELBURNE -- Stevenson, Kenyon
Shelburnes of Old Virginia: from the arrival of Thomas, the emigrant, in 1607 to the time when the children of Augustine came from Kentucky to Indiana. Akron, Ohio.

SHELLY -- Whitley, Edythe
Shelly family of Scott County, Virginia and Franklin County, Tennessee. 1964.

SHELOR -- Shelor, Susan Jefferson
Pioneers and their coat of arms of Floyd County; genealogies of prominent early settlers of the Blue Ridge Plateau of Virginia. Winston-Salem, N.C. 1961.

SHELTON -- Shelton, Frank H.
Thomas Shelton family in early Virginia: genealogy of a Shelton family. Colorado Springs, Colo. 1981.

SHEPARD -- Hedrick, Ralph W.
William G. Shepherd family story and genealogy, 1778-1970. Parkersburg, W. Va. 1970.

SHEILD -- Vick, Dollie Hughes
A Virginia genealogy. 1965.

SHIELDS -- Raber, Nellie M. R.
William Shields of Augusta County, Virginia and Trumbull County, Ohio. Lakewood.

SHIELDS -- Woodward, Lloyd A.
A history of the ancestors and descendants of Wilford A. and Sarah E. (Shields) Dean, Married 1877. McLean. 1981.

SHIPLEY -- Hall, Frank Nelson
A Story of the Shiplett (Shipley) family of Muskingum County, Ohio (near Zanesville) and related families: David Roland Shiplett from Culpepper, Virginia, Charles Franklin from Maryland, Catherine Councilman (Franklin) from Baltimore, Maryland, William Perley (Caleb) Hughes from New Jersey, Amy Allen (Hughes) from New Jersey, Fred Hall of Belvidere, Ill. The descendants of Nelson and Ephraim Shiplett. Denton, Tex. 1962.

SHUMAKER -- Funai, Clara McLaughlin
A Weaving. Lynchburg. 1977.

SHIRLEY -- King, Harry Tracy
John Shirley and his descendants of Virginia and South Carolina. Roby,
Tex. 1972.

SHIVELY -- Andrews, George William
Schaublin (Shively) families from the District of Waldenburg, Baselland,
Switzerland. Alexandria. 1978.

SHORT -- Baer, Mabel Van Dyke
Short families of Kentucky and Virginia. 1966.

SHORT -- Lynch, Josephine S.
Short, an early Virginia family. Richmond: Whittet & Shepperson, 1970.

SHORTER -- More light on the Va. Shorter family: other families treated are
Clarks, Kennedys, Towles, Sampsons, Bankstons, Battles, Watkinses,
Billingsleas, Fannins, Cowles, Aldredges, Humes. Contributed from
Saunder's book "Early settlers of Alabama"; with corrective and
explanatory notes by George Magruder Battey, III. Newton, Pa. 1953.

SHOWALTER -- Brubaker, Jacob D.
Jacob W. and Margaret Heatwole Showalter family history. Harrisonburg.
1970.

SHOWALTER -- Showalter, Elizabeth A.
Descendants of George Branner Showalter and Elizabeth Ellen Blosser.
Harrisonburg. 1974.

SHOWALTER -- Showalter, Vada E.
Anthony Showalter family. Harrisonburg. 1974.

SHRIVER -- Seegrist, Nellie Schryvers
The Schryvers-Rysdam story: a family history, 1575-1978. McLean. 1978.

SHUFFELTON -- McBrise, Nancy S.
Shuffelton kinship. Verona. 1977.

SHULTZ -- Bushman, Katherine G.
Shultz of Augusta County, Virginia; being a supplement to the material
record in the Genealogical Record of the Schwenkfelder Families, edited
by Samuel E. Brecht, 1923. 1974.

SHUMAKER -- Funai, Clara McLaughlin
A Weaving. Lynchburg. 1977.

SIBLEY -- Burton, Violet S.
Virginia was their home: Fowlkes, Wooten, Ellis, Jennings and related lines.
Fort Smith, Ark.

SILER -- Siler, A. O.
   The Siler family, a compilation of biographical and historical sketches
   relating to the descendants of Plikard Dederic and Elizabeth Siler, with
   genealogical chart. Charleston, W. Va. 1922.

SILVIUS -- Silvious, Stephen Calvin
   Descendants of Isaac Silvious of Virginia: a brief study. 1979.

SIMME -- Chappell, Wilma
   The Simms family of Stafford County, Virginia. A record of the descen-
   dants of three brothers ... Richard Simms (1752-1850) of Clay County,
   Missouri; Presley Simms (ca. 1754-1852) of Montgomery County, Indiana;
   Rhodam Simms (1756-1853) of Ralls County, Missouri. St. Louis. 1969.

SIMMONS -- Graham, Ruth Maxwell
   Descendants of John Simmons. Arlington. 1975.

SIMMONS -- McCall, Ettie Augusta Tidwell
   William Simmons of James City County and Surry County, Virginia. 1953.

SIMMONS -- Simmons, R. Daniel
   Simmons family genealogy with some connecting lines, 1793-1984. St. Marys,
   W. Va. 1984.

SIMMS -- Hall, William K.
   The Simms of Stafford County, Virginia. St. Louis, Mo. 1969.

SIMPSON -- Johnson, Katherine Baker
   The family of John Simpson of Montgomery and Halifax Cos., Virginia. 1940.

SIMS -- Prewitt, Lela Wolfe
   Ancestors & descendants of Thomas Sims of Culpeper County, Virginia,
   Edmund Butler of Virginia and Kentucky with allied families & other
   Culpeper data. Fairfield, Iowa. 1972.

SIMS -- Sims, Henry Upson
   The genealogy of the Sims family of Virginia, the Carolinas and the gulf
   states. Kansas City, Mo. 1940.

SINCLAIR -- Selden, Jefferson Sinclair, Jr.
   The Sinclair family of Virginia; descendants of Henry Sinclair, born in
   Aberdeen, Scotland, the second son of the Earl of Caithness, and his son
   John Sinclair, 1755-1820, and allied families. Hampton. 1964.

SINCLAIR -- Sinclair, Dohrman, J.
   Ancestors and descendants of Dohrman J. Sinclair and Mary Donaldson
   Sinclair. Strasburg: Shenandoah Pub., 1970.

SINK -- Sinks, John D.
   Sinks, a family history. Arlington. 1980.

SINK -- Sinks, John D.
Sinks update--1980. Arlington. 1980.

SISK -- Sisk, Luther L.
The Sisk family: Virginia--North Carolina--South Carolina--Kentucky--
Alabama--Tennessee--Georgia--Missouri--Texas. Escondido, Calif. 1980.

SITTON -- Sitton, Enid W.
Sitton and Gibson genealogy; descendants of three Revolutionary War
soldiers: Joseph Sitton, North Carolina; Guyon Gibson, South Carolina,
Thomas Kennedy, Virginia. Houston, Tex. 1967.

SKELTON -- Baskervill, P. Hamilton
The Skeltons of Paxton, Powhatan County, Virginia, and their Connections,
including sketches of the families of Shelton, Gifford and Crane.
Richmond: Old Dominion Press, Inc., 1922.

SKILLERN -- Appell, Darlene R. and Ethelmae Eylar Carter
Skillern family history and genealogy; descendants of William and Elizabeth
Skillern of Virginia, including the family of John and Rebecca (Maxwell)
Anderson and their descendants. Pleasant Hill, Calif. 1971.

SKINNER -- Holcombe, Lester Granville
Descendants of Richard Alexander Skinner of Loudoun County, Virginia.
Bourbonnais, Ill. 1972.

SLACK -- Keeney, Roscoe C.
6,474 Slack relatives: a detailed listing of the descendants of John and
Nancy Huddleston Slack and a resource guide to other Slack families in
the Kanawha and Elk Valleys. Parsons, W. Va.: McClain Print., 1984.

SLAPPEY -- Hargrett, Felix
The Slappeys of South Carolina and Georgia: a sketch with a glance at the
allied family Hatfield. Lynchburg. 1984.

SLAUGHTER -- du Bellet, Louise Pecquet
Slaughter family; descendants of Robert Slaughter and Frances Anne Jones,
of St. Marks Parish in Va.

SLAUGHTER -- Ficklin, Slaughter W.
Genealogy of the Slaughter Family since 1720. Charlottesville: James
Alexander, 1870.

SLAVENS -- Slavens, Thomas H.
Descendants of John Slavin, born County Tyrone, Ireland, 1723, settled
in Va. 1740, died Hiland County, Va., 1788. San Antonio, Tex. 1940.

SLOAN -- Schroeder, Lyra
The story of one of the Sloan families. Roanoke. 1977.

SMALLWOOD -- McDonnell, Mildred A.
The Smallwood family of Maryland and Virginia. 1970.

SMITH -- Battey, George Magruder, III
Mayos of Virginia and kinsmen, Smiths of Virginia and others of the connection. Washington. 1940.

SMITH -- Brownlee, Francis Smith
From 1677 to 1955, a genealogical, historical and reminiscent account of one of the many John Smiths from Virginia and of his descendants. Wichita, Kans. 1955.

SMITH -- Hartman, Blanche T.
The Smiths of Virginia; a history and genealogy of the Smiths of "Big Spring plantation", Frederick County, Virginia, together with a chronicle of the Drugan and the Carnahan families of Pennsylvania and Ohio. Pittsburg, Pa. 1929.

SMITH -- In memoriam: to the memory of the faithful and beloved husband and father, Francis Lee Smith (1808-1877). Alexandria. 1877.

SMITH -- Hieronymous, Goldie Smith
Descendants of Elijah Smith and Polly (Wiley) Smith's eldest sons and daughter: William Smith and Nancy Jane Sutton, Lucinda Smith and George Petrey, Robert Smith and Mary Ann Sutton, John Smith and Ollie Jones, and descendants of Moses Foley, Sr. Falls Church. 1980.

SMITH -- Hieronymous, Goldie Smith
Descendants of Nathaniel Smith, Knox/Whitley County, Kentucky, son of Elijah Smith--Revolutionary War patriot from New Jersey and Virginia: documentary research and compilation of family information. Falls Church. 1982.

SMITH -- Highland, Scotland G.
Fourth annual Christmas Plea. Dedicated by the author to his maternal ancestor John Smith, born 1655, great grandfather of Robert Fulton, born at Fulton house, Fulton (then little Britain) Township, Lancaster County, Pennsylvania, November 14, 1765; died in New York, February 24, 1815. An historical and genealogical narrative. Clarksburg, W. Va. 1926.

SMITH -- Hill, George Canning
Capt. John Smith; a biography. Boston. 1858.

SMITH --Jensen, Nephi
Journal of Jesse N. Smith. Salt Lake City. 1940.

SMITH — Price, Lucy Montgomery Smith
The Sydney-Smith and Clagett-Price genealogy, with the Lewis, Montgomery, Harrison, Hawley, Moorhead, Rixey, Doniphan, Waugh, Anderson, Randolph, Mott, Drake, Butcher, Triplett, Humphrey, Ball, Porter, Brown, Dorsey, Cooper, Stuart, Strother, families with whom they intermarried, and some of their descendants. Strasburg. 1927.

SMITH -- Genealogy of the Smith Family of Essex County, Virginia.

SMITH -- Simms, W. Gilmore
    The life of Captain John Smith. The founder of Virginia. Boston. 1846.

SMITH -- Smith, Guy R.
    One branch of the Capt. John and Margaret Smith family of Augusta County,
    Virginia Colony. Novi, Mich. 1979.

SMITH -- Smith, Pearl O.
    Peter Smith: some of his Virginia, North Carolina, and Kentucky descendants.
    Washington. 1976.

SMITH -- Wulfeck, Dorothy Ford
    Smith of Virginia. Naugatuck, Conn. 1969.

SMOCK -- Smock, David L.
    Smocks in the American Revolutionary War. McLean. 1982.

SMOCK -- Smock, David L.
    Henry Smock and Anna DeBaun: their ancestors and descendants. McLean.
    1983.

SMOOT -- Newman, Harry Wright
    The Smoots of Maryland and Virginia; a genealogical history of William
    Smute, boatright, of Hampton, Virginia, and Pickawaxon, Maryland, with
    a history of his descendants to the present generation. Lynchburg.
    1936.

SNEAD -- Cox, Virginia DeMott
    The Sneads of Fluvanna. Fork Union. 1959.

SNEAD -- Hatcher, Virginia Snead
    The Sneads of Fluvanna. Roanoke: The Stone Printing & Mfg. Co., 1910.

SNEAD -- Srokes, William E., Jr.
    An American saga; the story of the Snead family of Accomac County, Virginia,
    and of Kentucky. North Garden. 1952.

SNIPES -- Fisher, James W.
    The ancestors and descendants of Elbert Monroe Snipes in England, Virginia,
    North Carolina, South Carolina. 1984.

SNIPES -- Truett, Earl A.
    The descendants and ancestors of Young Snipes. Reston. 1982.

SOMMERS -- Wyatt, Lucile Rebecca Douglas
    The Sommers memorial. Danville: J. T. Townes Printing Co., 1967.

SOUTH -- Gee, Christine South
    Genealogical notes on the South family from New Jersey, Pennsylvania,
    Maryland, Virginia, South Carolina, Kentucky and Texas. Greenville,
    S.C. 1963.

SOUTHWEST VIRGINIA -- Summers, Lewis Preston
   Annals of Southwest Virginia, 1769-1800 (Botetourt, Fincastle, Montgomery, Washington, Wythe). Abingdon. 1929.

SOUTHWEST VIRGINIA AND THE VALLEY -- Historical and Biographical. Roanoke: A. D. Smith & Co., 1892.

SOWERS -- Tobin, Richard W.
   Sours family of Page County, Virginia. Gainesville. 1983.

SPEARS -- Kennette, Mary Spiers
   Descendants of Henry Spiers, pioneer Scotsman, Prince George County, Virginia, 1744-1979. 1979.

SPEARS -- Spears, Joseph F.
   The Spears saga. Alexandria. 1982.

SPICER -- Spicer, Florene LeVan
   Genealogical record of the Spicer family: descendants of John Spicer of Virginia, Maryland, and Delaware, including some of the related Kerby and Ralph families and miscellaneous Spicers. Eugene, Ore. 1980.

SPOTSWOOD LETTERS -- The Official Letters of Alexander Spotswood, etc. Richmond: Virginia Historical Society, 1882.

SPOTSWOOD -- Campbell, Charles
   Genealogy of the Spotswood Family in Scotland and Virginia. Albany, N.Y.: J. Munsell, 1868.

SPOTSWOOD -- Fontaine, Wm. Winston, A.M.
   The descent of General Robert E. Lee, from King Robert the Bruce, of Scotland. A paper before the Southern historical association, of Louisville, Ky., March 29, 1881. 1881.

SPRINGSTON -- Lockhart, Roy L.
   The Springston family. Parkersburg, W. Va. 1973.

SPRUANCE -- Spruance, W. C.
   The Spruance family in Delaware, 1733-1933 with collateral relations and ancestral lines including the Spotswood family in Virginia and the Willing family in Pennsylvania. Wilington, Del. 1933.

SPURR -- Spurr, Richard A. G.
   Spurrs from Virginia to Indiana, 1800-1973. Bedford, Ind. 1973.

STAATS -- Staats, Harold
   Genealogy of the Staats family. Ripley, W. Va. 1921.

STAATS -- Jensen, Verl S.
   Genealogy of the Staats Family, by Harold Staats, Ripley, W. Va., 1921.
   Index to selected parts, namely, those parts dealing with the West
   Virginia branch, Jackson County, W. Va. the Casto Family. Portland,
   Ore. 1977.

STALLARD -- Roy, Nancy R. and Kay Hampton
   Notes on the Stallard family of Virginia. Santee, Calif. 1966.

STALLINGS -- Parham, D. E. H.
   Stallings, Virginia to Alabama. W. Palm Beach, Fla. 1967.

STANFIELD -- Hieronymus, Goldie Smith
   Descendants of Sampson Stanfield. Falls Church. 1981.

STANLEY -- Barnhill, Celeste Terrell
   Virginia Quaker Stanleys and descendants. Miami Beach, Fla. 1931.

STANLEY -- Flaherty, Elnora S.
   Whither thou goest; a story of the Stanley family in Virginia, North
   Carolina, Kansas and Oklahoma. Irving, Tex. 1973.

STANLEY -- Pence, Richard Allen
   Our Stanley ancestors in America. Fairfax. 1970.

STAPLES -- Kroll, Gretchen Elizabeth Staples
   Our family. Fairfax. 1979.

STAPLETON -- Stapleton, Harriet L.
   Stapleton family history, the descendants of Thomas and Mary Stapleton.
   Arlington. 1972.

STARK -- Abbott, Jane H.
   James Stark, Jr. with wife "Cathron" of Virginia. "Died in the Carolina."
   Genealogical notes and records. 1929.

STARK -- Abbott, Jane H.
   Thomas Stark, of Virginia, to South Carolina, South Carolina to Tennessee
   and returned to South Carolina. Genealogical notes and records. 1929.

STARK -- Abbott, Jane H.
   Jeremiah Stark of Culpeper County, Va., later of Allen County, Ky. and
   some descendants. Genealogical notes and records. 1930.

STARK -- Harris, Mary Kathryn
   James Stark of Stafford County, Virginia and his descendants. Fort Worth,
   Tex. 1985.

STARK -- Stark family of N.H., Va., Ky., and Conn.

STARKWEATHER -- Starkweather, Carlton Lee
A brief genealogical history of Robert Starkweather of Roxbury and
Ipswich, Massachusetts. Occoquan. 1904.

STATES -- Staats, Harold
Genealogy of the Staats family. Ripley, W. Va. 1921.

STEEL -- Goeller, Mildred L. S.
Steeles of Steeles Tavern, Virginia and related families: Moore, Moon,
Calvert, Massie, Strother and Searson. 1974.

STEELE -- McCrary, Dixie Lee
Robert Steele of the New River Valley in Virginia. 1976.

STEELE -- Steele, Donley M.
A genealogy of the descendants of James Steele and his wife Mary.
Morgantown, W. Va. 1919.

STEELE -- Steele, Donley M.
A genealogy of the descendants of James Steele and his wife Mary, late
of Clinton district, Monongalia County, Virginia (now West Virginia)
for the entertainment and instruction of the family and for handy
reference. 1919.

STEMPLE -- Stemple, Jay
History of the Stemple family, 1660-1960. Salem. 1960-66.

STEMPLE -- Stemple, Jay
A genealogy of the Stemple family. Richmond: Whittet & Shepperson, 1966.

STERRETT -- Starrett, Elizabeth Regenstein
Starrett and allied families: including the Virginia and Kentucky ancestry
of Elizabeth Regenstein Starrett and over 40 other early American connections. Berryville. 1981.

STERRETT - Sterrett, T. Woods
The Sterrett genealogy; families of Pennsylvania, Virginia, Canada & others.
New Haven, Conn. 1930.

STEVENS -- Stevens, Albert C.
Record of the family of John Stevens, Staten Island, N.Y., Orange Co.,
Va., and Shelby Co., Ky. Louisville, Ky. 1961.

STEVENS -- The Stevens family. Arlington: The American Genealogical Research
Institute, 1972.

STEVENS -- Stephens, Robert W.
Stephens family history: ancestry and descendants of revolutionary soldier Robert Stephens and his wife, Sarah Farmer, of Virginia through their son Josiah Stephens. Dallas, Tex. 1982.

STEWART -- Baker, Gordon C.
The descendants of Daniel and Rebecca Stewart of Stewartstown, West Virginia. Rockville, Md. 1977.

STEWART -- Blakemore, Mary S.
Genealogy of the Stewarts of Sequatchie Valley, Tennessee, and allied families. Richmond: Dietz Press, 1960.

STEWART -- Dickerson, Florence S.
The James Stewart family of early Augusta County, Virginia, and descendants, 1740-1960. Parsons, W. Va. 1966.

STEWART -- Dickerson, Florence Smith
The James Stewart family of early Augusta County, Virginia. Amelia. 1966.

STEWART -- Mott, J. P.
Some descendants of John Stewart of Amherst County, Virginia. 1948.

STILES -- McSwain, Eleanor O.
Styles - Frankling, Stiles - Franklin; some descendants of Joseph Styles, attorney, New Kent Co., Va., 1680, and James Frankling, planter, Henrico Co., Va., 1643 - 1704. Macon, Ga. 1975.

STOCKTON -- Johnson, Leona Irene Smith
David Stockton of Virginia. Albuquerque, N.M.; Houston, Tex. 1972.

STONE -- Stone, Dolly Mary
Samuel Stone and his wife, Mary Ann Chunn; a story of their lives, including early residence in Virginia, Tennessee, and Alabama, their migration to Missouri and later to the Republic of Texas, with data concerning their family and descendants, and also including some genealogical history proving the ancestry of Mary Ann Chunn. San Antonio, Tex. 1955.

STONER -- Stoner, Vera Barnhart
The family of Jacob Stoner II of Botetourt County, Virginia, with historical and genealogical records, 1732-1965. Ladoga, Ind. 1965.

STORY -- Murphy, Sharon B.
Story, 1788-1973, with information about the families of Tupper, McDowell, Craig. Reston. 1973.

STOVALL -- Smith, Carmae Massey
The Stovall family in America: descendants of Bartholomew of Henrico County, Virginia, 1684. Houston, Tex. 1979.

STOWE -- Hoke, Tachel Hanna
The Stowe family: descendants of William and Mary Stowe, from Virginia to North Carolina, 1718-1976. Myrtle Beach, S.C. 1977.

STRACHAN -- Strahin, Richard D.
The family Strahin. Parsons, W. Va.: McClain Print, 1982.

STRAIGHT -- Murrow, Charles H.
Ephraim Straight, b. ca. 1800 in Virginia and James Fredregill, b. ca. 1795. Des Moines, Iowa. 1974.

STRAITH -- Lawrence, Schuyler
A genealogical memoir of the Straith-Strath family of Scotland and Virginia, 1764-1934; and a special record of the descendants of Dr. Alexander Straith. Towans, Pa. 1934.

STREET -- Trembly, W. C.
Genealogy and other information about the family of General Joseph Montfort Street, born Dec. 18, 1782 in Lunenburg County, Va., died May 5, 1840 at Sac and Fox, Agency, Iowa. Agency, Iowa. 1976.

STRICKLER -- Forerunners: a History or Genealogy of the Strickler Families, Etc. Harrisonburg. 1925.

STRICKLER -- Strickler, Harry M.
Forerunners; a history or genealogy of the Strickler families, their kith and kin, including Kauffmans, Stovers, Burners, Ruffners, Beavers, Shavers, Brumbachs, Zirkles, Blossers, Groves, Brubakers, Neffs, Rothgebs, and many other early families of Shenandoah, Rockingham, Augusta, Frederick and Page counties of the Shenandoah Valley; a memorial to those who have gone before. From about 1700 to the present time, 1924. Harrisonburg. 1925.

STRICKLER -- Nicholson, Kenneth J.
Daniel and Mary Strickler, pioneers. Arlington. 1964.

STRICKLER -- Strickler, Harry M.
Forerunners. Harrisonburg. 1924.

STRONG -- Rolff, James Robert
Strong family of Virginia and other southernstates. Oak Forest, Ill. 1982.

STROSNIDER -- Strosnider, Ruth C.
The Strosnider family in America, 1751-1981. Blacksville, W. Va.: McClain Print, 1982.

STROTHER -- Merrill, Carol R.
The Strother family: Charlottesville to Ardmore. 1983.

STROTHER -- Owen, Thomas McAdory
    William Strother of Virginia, and his descendants.

STUART -- Baker, Gordon C.
    The descendants of Daniel and Rebecca Stewart of Stewartstown, West
    Virginia: including a history of the Blosser, Huggans, and Cowell
    families, and three other Stewart clans in the area. Rockville, Md.
    1977.

STUART -- Life of General J. E. B. Stuart.

STUART -- History of Stuart family; by Essie W. Stuart in loving memory of
    her late husband Walter Stuart. West Union, W. Va. 1950.

STUART -- Robertson, Alexander F.
    Alexander Hugh Holmes Stuart, 1807-1891. Richmond. 1925.

STUBBS -- Stubbs, William Carter
    The descendants of John Stubbs of Cappahosic, Gloucester County, Virginia,
    1652. New Orleans. 1902.

STUBBS -- Stubbs, William Carter
    The descendants of John Stubbs of Cappahosic, Gloucester County,
    Virginia, 1652. Corpus Christi, Tex. 1966.

STULTING -- Smith, Grace Stulting
    The Stulting family. Charlottesville. 1974.

STUMP -- Hardman, Paul
    The Stumps, descent of the four Michaels. Charleston, W. Va. 1940.

STUMP -- Stump, Joseph & J. Milton
    History or record of the descendants of Peter Stump of Hampshire County,
    West Virginia ... with a biographical sketch of some of the descendants.
    Staunton: Campfield Print., 195-.

STUMP -- Stump, Thirman
    Michael Stump, Sr. of Virginia, 1709-1768: a treatise on the origin and
    ancestry with surname armorials. Parsons, W. Va.: McClain Print, 1975.

STURGES -- Danforth, Art
    A Sturges family story: the ancestors and all identified descendants of
    Aaron ('Old Sturge') Sturges, 1803-1890, with historical, social, and
    geographic background. Falls Church. 1982.

STURM -- Sturm, Alan
    A partial history of the Sturm family of Barbour County, West Virginia.
    Buckhannon, W. Va. 1973.

STURM -- Sturm, Lloyd Elmer
Genealogy of the Sturm family; a record of the descendants of Jacob Sturm
of Sharpsburg, Maryland, from 1750 to 1936. Clarksburg, W. Va. 1938.

STURMAN -- Thomas Sturman and Ann; Col. William Hardiwck and Elizabeth
Sturman; Jeffrey Johnson and Margaret of Virginia, and their descendants
in North Carolina and Knox County, Tennessee. 1974.

STUTLER -- Hoffman, Gladys S.
Stutler, Hughes, Jackson: pioneer families of West Virginia. Atlanta.
1968.

SUBLETT -- Sublett, S. S.
A Partial History of the French Huguenot by name Soblet. Richmond. 1896.

SUMMERS -- De Groat, Elizabeth
Ledger and family records of Summers family, northern Virginia, 1762-1980.
1981.

SURBER -- Vance, Vida Surber
The Missouri & Kentucky Surbers & their descendants: a study of the
ancestry and posterity of Henry Surber: a Virginia colonist of the
eighteen(th) century, from ca. 1700 to 1978. Mexico, Mo. 1985.

SURRATT -- Hoch, Beverly Repass
The Surratt family of Southwestern Virginia. Darnestown, Md. 1979.

SURRATT -- Surratt, Walter Millard
The Surratt family of southwestern Virginia. Darnestown, Md. 1979.

SUTER -- Suter, Mary Eugenia
Memories of yesteryear; a history of the Suter family. Waynesboro.
1959.

SUTHERLAND -- Ball, Bonnie
Pioneer doctor of the Frying Pan. Southwest Virginia Historical Society,
1972.

SUTHERLAND -- Hudson, Florence Sutherland
"We cousins" (Virginia to Texas). A genealogy of several of the families
comprising the Alabama settlement of Austin's Colony, 1830 and 1831, now
Texas, and including the other Virginia lines of the Sutherland family.
San Benito, Tex. 1957.

SUTHERLAND -- Sutherland, Henry C.
Sutherland records, found in Georgia, Illinois, Indiana, Kentucky,
Maryland, North Carolina, Suth Carolina and Virginia. Crown Point,
Ind. 1968.

SUTTENFIELD -- North, Mae Belle Barrow
History of the Suttenfield and Taylor families of Virginia and North
Carolina. Summerfield, N.C. 1973.

SUTTON -- Sutton, T. Dix
The Suttons of Caroline County, Virginia. Richmond: Richmond Press, 1941.

SWARTZ -- Swartz, B. K.
The descendants of John Swartz, Sr. (1760-1817) of Saumsville, Shenandoah County, Va. Muncie, Ind. 1970.

SWARTZ -- Swartz, Philip A.
The Swartz family of the Shenandoah Valley, Va. Poughkeepsie, N.Y. 1955.

SWEARINGEN -- Family Historical Register. Compiled by a member of the family. Washington. 1894.

SWIGER -- Swiger, Ira L.
A genealogical and historical history of the Swiger family. Fairmont, W. Va.: Fairmont Printing & Pub. Co., 1916.

SWITZER -- Switzer, George Frederick
The descendants of John Andrew Switzer, Harrisonburg, Virginia. Harrisonburg. 1951.

SYDNEY -- Price, Lucy Montgomery Smith
The Sydney-Smith and Claggett-Price genealogy. Strasburg: Shenandoah Pub. House, 1927.

SYDNOR -- Sydnor, William Edward
The Sydnor family history: the descendants of Col. Edward Sydnor of Hanover County, Virginia. San Luis Obispo, Calif. 1984.

SYKES -- Sykes, Joseph Royal
Sykes generation. Galax. 1978.

TABER -- Taber, Russel
The genealogy of the Taber family. Wheeling, W. Va. 1893.

TACKETT -- Johnson, Erna Young
The Tacketts in Kanawha County, Virginia. Charleston, W. Va. 1969.

TAFT -- Taft family bulletin. Falls Church: Taft Family Assoc.

TALBOT -- Fletcher, Robert Howe
Genealogical sketch of certain of the American descendants of Mathew Talbot, gentleman. Leesburg. 1956.

TALBOT -- Knight, Rosa Talbot
Genealogy of the Talbot and Wingfield families of Virginia and Georgia. 1924.

TALIAFERRO -- McGroarty, W. B.
    Genealogical chart of the Taliaferro family. Falls Church. 1927.

TANDY -- Sanders, Walter R.
    Smyth Tandy, 1741-1823, Virginia gentleman & Kentucky pioneer.
    Litchfield, Ill. 1948.

TANKARD -- Fitzhugh, Georgianna
    The life of Dr. John Tankard. Hampton: Hampton Institute Press, 1907.

TANKARD -- Fitzhugh, Georgianna
    The life of Dr. John Tankard. Onancock: Eastern Shore of Virginia
    Historical Society, 1965.

TANNER -- Hussey, Marguerite Carleton
    The family of Rev. John Tanner - Baptist preacher; Virginia - North
    Carolina - Kentucky - Missouri. Berkeley, Calif. 1972.

TANNER -- Lloyd, Emma Rouse
    Tanner family of Virginia and Kentucky.

TARR -- Johnson, Hugh A.
    The ancestry and descendants of Josiah Mendum Tarr and Mary Delia Sawyer.
    Annandale. 1976.

TATE -- Bushman, Katherine Gentry
    The Tate family of Augusta County, Virginia. 1963.

TATE -- Updike, Ethel Speer
    Tate family of Washington and Russell County, Virginia. Phoenix,
    Ariz. 1984.

TATTERSON -- Tatterson, Clerissa H.
    History and genealogy of the Poling family. Parsons, W. Va.: McClain
    Print Co., 1978.

TAYLOE -- Tayloe, W. Randolph
    The Tayloes of Virginia and allied families. Berryville. 1963.

TAYLOR -- Carte, Carrie Cathern
    The forebears and descendants of William Taylor and Mahala Cromwell.
    Parsons, W. Va.: McClain Print Co., 1980.

TAYLOR -- Smith, Cora Taylor Younger
    People and places here and there with facts and memories: the Reverend
    Daniel Taylor, Senior, of Virginia. Florence, S.C. 1981.

TAYLOR -- Taylor, James H.
    The James Taylor family; Orange County, Va. 1936.

TAYLOR -- Taylor, Reubemia
    The Taylor family in Virginia and Kentucky, 1650-1900. 1953.

TAYLOR FAMILY OF VIRGINIA, 1898.

TAZEWELL -- Grigsby, H. B.
Life and Character of Hon. Littleton Waller Tazewell. Norfolk. 1860.

TEMPLE -- Temple, Lucy Temple
William Temple of Prince George County, Virginia and his descendants.
Richmond. 1978.

TEMPLEMAN -- Templeman, Eleanor Lee
Chart showing the ancestry of Robert Morris Templeman. 1943.

TENNANT -- Tennant, Richard
Memories of J. Ross Tennant and a genealogy of the family. Pentress,
W. Va. 1948.

TENNYSON -- Tennyson, Emily Sellwood Tennyson, Baroness
Lady Tennyson's journal. Charlottesville: University Press of
Virginia, 1981.

TERRELL -- Barnhill, Celeste Jane Terrell
Richmond, William and Timothy Terrell, colonial Virginians. Greenfield,
Ind. 1934.

TERRELL -- Battey, George Magruder
Terrell notes (on the English Terrells who settled in Virginia, the
Carolinas and Georgia). Washington. 1943.

TERRELL -- Lamb, Georgia Wharton
Following the trail; a genealogical study of the Terrell and related
families. Manassas. 1939.

TERRELL -- Terrell, Edwin H.
Genealogical Notes on the Tyrrall and Terrell Family of Virginia. San
Antonio, Tex. 1907.

TERRELL -- Terrell, Edwin H.
Further genealogical notes on the Tyrrell-Terrell family of Virginia
and its English and Norman-French progenitors. San Antonio, Tex. 1909.

TERRELL -- Tyrrell, Joseph Henry
The genealogy of Richmond and William Tyrrell or Terrell (descended from
the family of Tyrrell of Thornton Hall, Buckingshire, England), who
settled in Virginia in the seventeenth century. 1910.

TERRELL -- Terrell, Roy Lee
A genealogy line of the Tyrrell, Terrell and Terrill family of Virginia
and Texas, and its English and Norman progenitors. Grass Valley,
Calif. 1934.

TERRY -- Ingmire, Frances T.
Terry and allied families of Virginia, Kentucky, Illinois, Texas. Creve
Coeur, Mo. 1976.

TERRY -- Bushnell, Edna Harris
Terry records of Virginia. Owensboro, Ky. 1980.

TERRY -- Moon, Maude Terry and Gifford Clark Terry
Genealogy of the James Terry 1701 branch of the Virginia-North Carolina
Terry family tree. With special emphasis on the descendants of William
H. and Jemima Norwood Terry, 19th cent. residents of Chatham County, N.C.
Sandwich, Ill. 1964.

TETER -- Kellogg, Joseph M.
Kellogg notebooks on West Virginia families: The Teter Family. Lawrence,
Kans. 1958.

THOMAS -- Gilbert, Betty Jane
Robert Thmas, d. 1768, Fairfax Co., Va. and his descendants. Decorah,
Iowa: Anundsen Pub. Co., 1981.

THOMAS HARDAWAY -- Hubert, Sarah D.
Thomas Hardaway of Chesterfield Co. Richmond. 1906.

THOMAS -- Mihlbach, Carolyn Thomas
Thomas family record: descendants of David and Mary Thomas. Ravenswood,
W. Va. 1981.

THOMAS RITCHIE -- Ambler, Charles Henry
A Study in Virginia Politics. Richmond: Bell, Book & Stationery Co., 1913.

THOMASON -- Emerson, K. C.
Thomason-Thompson. Arlington. 1978.

THOMASSON -- Burdette, Elizabeth Y.
John Thomasson, Sr. (1753-1840) of Louisa County, Virginia. 1971.

THOMPSON -- Eberle, Marie Thompson
Thompson twigs: some descendants of Sheldon and Ann Thompson of
Washington County, Virginia: with allied families of Allen/Daily,
Bowman/Whitaker, Crawford, Johnson/Dickenson, Linder, McCulloch, White.
Edwardsville, Ill. 1981.

THOMPSON -- Johnson, Katherine Baker
The Thompson, Epperson, Langford and Haynes families of Albemarle
County, Virginia, and Knox County, Tennessee. 1940.

THOMPSON -- Johnson, Patricia Givens
Springfield saga: the Thompsons of Fort Thompson on New River, Pulaski
County, Virginia. Christianburg. 1985.

THOMPSON -- Kendall, John Smith
    The Thompson family of West Virginia and California. With notices of
    the families allied to it through marriage. Berkeley, Calif. 1942.

THOMPSON -- Lockhart, Henry
    Thompsons, mainly of Hanover & Louisa Counties, Virginia. Oxford, Md.
    1960.

THOMPSON -- RYAN, Polly T.
    Journey in Virginia: a history of 300 years. Oakton. 1975.

THOMPSON -- Stercula, Beverly M.
    The Thompson families of Hanover, Louisa, Albemarke, Goochland, Amelia
    and Fluvanna Counties in Virginia. Fullerton, Calif. 1966.

THOMPSON -- The Thompson family. Arlington: American Genealogical Research
    Institute, 1972.

THOMSON -- Earle, Mary E.
    John Thomson of Hanover County, Virginia. 1973.

THORNTON -- Thornton family wills, deeds, etc. Family from Virginia.

THORNTON -- Whitley, Edythe R.
    Thornton family of Virginia. Nashville, Tenn. 1934.

THOROWOOD -- Creecy, John H.
    Thorowood family of Princess Anne County, Va. Richmond. 1971.

THORPE -- King, Edward Thorp
    Genealogy of some early families in Grant and Pleasant districts,
    Preston County, West Virginia, also the Thorpe family of Fayette
    County, Pennsylvania, and the Cunningham family of Somerset County,
    Pennsylvania. Marshalltown, Iowa. 1933.

THREADGILL -- Miller, Janis Heidenreich
    Threadgills in America; a colonial Virginia family. Francis Dycus
    Threadgill. Baltimore. 1971.

THROCKMORTON -- Sitherwood, Frances Grimes
    Throckmorton family history, being the record of the Throckmortons in
    the United States of America with cognate branches, emigrant ancestors
    located in Salem, Massachusetts, 1630, and in Gloucester County, Virginia,
    1660. Bloomington, Ill. 1929.

THROCKMORTON -- Throckmorton, Charles Wickliffe
The descendants of the Honorable Thomas Throckmorton, born 1739 in
Virginia, and died at "Rich Hill", Kentucky, 1826. New York. 1898.

THROCKMORTON -- Throckmorton, C. Wickliffe
A genealogical and historical account of the Throckmorton family in
England and the United States, with brief notes on some of the allied
families. Richmond. 1930.

THROCKMORTON -- Throckmorton, Charles W.
Genealogical chart with description of the quarterings of the arms of
Gabriel Throckmorton, of Ware Parish, Gloucester Co., Va. New York.
1933.

THURMAN -- Crouch, Kenneth E.
The Thurman family; ancestry of John S. and Bevie Saunders Thurman and
allied families of Bedford County, Virginia. 1956.

THURMAN -- Humphries, John D.
Descendants of John Thurman of Virginia, William Graves of Virginia
and James Jones of South Carolina. Atlanta. 1938.

THURMAN -- Thurmond, John William Wesley
Thurmond, the ancestry and descendants of James Thurmond of Albemarle
and Nelson Counties, Virginia and other related material. Richmond:
Gatewood Pub. Co., 1983.

THURMAN -- Witschey, Walter Robert Thurmond
The Thurmonds of Virginia. Richmond: Gatewood Co., 1978.

THURMOND -- Donnelly, Shirley
The Thurmonds; a study in the genealogy and history of Philip Thurmond
of Amherst County, Virginia and his descendants. Oak Hill, W. Va. 1939.

TICE -- Dowling, Wilfrid S.
A genealogy of a division of the Tice family in America. Arlington. 1953.

TIDWELL -- Tidwell, W. A., Jr.
Presley Tidwell: a memorial to the Presley family role in the establishment
of Kinsdale, Virginia. 1972.

TILLMAN -- Tillman, Stephen Frederick
The Tillman family. Richmond: William Byrd Press, 1930.

TINCHER -- Dorsey, Lois Tincher
The Tincher tribe and Caesar's Tencteri tribe: (chronicles of a pioneer
family in the valley of Virginia, 1750, and some who migrated westward).
Chicago: Adams Press, 1975.

TIPTON -- Heinemann, Charles Brunk
Tipton family of Maryland, Virginia, Tennessee, Kentucky, Ohio, Indiana,
Illinois, Missouri. Washington. 1934.

TODD -- Rubey, Ann Todd; Florence Isabelle Stacy, and Herbert Ridgeway Collins
Speaking if families: The Tod(d)s of Caroline County, Virginia, and their
kin. Columbia, Mo. 1960.

TODD -- Todd, Mary L. B.
Some notes of the Todd family; lineage of Rev. John Todd of Louisa
County, Virginia. Forwst, Ill. 1966.

TODD -- Whitcradt, J. R.
The Virginia Todds. Philadelphia: Frankford Disptach Publishing House,
1913.

TORRENCE -- Bachman, Audrey Torrence
Torrence family. Reston. 1979.

TOCUHTONE -- Sandel, Mary Eleanor and Elias Wesley Sandel
The Touchtones of Maryland, Virginia, North & South Carolina, Georgia,
Mississippi, and Louisiana. 1972.

TOWELS -- Kirk, H. I.
Towels family of Virginia. Baltimore. 1929.

TOWLER -- Towler, Juby E.
Genealogy; From the fruit of the garden. Danville. 1968.

TOWELS -- Purcell, Hester Towles and Jean Bryon Johnson
The Towels story from Henry, the emigrant of Accomac County, Virginia,
to Hester Towles and Jean Bryan Johnson. Kansas City, Mo. 1957.

TOWNSEND -- Miles, Frances Townsend
Some descendants of Nathaniel C. Townsend & Sarah H. Austin of Nelson
County, Virginia. Bartlesville, Okla. 1976.

TRABUE -- Colwell, Pauline Trabue Groves and Osee Johnson Knouf
Trabue family history; ancestry and known descendants of David Trabue,
Jr., born Oct. 9, 1768, Manikintown, Virginia, died Apr. 8, 1842,
Jessamine Co., Kentucky. Champaign, Ill. 1968.

TRACY -- Tracy, Dwight
Recently discovered English ancestry of Governor William Tracy of
Virginia, 1620, and of his only son - Lieutenant Thomas Tracy of Salem,
Massachusetts, and Norwich, Connecticut. New Haven. Conn. 1908.

TREADWAY -- Lewis, Ailene Fitch
The Tredway, Gooch, Embry, Cyphers, and allied lines, from England to
Maryland, Virginia, Ohio, Kentucky, Illinois: west to north Missouri,
Kansas, 1597-1983. Holden, Mo. 1948.

TRENT -- Benns, Martha A.
Notes on Trent family of Virginia. 1929.

TRENT -- Trent, Ivan
May we remember--: a history of the Trent and Painter families of Virginia. Columbus, Ohio. 1981.

TREVETT -- Turman, Nora Miller
The E. John Trevvett family of Virginia, 1880-1977, with some English ancestors. Glen Allen, Pa. 1978.

TRIMBLE -- Trimble, John Farley
Trimble families of America. Parsons, W. Va.: McClain Print. Co., 1973.

TRIMBLE -- Trimble, David B.
Hiestand family of Page County, Virginia. San Antonio, Tex. 1974.

TRIPLETT -- Abbott, Hortense E.
Descendants of the Triplett families of Virginia, North & South Carolina. Hemet, Calif. 1982.

TRIPLETT -- Lytle, Leonard
The descendants of Joseph Triplett of Hardy County, West Virginia, and Summit and Licking Counties, Ohio. Ballycastle, N.J. 1955.

TROTTER -- Trotter, Mrs. Isham Patten, Jr.
Trotter genealogy, the Virginia-Tennessee-Mississippi Trotter line, 1725-1948. Louisville, Ky. 1948.

TROTTER -- Wilkinson, William W.
Early Trotters of Brunswick County, Virginia, and all the descendants of Colonel Isham Trotter. La Crosse. 1950.

TUCKER -- Coleman, Mrs. George P.
The story of a portrait. Richmond: Dietz Press, 1935.

TUCKER -- Coleman, Mary Haldale (Mrs. George P. Coleman)
St. George Tucker, citizen of no mean city. Richmond. 1938.

TUCK -- Macon, Aletha Jane
John and Edward Tuck of Halifax County, Virginia and some of their descendants. Macon, Ga.: Southern Press, 1964.

TUCKER -- Tucker, Beverley Randolph
Tales of the Tuckers; descendants of the male line of St. George Tucker of Bermuda and Virginia. Richmond. 1942.

TUCKER -- Tucker, Reuel Walter
Memoirs and history of the Peyton Tucker family; ancestors and descendants of England, Wales, Vermont, Massachusetts, Maryland, Virginia, the Carolinas, Georgia, Tennessee, Kentucky, Illinois, Missouri, Arkansas, Louisiana, Texas, Oklahoma, and California; and genealogy. Baltimore: Gateway Press, 1975.

TUGGLE -- Tuggle, Vivian S.
The Tuggle family of Virginia; Thomas Tuggle of Middlesex County, Virginia and his descendants, 1630-1967. Baltimore: Gateway Press, 1970.

TULLIS -- Little, Lawrence
A record of descendants of Moses Tullis, Sr., of Berkeley Co. Va., and Thomas Little of Hunterdon Co., N.J. Urbana, Ohio. 1972.

TUNSTALL -- Morris, Whit
The first Tunstalls in Virginia. San Antonio, Tex. 1950.

TURLEY -- Collins, Ruth Turley
William Turley (c. 1749-1819) of Fauquier County, Virginia. Alexandria. 1977.

TURLEY -- Mitchell, Beth
Turley family records. Alexandria: Turley Family Historical Research Association, 1981.

TURNER -- Lloyd, Emma Rouse
Turner family of Virginia and Kentucky.

TURNER -- Turner, Louise Patton Richardson
Some Turners of Virginia. Tulsa, Okla. 1965.

TURNER -- Charts of the descendants of Thomas Turner, of England, who came to Virginia about 1650. 1950.

TUTTLE -- Gaylord, Mary Tuttle
The Tuttles, branch of Simon. Lexington. 1981.

TWO FAMILIES -- Stubbs, Dr. and Mrs. W. C.
A History of Two Virginia Families Transplanted from County Kent, England. Thomas Baytop. John Catlett. New Orleans.

TYLER -- Beaman, Chester E.
The Tyler family of Virginia and Missouri. Alexandria. 1977.

TYLER -- Brigham, W. Tyler
The Tylers of Mass., Conn., R.I., Va., and N.J.

TYLER -- Brophy, John P.
Ancestry of Elizabeth Warren Tyler of Virginia, wife if John P. Brophy. New York: Brophy & Sons, 1911.

TYRRELL -- Terrell, Edwin H.
Genealogical notes on the Tyrrell and Terrell family of Virginia and its English and Norman progenitors. San Antonio, Tex. 1907.

UPCHURCH -- West, Belle Lewter
Upchurch family of England, Virginia and North Carolina. Durham, N.C.
1972.

UPDIKE -- Craig, Robert S.
The Virginia Updikes-Updykes. Parsons, W. Va.: McCalin Print, 1985.

UPSHAW -- Selleck, B.
Drury Upshaw of Virginia and some of his descendants, 1767-1930. 1930.

UPSHAW -- Upshaw, Sophie W.
Captain William Upshaw, gent., planter of Virginia: some of his Georgia
descendants and allied families, Francis, Wright, MacAllen, Bardwell,
Daves, Chalmers. Baltimore: Gateway Press, 1975.

UPSHUR -- Upshur, John Andrews
Upshur family in Virginia. Richmond: Dietz Press, 1955.

UTTERBACK -- Utterback, William I.
The history and genealogy of the Utterback family in America.
Huntington, W. Va.: Gentry Bros. Printing Co., 1937.

VADEN -- Inman, Joseph Francis
Ancestors and descendants of Robert Augustus Vaden and Cora Margaret
Drawbaugh. Richmond. 1968.

VALENTINE -- The Edward Pleasant Valentine Papers. Four volumes.
Published by the Valentine Museum. Richmond: Whittet & Shepperson.

VALENTINE -- The Edward Pleasants Valentine papers, abstracts of records in
local and general archives of Virginia relating to the families of Allen,
Bacon, Ballard, Batchelder, Blouet, Brassieur (Brashear) Cary, Crenshaw,
Dabney, Exum, Ferris, Fontaine, Gray, Hardy, Isham (Henrico County)
Jordan, Langston, Lyddal, Mann, Mosby, Palmer, Pasteur, Pleasants, Povall,
Randolph, Satterwhite, Scott, Smith (the family of Francis Smith of
Hanover County), Valentine, Waddy, Watts, Winston, Womack, Woodsen ...
Richmond. 1927.

VANCE -- Dixon, Elizabeth Williamson
The Vance family of Virginia, Pennsylvania, North Carolina, Tennessee;
the Brank family of North Carolina and Kentucky. 1958.

VANDEUSEN -- Van Deusen, Roe G.
Van Deusen journal. Alexandria. 1975.

VAN DEVENTER -- Vandevander, Paul J.
The Van Deventer family, 1550-1977. Parsons, W. Va.: McClain Print. 1978.

VAN LANDINGHAM -- Van Landingham, Florence
Van Landingham. Transcribed from microfilm and record books in the Va.
State Library at Richmond, Va. West Palm Beach, Fla. 1976.

VANNOY -- Witte, Forest B. Vannoy
The Vannoy family history. Bridgeport, W. Va. 1960.

VANVLEECK -- Van Vleck, Jane
Ancestry and descendants of Tielman Van Vleeck of New Amsterdam. Richmond.:
William Byrd Press, 1955.

VAN ZANDT -- Dean, Ralph H.
Our Dutch ancestors: Van der Grift, Van Zandt, Van Horn and the Lee (Lea)
family of North Carolina and Virginia. Woodland, Calif.

VARIAN -- Briggs, Samuel
The book of the Varian family. Richmond. 1980.

VAUGHAN -- Vaughan, Lewis Elmo
Vaughan pioneers: William and Fereby Vaughan of Russell County, Virginia,
and their descendants. Baltimore: Gateway Press, 1979.

VENABLE -- Eggleston, Dr. J. D.
Historic Slate Hill plantation in Virginia. Hampden-Sydney. 1945.

VENABLE -- Venable, Elizabeth Marshall
Venables of Virginia. Jacksonville, Fla. 1925.

VENABLE -- Venable, Eizabeth Marshall
Venables of Virginia; an account of the ancestors and descendants of
Samuel WoodsonVenable of "Springfield" and of his brother William Lewis
Venable of "Haymarket", both of Prince Edward County, Virginia. New
York. 1925.

VEST -- Sowers, Erma C.
Descendants of Littleberry Vest. Roanoke: E. C. Sowers, 1983.

VIALL -- Viall, Gary L.
Some descendants of John Viall (1618-1686) of Boston and Swansey. Falls
Church. 1972.

VIALL -- Viall, Gary L.
Some descendants of Jonathan Viall (1674-1724) and John Viall (1618-1686).
Falls Church. 1979.

VIRGINIA HERALDICA -- Edited by William Armstrong Crozier. Virginia County
Record Series. Published by The Genealogical Association. New York.
MDCCCCVIII.

VIRGINIA VALLEY RECORDS -- Wayland, John W. Dayton, Va.: Ruebush, Elkins
     Co. Harrisonburg. 1930.

VIRKUS -- The Abridged Compendium of American Genealogy. First Families of
     America. Edited by Frederick A. Virkus. A. N. Marquis & Company,
     Publishers. Chicago. Vol. I, 1925; Vol. II, 1926; Vol. III, 1928.

VIVION -- Heinemann, Charles Brunk
     Vivion family of Virginia. Chicago. 1936.

WADDELL -- Waddell, Jos. A.
     Waddell's Annals of Augusta Co., Virginia, from 1726 to 1871. Staunton.
     1902.

WADDEL -- Waddel, John N.
     Memorials of academic life: being an historical sketch of the Waddel
     family, identified through three generations with the history of the
     higher education in the South and Southwest. Richmond. 1891.

WADE -- Brand, Franklin Marion
     The Wade family, Monongalia County, Virginia. 1927.

WADE -- Posey-Wade-Harrison (Emison) and other Families of Maryland and
     Virginia, with supplement to The Emison Family.

WADE -- The Wades; the history of a family, dealing with the kith and kin
     of Zachary and Mary Hatton, their descendants and related lines, male
     and female, in Maryland, Virginia, Tennessee, South Carolina, North
     Carolina, and other States. Cairo, Ill. 1963.

WAGNER -- Waggener, Lawrence A.
     The Waggener trace: a genealogy of the Waggener family of Virginia,
     Kentucky, Nebraska, Colorado, Oregon, and California, USA. Protland,
     Ore. 1985.

WAITE -- Waitt, Robert W.
     Genealogical sketches of the Waitt family of Richmond, Virginia.
     Richmond. 198-.

WAITE -- Waite, Roy H.
     The Waites of Deanville. Richmond: Whittet & Shepperson, 1966.

WALKER -- Manton, Evelyn
     Walker, Eakin, Preston and allied families of Botetourt and Bedford
     Counties, Virginia. 1947.

WALKE -- Walke family in Virginia. Based upon data obtained from records in lower Norfolk and Princess Anne Counties, family Bibles, &c. 1897.

WALKER -- Walker, Legare
The Walker family, originally of the Wycomico River section of Northumberland (subsequently Westmoreland) County, Virginia, stemming from William Walker, 1622/23-1657, and through one of his descendants, Joseph Rabley Walker, 1768-1816, who immigrated from Macklenburg County in that state to south Carolina, circa 1806, and settled in Edgefield County near the town of that name; also a correction of certain errors in a chart of the Adams family, with which Walkers are connected by marriage. Summerville, S.C. 1945.

WALL -- Reed, Ardelle McMillen
Wahl ancestors, descendants, and related families of Alsace and Butler County, Pennsylvania, 1632-1982. Richlands. 1982.

WALLACE -- Wallace, George Selden
Wallace; genealogical data pertaining to the descendants of Peter Wallace & Elizabeth Woods, his wife. Charlottesville. 1927.

WALTHALL -- Walthall, Ernest Taylor
Walthall Family. Richmond: Walthall Printing Co., 1906.

WALTHALL -- Walthall, Malcolm Elmore
The Walthall family; a genealogical history of the descendants of William Walthall of Virginia. Richmond. 1946.

WALTHALL -- Walthall, Malcolm Elmore
The Walthall family; a genealogical history of the descendants of William Walthall of Virginia. Charlotte, N.C. 1963.

WALTMAN -- Thoesen, Edith M. W.
Emanuel Waltman family of Lovettsville, Va. Denver, Colo.

WALTON -- Andrus, Lucius Buckley
1933 memoranda and 1934 supplement in re Walton families; (1) Robert Walton of St. Andrews, New Brunswick. (2) George Walton of Maine and New Hampshire. (3) George Walton of Virginia, signer of the Declaration of Independence. Indianapolis, Ind. 1934.

WALTON -- Black, Roy W.
Wal(l)ton family of Brunswick & Greenville Counties, Virginia and Morgan & Putnam Counties, Georgia. Bolivar, Tenn. 1955.

WALTON -- Black, William H.
Walton - Sims of Eastern Virginia. 1961.

WALTONS OF VIRGINIA -- Stubbs, Mrs. W. C.

WALTONS -- Tinney, Joe C.
   The Walltons of Brunswick County, Virginia: descendants of George and Elizabeth (Rowe) Walton. Waco, Tex. 1983.

WALTON -- Walton, Chas. Cortlandt, Jr.
   Notes on the family of Edward Walton, and some of its connections. Williamsburg. 1925.

WAMPLER -- Huffman, Glenn
   Wampler: the descendants of Ben Wampler and Elizabeth Beery of Augusta County, Virginia, including some record of their ancestry 1701-1982. Washington, D.C. 1982.

WARD -- McGhee, Lucy K.
   Ward family history of Virginia, showing their links with the states of North Carolina, Tennessee and Kentucky branches of Wards. Washington. 1957.

WARDER -- Warder, Walter
   Warder family in Virginia, Kentucky and Illinois. Cairo, Ill. 1934.

WARMAN -- A history of the Warman and related families, chiefly of Monongalia County, West, Va. Columbus, Ohio. 1972.

WARNER -- Davis, Elizabeth Warner Holliday
   "You should meet them": your ancestors and descendants of Warner, Sanderson, Dickinson, Lewis, Martin, Payne, Daniel, Holliday, Bickel, Murdy, Davis, Massie, 1600-1983 and historical accounts. Vienna. 1983.

WARREN -- The Warren Family. Arlington: The American Genealogical Research Institute, 1973.

WARREN -- Palmer, Sarah
   The Waring family of Virginia 1680. Jacksonville, Fla. 1979.

WARTMAN -- Wartman, William Bechmann
   Genealogy of John and Rosina Schmid Wartman and connected families. Charlottesville. 1980.

WARWICK -- Notes on some of the Warwicks of Virginia. New Haven, Conn. 1937.

WASHINGTON -- Ball, G. W.
   Maternal Ancestry and Nearest of Kin of Washington. A Monograph. Washington. 1885.

WASHINGTON -- Bourne, Miriam Anne
   First family: George Washington and his intimate relations/Miriam Anne Bourne. New York: Norton, 1982.

WASHINGTON -- Branscombe, Arthur
   The cradle of the Washingtons and the home of the Franklins. London and New York. 1901.

WASHINGTON -- Castleman, H. B.
A chart of the Washington family, outlined with especial reference to the
ancestors and descendants of Augustine Washington, the father of General
George Washington. Phila(delphia), Pa. 1932.

WASHINGTON -- Carnevale, Alphonse Joseph
A genealogical historiography of General Washington. East Elmhurst,
N.Y. 1959.

WASHINGTON -- Chamberlin, Katharine Beecher Stetson
Pedigree of George Washington. Pasadena, Calif. 1932.

WASHINGTON -- Darden, Newton J.
The Pargiter-Washington English ancestry of the Washington families of
Virginia during Colonial times, 1654-1700. 1930.

WASHINGTON -- Direct line of living descendants of the Washington family.
Washington. 1933.

WASHINGTON -- The English ancestry of Washington, the genealogical portion
of same furnished by Albert Welles ... collated by James Phillipse,
esq., of London. 1876.

WASHINGTON -- Family tree of George Washington. The descendants of George
Washington from King John and nine of the twenty five barons sureties
of Magna Carta. 1972.

WASHINGTON -- Felder, Paula S.
George Washington's relations and relationships in Fredericksburg,
Virginia. Fredericksburg: Historic Publications of Fredricksburg, 1981.

WASHINGTON -- Fleming, Mrs. Vivian Minor
The Kenmore mansion, built 1752, home of Colonel Fielding Lewis and his
wife, Betty Washington. Fredericksburg. 1924.

WASHINGTON -- A Genealogical History of Thornton A. Washington. Washington.
1871.

WASHINGTON -- Genealogy of the Washington family. Los Angeles, Calif. 1900.

WASHINGTON -- Gunderson, Carl M. Ringen
Norwegian forefathers of General George Washington. 1st President of
the United States. Los Angeles, Calif. 1981.

WASHINGTON -- Hayden, Horace Edwin
Experimental pedigree of the descendants of Lawrence Washington,
1635-1677, of Virginia. Reprinted from his volume of "Virginia
genealogies." Wilkes-Barre, Pa. 1891.

WASHINGTON -- Hoppin, Charles Arthur
The Washington ancestry and records of the McClain, Johnson, and forty
other colonial families, prepared for Edward Lee McClain. Greenfield,
Ohio. 1932.

WASHINGTON -- Hoppin, Charles Arthur
 Some descendants of Colonel John Washington and of his brother Captain
 Lawrence Washington, founders of the Washington family of Westmoreland
 County, Virginia, and records of the allied families of Wheelwright,
 Hungerford, Pratt, Dodge, Conant, Chilton, Gwinn, Barton, Birkett,
 Warren, Wickliffe, Bailey, Massey, Pope, Townshend, and others. New
 York. 1932.

WASHINGTON -- Jackson, Cordelia
 Edward Washington and his kin. Washington. 1934.

WASHINGTON -- Longden, H. Isham
 The history of the Washington family. Reprinted from "the Genealogists'
 magazine". Northampton. 1927.

WASHINGTON -- Lossing, B. J.
 Mary and Martha Washington. New York. 1886.

WASHINGTON -- Nordham, George Washington
 George Washington's women: Mary, Martha, Sally, and Waters family.
 146 others. Philadelphia, Pa.: Dorrance, 1977.

WASHINGTON -- Pape, T., B.A.
 Warton and George Washington's ancestors. Morecambe. 1913.

WASHINGTON -- A preliminary investigation of the alleged ancestry of George
 Washington; first president of the United States of America; exposing
 a serious error in the existing pedigree. By Joseph Lemuel Chester ...
 (Reprinted from the Herald and genealogist, London, and the Heraldic
 Journal, Boston.) H. W. Dutton & Son, 1866.

WASHINGTON -- Sipe, Chester H.
 Mount Vernon and the Washington family; a concise handbook on the
 ancestry, youth and family of George Washington, and history of his
 home. Butler, Pa.: Ziegler Print., 1929.

WASHINGTON -- Smith, Gloria L.
 Black Americans at Mount Vernon: genealogy techniques for slave group
 research. Tuscon, Ariz. 1984.

WASHINGTON -- Toner, Joseph M., M.D.
 Wills of the American ancestors of General George Washington, in the
 line of the original owner and the inheritors of Mount Vernon. From
 the original documents and probate records. Boston. 1891.

WASHINGTON -- Washburn, Mabel T. R.
 Washington's old world ancestry: historic past of the race - blood
 royal of the man who changed a king's colony into a nation.

WASHINGTON -- Washingtin, George S. H. L.
 The earliest Washingtons and their Anglo-Scottish connexions.
 Cambridge, England. 1964.

WASHINGTON -- Washington, Thornton Augustin
A genealogical history, beginning with Colonel John Washington, the emigrant, and head of the Washington family in America. Washington. 1891.

WASHINGTON -- Waters, Henry F.
An examination of the English ancestry of George Washington, setting forth the evidence to connect him with the Washingtons of Sulgrave and Brington. Boston. 1889.

WASHINGTON -- Welles, Albert
The pedigree of the Washington family: derived from Odin, the founder of Scandinavia, B.C. 70, involving a period of eighteen centuries, and including fifty-five generations, down to General George Washington, first president of the United States. New York. 1879.

WASHINGTON -- Wells, William C.
George Washington's ancestors, the Washingtons of Sulgrave and Brington. London. 189-.

WASSON -- Sands, John A.
Wasson. Arlington. 1976.

WATERS -- Smith, Gladys E. B.
Waters family of Maryland and Virginia. Virginia Beach.

WATERS -- Upshur, Thomas T.
Pedigree of Francis Edward Waters of Baltimore, Maryland: Waters line. Nassawadox. 1906.

WATKINS -- Allen, Jane McMurty
Henry Watkins of Henrico County: his descendants and their allied families. Baltimore. 1985.

WATKINS -- Watkins, Francis N.
A catalogue of the descendants of Thomas Watkins of Chickahomony, Va., who was the common ancestor of many of the families of the name in Prince Edward, Charlotte, and Chestefield Counties, Virginia. New York. 1852.

WATKINS -- Watkins, Francis N.
Catalogue of the descendants of Thomas Watkins of Chickahomony, Virginia; who was the common ancestor of many of the families of the name in Prince Edward, Charlotte, and Chestefield Counties, Va. Henderson, N.C.: Atlas Print, 1899.

WATKINS -- Watkins, Marie Oliver and Helen Hanacher Watkins
Tearin; through the wilderness; Missouri pioneer episodes, 1822-1885, and Genealogy of the Warkins family of Virginia and Missouri. Charleston, W. Va. 1957.

WATKINS -- Watkins, Virginia S.
Watkins family in Virginia. Honolulu, Hawaii. 1960.

WATSON -- Descendants of John Watson who landed in Elizabeth City, Va. in
     1620, and died there in 1640.

WATSON'S ROYAL LINEAGE -- Watson, A. R.
     A Royal Lineage. Alfred the Great. Richmond. 1901.

WATTS -- Heinemann, Charles Brunk
     Watts families descended from early immigrants who settled in the
     Tideater counties of Virginia. Washington. 1940.

WAY -- Way, Charles G.
     Virginia Way family.

WAYMAN -- Gottschalk, Katherine Cox
     Wayman family of Virginia and Missouri. 1958.

WEAKLEY -- Weakley, Samuel Anderson
     The southern Virginia Weakley families and their descendants. 1963.

WEAS -- Jones, Lizzie E. B.
     Ancestry and descendants of Catherine Weas of West Virginia. Des
     Moines, Iowa. 1920.

WEAVER -- Weaver, Dorothy Lee
     John George Weaver family, Shenandoah Valley of Virginia. Locust Grove.
     1980.

WEAVER -- Weaver, Robert B.
     William Weaver, Jr. and his descendants. Lexington. 1981.

WEBB -- Turner, Ronald R.
     Webb families of the Virginias. Fairview Park, Ohio. 1983.

WEEKS -- Weeks, Jesse O.
     Genealogy of the family of James Elmichael Weeks, 1768 and Isabelle Sharp
     Weeks, 1778 of Virginia and their descendants. Kansas City, Mo. 1935.

WEISIGER -- Wesisiger, Benjamin B.
     The Wiesiger family: an account of Daniel Weisiger, the immigrant, of
     Henrico and Chesterfield Counties, Virginia and his descendants.
     Richmond. 1984.

WELCH -- Welch, Alexander McMillan
     Philip Welch of Ipswich, Massachusetts, 1654, and his descendants.
     Richmond: W. Byrd Press, 1947.

WELLMAN -- Lane, Herbert V.
     A genealogical record of some descendants of Bennett Wellman of Maryland,
     Virginia, West Virginia, Kentucky, and North Carolina. Bradenton, Fla.
     1978.

WELLS -- Grant, Howard B.
Phineas Wells of New York and Virginia. Philippi, W. Va. 1935.

WENTZ -- Miller, Lemoyne Wentz
Footprints in the hills. Buckhannon, W. Va.: Ralston Press, 1984.

WEST -- Ayres, Margaret McNeill
The noble lineage of the Delaware-West family of Virginia, through Col.
John West, his sons, and his daughter Anne West who married Henry Fox.
Memphis. 1958.

WEST -- Brown, Alexander
Old Virginia blood. Ancestry of the distinguished family of West.
Minneapolis: Snead-Winston Co., 1926.

WEST -- Fox, Ann W.
The royal lineage of Anne West who married Henry Fox of "Huntington",
King County, Virginia. 1941.

WEST -- Fox, Ann Woodward
The noble lineage of the Delaware West family of Virginia. Memphis,
Tenn. 1958.

WEST -- Gregory, George
West Chart - Sir Thomas West, 2nd Lord De La Warr. Richmond. 1926.

WEST -- West, Elmer D.
Some descendants of Anthony West of Accomack, Virginia. Silver Spring,
Md. 1980.

WEST -- Wilson, Loretta West
Claiborne Dandridge West of Buckingham County, Virginia, his ancestors
and descendants. Dallas, Tex.: Southern Methodist University Printing
Dept., 1967.

WESTFALL -- Durett, Ralph
Westfall family of New York, Virginia, West Virginia and Ohio. 1974.

WEYBRECHT -- Genealogy of Martin Weybrecht, Bavaria 1689 - Lancaster County,
Pa., 1732, Weybright-Waybright; also Martin Weybright, Highland Co., Va.
1800.

WHALEY -- Barton, W. Baynard and Fannie May Dooley Barton
A limited genealogy study of descendants of Maj. Gen. Edward Whalley
(the Regicide) Featuring Private Thomas Whaley, Lieut. Archibald Whaley
of 1776 era descendants, Edward Charles Whaley, Joseph Whaley of Edisto
Island, S.C. and descendants of Nathaniel Whaley in Delaware, Virginia,
and Maryland with appropriate ancestral review, discussion and history
1067-1956. Stonega. 1956.

WHALLEY -- Cramb, Levi Kelsey
Preliminary notes on the Whaleys of Loudoun County, Virginia, and of
their descendants who migrated to Kentucky. Fairbury, Nebr. 1943.

WHALEY -- Foelsch, Donald H.
An index to Levi Kelsey Cramb's Preliminary notes on the Whaleys of
Loudoun County, Va. Williamsport, Pa. 1982.

WHEATLEY -- Kirby, Helen Ballard
The Wheatley family of Logan and Boone Counties, West Virginia. 1982.

WHELAN -- Wayland, John Terrill
Wayland families of nineteenth century Misssouri: with additions to
the original Virginia line. Longview, Tex. 1982.

WHITAKER -- Whitaker, Mildred Campbell
Genealogy of the Campbell, Noble, Gordon, Shelton, Gilmour and Byrd
Families, etc. St. Louis, Mo. 1927.

WHITE -- Cochran, Wes
The White-Hayes families, 1825-1978. Parkersburg, W. Va. 1978.

WHITE -- Kaufmann, Eva E.
The White saga, or, Two hundred years in Loudoun County, Virginia.
Gaithersburg. 1977.

WHITE -- Stewart, Charles L.
Raymond Arthur White ancestry; Illinoisan, Virginian, and European;
Acel, de Arches, Beaumont, Bigod. Urbana, Ill. 1965.

WHITE -- White, Gifford E.
James Taylor White of Virginia and some of his descendants into Texas.
Austin, Tex. 1982.

WHITE -- White, Rev. H. M.
Rev. William S. White, D.D., and his times (1800-1873). An autobiography.
Richmond. 1891.

WHITE -- White, Roscoe R.
White family records; descendants of Peregrine White, son of William
and Susanna (Fuller) White, 1620 to 1939. Clarksburg, W. Va. 1939.

WHITE -- White, Stanley R.
White connections, Loudoun County, Virginia: a genealogy of White,
McIlhany, Vanandy, Roberts, Hunter, Tamblin, Ransom. Long Beach,
Calif. 1981.

WHITEHEAD -- Dimond, E. Grey
The Reverend William W. Whitehead, Mississippi pioneer: his antecedents
and descendants: including some notes concerning the Whiteheads of the
Isle of Wight and Southampton, Virginia, Edgecombe, Halifax, Nash, and
Wake, North Carolina, Wayne, Indiana, Terriroty, La Porte, Indiana,
points west, and those massaced in the Nat Turner slave uprising of 1831.
St. Louis, Mo. 1985.

WHITESIDE -- Whiteside, Don
Male Whiteside(s) names in Virginia from selected sources, 1663-1895.
Edmonton. 1970.

WHITFIELD -- Whitfield, Vallie J. F.
Virginia history and Whitfield biographies. Pleasant Hill, Calif. 1976.

WHITING -- Davis, Joseph N.
A brief genealogy of the Whiting family of Virginia. Wahoo, Nebr. 1966.

WHITLEY -- Strader, Helen Whitley and Routh Whitley Benbow
Our wandering Whitleys; descendants of Sharp R. Whitley & John Saunders
Whitley of Virginia, Kentucky, Tennessee, Illinois, Missouri and Texas
and allied families. Clovis, N.M. 1974.

WHITMAN -- Bedwell, Mary Elizabeth
A genealogical history of the Whitman, Bedwell, and related families.
Blacksburg. 1974.

WHITTET -- Whittet, William and Robert Whittet
Whittet: a family record. 1657-1900. Richmond: Whittet & Shepperson,
1900.

WILKES -- Bass, Ivan Ernest
Wilkes family history and genealogy. Boyce. 1965.

WILKINSON -- Wilkins, James Richard
Pioneers and patriots: a history of the John Wilkins and some related
families of Virginia: Tuck, Hite, Wall, Winn and others. Winchester.
1980.

WILKINSON -- Wilkinson, Sam F.
The Wilkinson family history of Virginia, Missouri and Oklahoma. Nowata,
Okla. 1950.

WILLIAMS -- Hunt, June Perkins
John Williams of Isle of Wight, Virginia. 1973.

WILLIAMS -- Savage, Bertha Williams
We are the Williams: descendants of Thomas Williams of Virginia.
Wurtland, Ky. 1978.

WILLIAMS -- Smith, Ella W.
Tears and laughter in Virginia and elsewhere. Verona: McClure Press,
1972.

WILLIAMS -- Williams, Edwin A.
Plain facts about some Virginians. Baltimore. 1925.

WILLIAMS -- The Williams family of Virginia. Chattanooga. 1917.

WILLIAMS -- Williams, Herman Joseph
The George Philip Williams of Craig County, Virginia and Aylett Weaver
of Monroe County, West Virginia: genealogical compilation. Portsmouth,
Ohio. 1981.

WILLIAMS -- Williams, James Lawrence Basil
The Williams of Upshot in Virginia, 1613-1976: and some family connections.
Verona. 1976.

WILLIAMSON -- Alley, Joseph W.
Alden Williamson genealogy; a genealogical record of Alden Williamson's
family in Pike, Martin, Floyd, Johnson, Lawrence and Boyd Counties in
Kentucky and Mingo, Wayne, Logan, Lincoln, Cabell and Wyoming Counties
in West Virginia. Prichard, W. Va. 1962.

WILLIS -- DeHuff, E. W.
Descendants of John Willis in Richmond County, Va., 1917. Augusta,
Ga. 1962.

WILLIS -- DeHuff, E. W.
Additional data on John Willis, son of Henry Willis of Fredericksburg,
Va. Augusta, Ga. 1965.

WILLIS -- Potter, Maud
The Willises of Virginia; a genealogical account of the descendants of
Colonel Francis Willis of Gloucester County, Virginia. Colonel Willis
of Fredericksburg and William Willis of Southside Crany Creek. Mars Hill,
N.C. 1964.

WILLIS -- Willis, Byrd Charles
A sketch of the Willis family, Fredericksburg branch. Richmond: Whittet &
Shepperson, 1909.

WILLIS -- Willis, Byrd Charles and Richard Henry Willis
A sketch of the Willis family of Virginia, and of their kindred in other
states. With brief biographies of the Reades, Warners, Lewises, Byrds,
Carters, Champes, Bassetts, Madisons, Daingerfields, Thorntons, Burrells,
Taliaferros, Tayloes, Smiths, and Amblers. Richmond: Whittet &
Shepperson, 1898.

WILLIS -- Willis, Byrd C.
A sketch of the Willis family. Richmond: Whittet & Shepperson, 1909.

WILLIS -- Willis, Charles Ethelbert and Frances Caroline Willis
A history of the Willis family of New England and New Jersey and their
ancestors, comprising the families of Farrand, Ball, Kitchell, Cook, Ward,
Fairchild, Plume, Brune, Smith, Treat, Pierson, Crane, Cooper, Sanford,
Sheafe and others; to which is added a history of the family of John
Howard, esq., of Richmond, Virginia, and the Harris and Macleod families
of Georgia. Richmond: Whitmore & Garrett, 1917.

WILLIS -- The Willis family of Virginia and some of their descendants. With
brief biographies of their ancestors: the Martiaus, Reades, Warners,
Lewises, Washingtons, Byrds, Carters, Randolphs, Carys, Jacquelin-Amblers,
and a few later kin: the Randolph-Hackleys, Garniers, Shippeys, Barkelys,
Dorrs, Sawyers, Savages, Hogues, and Haywards. Mobile, Ala. 1967.

WILLOUGHBY -- Walter, Alice G.
Family charts: Capt. Thomas Willoughby, Carraway-Foster-Williams(on)
and Bartholomew Hoskins (1601-1706), Robyns/Robins, Thomas Sayer.
Virginia Beach. 1968.

WILSON -- Buland, Geraldine Brown
Descendants of Isaac Wilson and Ann States of Augusta County, Virginia.
Sapulpa, Okla. 1973.

WILSON -- Crocker, James Francis
The Wilsons. Portsmouth: Whitson & Shepherd, 1914.

WILSON -- Konopa, Leola Wilson
Descendants of Wilsons and Garners of Virginia. Columbia, S.C. 1970.

WILSON -- Rowland, Ralph S.
Wilsons and Burchells and related families, 1608-1976. Fairfax. 1976.

WILSON -- Stonestreet, Elizabeth Wilson
Ancestors and descendants of Isaac and Elizabeth C. Wilson. Harrisonville,
W. Va. 1979.

WILSON -- The Wilson family. Arlington: American Genealogical Research
Institute, 1972.

WILSON -- Wilson, Barr
Descendants of John Wilson, 1756-1827 (brother of Colonel Benjamin).
Parsons, W. Va.: McClain Print. Co., 1975.

WILSON -- John Wilson, 1740-1820, of Pittsylvania County, Va. Data collected
by Daniel Coleman of Norfolk, Va., member of "Virginia Historical
Society", extending over a period of thirty years; revised and arranged
by L. L. Cody of Macon, Ga. 1929.

WILSON -- Wilson, Le Grand
History of a Southern Presbyterian family. Richmond: Whittet &
Shepperson.

WILSON -- Wilson, Merritt
   The Wilson family of Western Maryland and West Virginia, and associated
   families: Ashby, Cresap, Harvey, Moon. Athens, Ohio: Lawhead Press,
   1971.

WILSON -- Wilson, York Lowry
   A Carolina-Virginia genealogy. Aldershot, England: Gable & Polden,
   Ltd., 1962.

WINDHAM -- Windham, Amasa Benjamin
   The Windham family of England, Virginia, North Carolina, South Carolina,
   Alabama, Mississippi, and Texas. Sandy Srpings, Ga. 1982.

WINE -- Wine, Jacob David
   The Wine family in America. Staunton: McClure Printing Co., 1952.

WINFREE -- Stubbs, Mrs. W. C.
   Winfree of Virginia. In Gulf State Historical Magazine.

WINGFIELD -- Wingfield, Linwood Davis
   History of the Wingfields of Virginia. Richmond. 1952.

WINGFIELD -- Wingfield, Marshall
   Pioneer families of Franklin County, Virginia. Berryville: Chesapeake
   Book Co., 1964.

WINSTON -- Claypool, Edward A.
   Descendants of James Winston, Jr., son of James Winston, the emigrant
   to Virginia. Chicago. 1900.

WINSTON -- Torrence, Clayton
   Winston of Virginia and allied families. Richmond: Whittet &
   Shepperson, 1927.

WISE -- Wise, Barton H.
   Life of Henry A. Wise of Virginia. By his grandson, the late Barton
   H. Wise. New York, N.Y.: The Macmillan Co., 1899.

WISE -- Wise, Jennings Cropper
   Col. John Wise of England and Virginia (1617-1695); his ancestors and
   descendants. Richmond. 1918.

WISE -- Wyse, Frederick Calhoun
   History of the Wise and Wyse family of South Carolina. Richmond. 1944.

WITHERS -- Gottschalk, Katherine Cox
   Withers family of the County Lancaster, England. Richmond: Dietz
   Priting Co., 1947.

WITHERS -- Williams, Edwin A.
Family of James and Elizabeth Keene Withers of Stafford County, Virginia;
incl. three generations of their descendants, 1680-1880.

WITHERS (Stafford) -- Withers, R. E.
Autobiography of an Octogenarian. Roanoke. 1907.

WOLVERTON -- Wolverton, Charles Evans
The old world, the new world, the Wolvertons, and West Virginia.
Clarksburg, W. Va. 1963.

WOLVERTON -- Wolverton, Charles E.
History, origin & heritage of the Wolverton and Woolverton family.
Clarksburg, W. Va. 1963.

WOOD -- Bayne, Margaret William
The Wood family of Fluvanna, Virginia, 1795-1969. Norfolk. 1984.

WOOD -- Lawler, Leo
Nehemiah Wood of Shenandoah County, Virginia: with forebear(s),
descendants, and allied families. Fredericksburg. 1980.

WOOD -- Peden, Henry C.
The William Wood and related families of Albemarle County, Virginia
and Barren County, Kentucky in the 1800's. Bel Air, Md. 1984.

WOOD VALLEY OF VIRGINIA -- Wood, James W.
History of the Wood family. Luray.

WOOD -- Wood, M. B.
A brief account of the Wood family in Virginia: containing a short
memoir of James O. Wood and his ancestors from their earliest settlement
in the colony of Virginia to his death. Philadelphia: J. B. Lippincott,
1893.

WOOD -- Wood, John Sumner
The Wood family index. Richmond: Garrett and Massie, 1966.

WOODING -- Wooding, Harry
The Woodings of Virginia. Danville. 1957.

WOODLEY -- Crocker, James Francis
The Woodleys of Isle of Wight County, Virginia. Portsmouth. W. A.
Fiske, Printer, 1914.

WOODRUFF -- Woodruff, Audrey L.
Tall tress in the forest; the Woodruff family of Virginia, Alabama,
and Missouri. 1966.

WOODS -- Esker, Katie Prince Ward
Archibald Woods of Albemarle County and Michael, son of Archibald
Woods. 1944.

WOODS -- Sampson, Anne Eliza Woods
Kith and kin, written, at their urgent request, for the children of
Mr. and Mrs. John Russell Sampson, by their mother. It includes records
of their ancestors bearing the names Baker, Baldwin, Breckinridge,
Brown, Bryson, Byrd, Curd, Dudley, Goodman, Horsley, Kennedy, Le Bruen,
McClanahan, McDowell, McKesson, Poage, Reed, Rogers, Thornton, Trice,
Sampson, and Woods. Richmond: William Byrd Press, 1922.

WOODWARD -- Woodward, Lloyd A.
A history of the ancestors and descendants of Elisha Woodward, 1589 to
1972. McLean. 1972.

WOOLFOLK -- Davis, W. F.
Genealogy of the male line of the ancestors of Sowyel Woolfolk, born in
Virginia, 1744, died in Woodford County, Ky., 1830. Kansas City, Mo.
1948.

WOOLDRIDGE -- Gardiner, Laurence B.
John Wooldridge, blacksmith. Troutville. 1980.

WOOTEN -- Wooton, Richard C.
Wooten and related families association quarterly. Arlington. 1981.

WOOTEN -- Wooten, Richard C.
The Wootens of Isle of Wight County, Virginia. Arlington. 1981.

WORD -- Word, Charles P.
Names of 1350 of our deceased relatives and friends, most of whom I
knew personally. Richmond: J. W. Randolph, 1887.

WORD -- Thompson, Mrs. Radiant B. Word
The ancestors of Benjamin Franklin Word. Fredericksburg. 1946.

WORTHINGTON -- Sims, Henry U.
The genealogy of the Worthington family of Alabama, South Carolina,
Virginia, and Ohio, being descendants of Robert Worthington, who
emigrated from Ireland to New Jersey in 1713, with an appendix on the
Symcock family of Pennsylvania down to 1716. Birmingham, Ala. 1937.

WORTHY -- Worthy, William Buford
The Worthy family from Virginia to Texas and some of their kin.
Columbia, S.C. 1984.

WRIGHT -- Grant, Robert N.
Untangling some of the Wrights of Bedford County, Virginia. Mountain
View, CaCif, 1977.

WRIGHT -- Perrine, Howland Delano
    Anthony Wright of Loudoun County, Virginia, and his descendants. New
York. 1925.

WRIGHT -- Powers, Negetha Gourley
    The Wright connection. Bristol. c1985.

WRIGHT -- Roehl, Katherine M.
    Enoch Wright and wife, Susan Abshire, their lineage, their lives, their
family; resided Va., Ohio, Ind., Calif. Lexington, Mich. 1971.

WRIGHT -- Wayne, Arthur Alvin
    Some early Wright families of the Colony and State of Virginia. Evanston,
Ill. 19--.

WRIGHT -- Wright, Carroll
    A genealogy: Wright-Mattison family. Charlottesville: Bailey Printing,
1981.

WRIGHT -- Wright, Jay B.
    Joseph and Elizabeth Wright of Bedford County, Va. and Columbiana
County, Ohio. DeWitt, N.Y. 1974.

WRIGHT -- Wright, Pauline Williams
    The Wright book: worthy heritage, enduring challenge: being the history
of some of the descendants of John Wright, 1745-1814, Bedford County,
Virginia. Baltimore: Gateway Press, 1974.

WYATT -- Wyatt, Pearl Spitzer
    The Wyatt family. Richmond. 1969.

WYATT -- Peters, Genevieve E.
    John Wyatt of Loudoun, Shenandoah and Franklin Counties, Virginia. 1969.

WYATT -- Wiatt, Alexander Lloyd
    The Wiatt family of Virginia: the descendants of John Wiatt, Jr.
(1732-1805) of Gloucester County, Virginia: with notes on Field,
Carter, Todd, Ball, Montague, and Jones families. Newport News.
1980.

WYATT -- Wyatt, Lucile Rebecca Douglass
    The Wyatt family records; the descendants of E. J. Wyatt, of Pittsylvania
County, Virginia, and his lineal descent from John Wyatt, early pioneer,
of Halifax County, who is presumanly the descendant of Adam Wyatt
through the Rev. Haute (Hawte) Wyatt, who emigrated from England to
Virginia, in 1621. Richmond: Dietz Press, 1957.

WYNKOOP -- Brockhurst, Robert H., Mrs.
    The Wynkoops of Loudoun County, Virginia. Pensacola, Fla. 1976.

WYSOR -- Wysor, William W.
    Old sherry; portrait of a Virginia family, by Frank J. Klingberg.
Richmond: Barrett and Massie, 1938.

YATES -- Clarke, Mrs. J. Brent (Elizabeth Waters)
   The Yates family in Virginia, descendants of George Yate(s) deputy
   provincial surveyor of Maryland (16-- - 1691). Washington. 1942.

YATES -- Daniel, Elizabeth
   John Yates of England and Virginia. His family and descendants.
   Charles Town, W. Va. 1936.

YATES -- Newman, Harry W.
   Notes on the descent of the Yates family of Virginia from George Yates I,
   of Maryland. Boulder, Colo. 1967.

YATES -- Terrill, A. E.
   Memorials of a family in England and Virginia. A.D. 1771-1851. London
   and Aylesbury: Hazell, Watson, & Viney, Ltd., 1887.

YATES -- Yates, Helen Kay
   Bartholomew Yates of Middlesex County, Virginia, and some of his
   descendants. Mechanicsville. 1980.

YATES (Caroline) -- Yates, Richard
   Family Chart of Michael Yates.

YEARDLEY -- Upshur, Thomas Teackle
   Sir George Yeardley, or Yardley, Governor and Captain General of
   Virginia, and Temperance (West) Lady Yeardley. 1896.

YEARDLEY -- Upshur, Thomas Teackle
   Sir George Yeardley or Yardley, Governor and Captain General of
   Virginia, and Temperance Lady Yardley and some of their Descendants.
   Nassawadox, Northampton Co., Va.

YONGE -- Gaskill, Bessie Alice Shurtlieff
   Captain Thomas Yonge, (1579 - after 1642) of London, England and
   Jamestown, Va. and some of his descendants; including Shurtlieff
   generations relative to his ancestry. 1966.

YOUNG -- Armstrong, William
   Partial family history of Young - Galbraith - and allied families of
   Pa., Va., and Tenn., from various family records.

YOUNG -- Cowles, C. D.
   Family Tree of Michael Cadet Young of Brunswick Co., Va.

YOUNG -- Hankins, Sherry Prillaman
   Young family history: an account of the descendants of William Thomas
   Young and Julia Hale Young of Franklin County, Virginia. Roanoke. 1978.

YOUNG -- Maxey, Elizabeth Young
    The family history of Isaac Snow and Sarah Fletcher Young. Spanishburg,
W. Va. 1978.

YOUNG -- Thomsen, Frances Draper
    Historical narrative and genealogy of the Parmiter, Young, Draper
families. Falls Church. 1958.

YOUNG -- Young, Walter Jorgensen
    The Young family of Bristol. Fredericksburg. 1937.

ZIEGLER -- Mason, Floyd R.
    John Zigler and Elizabeth Kline of Virginia. Alexandria. 1984.

ZIRKLE -- Bowie, Frank McKay
    History of the ancestry of Clairborne Joseph Zirkle and Frances Anne
Hite, the former formerly of New Market, Va., the latter formerly of
Luray, Va. Alexandria. 1948.

ZIRKLE -- Harpine, Jacob William
    A brief history of the first Zirkles, in Shenandoah and Rockingham
Counties, Virginia. 1962.

ZOLLMAN -- Zollman, Wikbur B.
    Descendants of William and Mary Bousman Zollman. Roanoke. 1942.

ZWINGLI -- Swingley, Joseph Albert
    Family record of the ancestors and lineage, various branches of the
Zwingli family of Switzerland. Norfolk. 1926.

BIBLIOGRAPHY

AVERY, Carrie W. Genealogical Records, Volume II. Privately printed. 1925.

BRAWNER, Henry N. Jr. United States of America Patent 1002127 - Emulsifying
     Apparatus for Milk or Cream. Washington: August 29, 1911.

BRAWNER, Henry N. Jr. United States of America Patent 1112594 - Methods or
     Processes of Homogenizing Cream. Washington: October 6, 1914.

KAMINKOW, Marion J. Genealogies In The Library Of Congress. Baltimore:
     Magna Carta Book Company, 1972.

KAMINKOW, Marion J. Genealogies In The Library Of Congress, Supplement
     1972 - 1976. Baltimore: Magna Carta Book Company, 1977.

KAMINKOW, Marion J. Genealogies In The Library Of Congress, Second Supplement
     1976 - 1986. Baltimore: Magna Carta Book Company, 1987.

KAMINKOW, Marion J. A Complement To Genealogies In The Library Of Congress.
     Baltimore: Magna Carta Book Company, 1981.

KURTZ, Thelma E. Brawner Family. Kearney, Missouri, 1976.

MAGRUDER, James M. Jr. Index to Maryland Colonial Wills 1634 - 1777.
     Baltimore: Genealogical Publishing Co., Inc., 1975. (Reprint of
     1933 Original.)

MICHAELS, Carolyn Leopold and Scott, Kathryn S. Library Catalog DAR Family
     Histories and Genealogies. Washington: National Society Daughters
     of the American Revolution, 1982.

MILLER, T. Michael. Alexandria and Alexandria (Arlington) County Virginia
     Minister Returns and Marriage Bonds 1801 - 1852. Bowie, Maryland:
     Heritage Books, Inc., 1987.

MILLER, T. Michael. Where Is It? Miller's Annotative Guide to Historical
     Source Material on Alexandria, Virginia. Alexandria: Lloyd House,
     Alexandria Library.

MILLER, T. Michael. Burials In St. Mary's Catholic Cemetery Alexandria,
     Virginia 1798 - 1893. Bowie, Maryland: Heritage Books, Inc., 1986.

SCHREINER-YANTIS, Netti. Genealogical and Local History Books In Print.
     Springfield: Genealogical Books In Print, 1985.

STEWART, Robert Armistead. Index To Printed Virginia Genealogies. Richmond:
     1930. (Reprinted by Genealogical Publishing Co., Baltimore, 1965.)

STRAHAN, Jean D. National Genealogical Society Library Book List. Washington:
     National Genealogical Society, 1978.

TAYLOR, George B. Record Of Progress Chestnut Farms Dairy. Washington:
     Privately Printed, 1929.

TORRENCE, Clayton. Virginia Wills and Administrations 1632 - 1800. Richmond:
     The National Society of the Colonial Dames of America, 1930.

WILLIAMS, Harrison. Legends of Loudoun. Richmond: Garrett and Massie, Inc.,
     1938.

VOGT, John and Kethley, T. William Jr. Virginia Historic Marriage Register
     Loudoun County Marriages 1760 - 1850. Athen, Georgia: Iberian
     Publishing Co., 1985.

This cross-reference table lists secondary names given in book titles listed in this bibliography.

FARRELL, 43
FASSITT, 41
FAULCONER, 163
FAUNTLEROY, 50 107 149
FAURE, 4 73
FAWCETT, 13
FAWLEY, 133
FEARNOW, 65
FEATHERSTONE, 73
FELTON, 49
FENNEL, 49
FERGUSON, 20 82 148 159
FERNEAT, 65
FERNO, 65
FERRELL, 43
FERRIS, 189
FERTH, 48
FETTY, 107 144
FICKLINING, 65
FIELD, 64 148 159 206
FINLEY, 16
FINNELL, 25
FISKE, 147
FITZGERALD, 139
FITZHUGH, 115
FLEET, 10 23
FLEMING, 72 148 159
FLETCHER, 208
FLOYD, 113
FOLEY, 171
FOLIOTT, 86
FONTAINE, 24 48 107 189
FOOKES, 69
FOOTE, 68
FORBES, 45
FORD, 4
FORTUNE, 84
FOSS, 67
FOSTER, 90 202
FOUTZ, 68
FOWKE, 132
FOWLKES, 168
FOX, 125 198
FRANCIS, 189
FRANKLIN, 28 70 167 176 193
FRANKLING, 176
FRANKS, 142
FRAY, 70
FRAZER, 70
FREDREGILL, 177
FRENCH, 65 75
FREYFOGLE, 78

FRIZZELL, 123
FRY, 60
FULLENWIDER, 71
FULLER, 44 199
FULLEWIDER, 71
FULTON, 171
FULWIDER, 71
FURLONG, 58
FUSON, 86
GAGER, 54
GAIN, 72
GALBRAITH, 207
GANDEE, 72
GANNAWAY, 1
GARDING, 86
GARDNER, 21 115
GARLAND, 48
GARNER, 202
GARNETT, 35 73
GARNIER, 202
GARRESTON, 125
GARRISON, 88
GARROTT, 73
GASKINS, 25 50 73
GATEWOOD, 42 73
GAY, 39 148 159
GEE, 48
GENTRY, 47 125
GEORGE, 73
GIBB, 166
GIBBENS, 74
GIBBS, 157 165 166
GIBSON, 170
GIFFORD, 170
GILES, 84
GILLELAND, 132
GILLESPIE, 53 164
GILLEY, 45
GILLMORE, 54
GILMER, 141
GILMOUR, 199
GIVENS, 39 145
GLADDEN, 164
GLASSCOCK, 75
GLASSELL, 76
GLAZEBROOK, 62 110
GLENDY, 51
GOAD, 50 77
GOCHENOUR, 44
GODDARD, 110
GODE, 77
GOMBIE, 28

GOOCH, 186
GOOD, 111
GOODMAN, 28 163 205
GOOLSBY, 1
GORDON, 6 121 148 159 199
GOTHARD, 43
GOULD, 75
GRADY, 60
GRAHAM, 26 39 47 107
GRANTHAM, 113
GRAVE, 166
GRAVES, 24 166 185
GRAY, 100 120 189
GRAYSON, 148 159 163
GREAVER, 80
GREEN, 11 75 146
GREENE, 146
GRIEVER, 80
GRIFFIN, 120 148 159
GRIFFING, 126
GRIGG, 80
GRIGSBY, 51
GRIMES, 3
GRIZZLE, 44
GROVE, 177
GROVER, 151
GRUBB, 69
GRUBBS, 141
GRUVER, 139
GRYMES, 66 115
GUIN, 81 82
GUTHRIE, 125
GWATHMEY, 117
GWIN, 39 82
GWINN, 195
GWUINN, 82
GWYN, 81 82
GWYNN, 81 82 120
GWYNNE, 82
HACKLEY, 202
HAGER, 10
HAHN, 111
HALDIMAN, 83
HALE, 7 207
HALL, 16 48 75 76 86 94 157 167
HAM, 84
HAMILTON, 155
HAMMAN, 84
HAMMER, 13
HAMPTON, 85
HAMRICK, 3
HANCOCK, 85

HANKS, 50
HANSON, 115 126
HARBER, 86
HARBOUR, 86
HARBUR, 86
HARDAWAY, 129 183
HARDEN, 39
HARDIWICK, 179
HARDON, 65
HARDWICK, 47
HARDY, 48 189
HARLOWE, 87
HARMON, 165
HARNEY, 121
HARPER, 39 151
HARRIS, 47 138
HARRISON, 25 85 141 148 148 159 171
191
HART, 57
HARTWELL, 122
HARVEY, 50 203
HARVIE, 89
HARWELL, 86
HASELL, 90
HATCHER, 12
HATFIELD, 170
HATTEN, 13
HATTON, 191
HAUTE, 206
HAWKINS, 13 48
HAWLEY, 171
HAWTE, 206
HAYDEN, 154
HAYES, 199
HAYMOND, 134
HAYNES, 183
HAYSLIP, 62
HAYWARD, 202
HAZELHURST, 90
HAZELRIGG, 58
HEADLEE, 82
HEADLEY, 82
HEARD, 114
HEATWOLE, 111 168
HELDRETH, 94
HELM, 113
HEMP, 111
HENDERSON, 24 39 98
HENDRICK, 120
HENDRICKS, 120
HENLEY, 10
HENRY, 65 107

HEREWARD, 89
HICKMAN, 1 107
HIESTAND, 187
HIGHLAND, 143
HIGHT, 84
HILL, 41 47
HILLMAN, 94 143
HILMAN, 94
HINDMAN, 60
HITE, 128 200 208
HITER, 77
HITT, 148
HOBSON, 48
HODGE, 58 95
HODGEN, 113
HOEHNS, 79
HOFFMAN, 133
HOGE, 76
HOGUE, 202
HOLDEN, 142
HOLDIMAN, 83
HOLEMAN, 83
HOLESTIN, 96
HOLLADAY, 76
HOLLAND, 83 122
HOLLIDAY, 35 193
HOLMAN, 105
HOLMES, 61 75 149 164
HOLSTINE, 96
HOLSTON, 96
HOLT, 137
HOOFFS, 95
HORD, 165
HORSLEY, 163 205
HOSKINS, 35 107
HOTSINPILLER, 26
HOTTLE, 70
HOUCHINS, 86
HOUNSELL, 97
HOUSTON, 90 125
HOUZE, 97
HOWARD, 39 48 82 125 202
HOWE, 125
HOWELL, 16 79
HOWSE, 97
HUBARD, 122 148 159
HUBBARD, 145
HUDDLESTON, 170
HUDGINS, 101
HUDSON, 79
HUES, 99
HUFFMAN, 133

HUGGANS, 178
HUGHES, 33 60 67 125 167 179
HUGHS, 99
HULL, 39
HULVA, 99
HULVER, 99
HUME, 168
HUMPHREY, 171
HUMPHRIES, 99 148
HUMPSTON, 100
HUMPSTONE, 100
HUMSTONE, 100
HUNDSBERGER, 100
HUNGERFORD, 195
HUNSBERRY, 100
HUNT, 8 54
HUNTER, 199
HUNTGATE, 38
HUNTON, 157
HUNTSBERRY, 100
HUNTZBERRY, 100
HURT, 120
HUSSEY, 125
HUTCHENS, 101
HUTCHESON, 101
HUTCHISON, 142
HYRE, 102
INGERSOLL, 1
INGOLD, 37
IREMONGER, 102
IRVINE, 125
ISHAM, 108 120 153 189
IVEY, 102
JACKSON, 48 91 179
JACOBS, 76
JACOCKS, 94
JACQUELIN, 202
JAMES, 130
JARRELL, 165
JARRETT, 134
JEFFREYS, 104
JEFFRIES, 123 124
JENKINS, 97
JENNINGS, 26 164 168
JENNISON, 75
JENNY, 39
JESSEE, 44
JETER, 165
JOHNSON, 57 113 125 165 179 183 186
194
JOHNSTON, 75 105
JOHNSTONE, 106

RICHARD, 58
RICHARDS, 33
RICHARDSON, 38 52 59
RIDDICK, 109
RIDDLE, 162
RIGGLE, 156
RILEY, 145
RITCHEY, 55
RITCHIE, 183
RIVES, 141 155
RIXEY, 171
ROBERTS, 199
ROBERTSON, 1 19 47 48 148 159
ROBESON, 155
ROBINSON, 28 75 76 147
ROBUCK, 159
RODES, 123 156
ROGERS, 38 110 157 163 205
ROHRABAUGH, 159
ROLFE, 148 159
ROMEY, 52
ROOK, 126
ROOKSLAND, 166
ROOTES, 160
ROSEN, 160
ROSENMULLER, 125
ROSS, 75 83 86
ROTHEGEB, 177
ROUT, 126
ROWLAND, 145
ROY, 35 120
ROYAL, 32
RUCKER, 157
RUDOLPH, 26
RUE, 5
RUFFIN, 162
RUFFNER, 177
RUPERT, 97
RUSSELL, 139 205
RYSDAM, 168
RYVES, 155 157
SAFENDORPH, 163
SAFFORD, 100
SAGE, 165
SALISBURY, 128
SALLE, 4
SALLIS, 86
SAMPSON, 4 75 163 168 205
SANBORN, 38
SANDERSON, 193
SANFORD, 202
SARGENT, 74

SATTERWHITE, 189
SAUNDERS, 82 185
SAVAGE, 120 202
SAWYER, 181 202
SAYER, 202
SCALES, 120
SCHAUBLIN, 168
SCHMID, 193
SCHOONHOVEN, 164
SCHREGARDUS, 164
SCHRYVERS, 168
SCHWENKFELDER, 168
SCOBEE, 56
SCOTT, 8 76 189
SEALE, 165
SEARSON, 175
SEAWELL, 122
SEGAR, 129
SEGENDORF, 163
SELDEN, 109
SELVEY, 130
SHACKELFORD, 95
SHANK, 91
SHANNON, 27
SHARP, 26 197
SHAVER, 177
SHEAFE, 202
SHED, 166
SHEETS, 142
SHELDON, 128
SHELTON, 170 199
SHEPHERD, 58 115 167
SHERROD, 133
SHIPLETT, 167
SHIPP, 35
SHIPPEN, 162
SHIPPEY, 202
SHIPPIN, 115
SHIRLEY, 1
SHIVLEY, 67
SHORT, 39 69 79
SHORTER, 101
SHOWALTER, 111
SHREVES, 165
SHREWSBURY, 131
SHUBRICK, 90
SILER, 169
SILVESTER, 5
SILVIOUS, 169
SIMMONS, 81
SIMMS, 52
SIMON, 73

TETER, 125
THOMAS, 33 60 135 138 157
THOMASON, 165
THOMSON, 124
THORNTON, 120 141 163 201 205
THRIFT, 84
THWEAT, 32
THWEATT, 101
TIGNOR, 50
TILFORD, 125
TILLMAN, 166
TOBIN, 82
TOBY, 138
TOD, 186
TODD, 60 206
TOLER, 129
TOMLINSON, 48
TOMPKINS, 125
TORRENCE, 3
TORTAT, 69
TOWLES, 186
TOWLE, 168
TOWNSHEND, 195
TRABUE, 24
TRAPIER, 90
TRAVERS, 100
TRAYNHAM, 8
TREAT, 202
TREVVETT, 187
TRICE, 163 205
TRIPLETT, 171
TRIPP, 73
TROLINGER, 51
TROUT, 110
TRUMBO, 129
TUCK, 200
TUCKER, 48 67 69
TUCKWILLER, 26
TUGGLE, 155
TUPPER, 176
TURBERVILLE, 115
TURMAN, 86
TURNER, 13 116 128 200
TUTTLE, 69
TWITTY, 48
TYLER, 100
TYNES, 109
TYRRALL, 182
TYRRELL, 182
UPDYKE, 189
UPSHAW, 17
UZZELL, 125

VALENTINE, 189
VANANDY, 199
VANCE, 76
VANDERGRIFT, 190
VANDYKE, 13
VANHORN, 190
VANMETER, 113
VANMETRE, 58
VANSCHOONHOVEN, 164
VAUGHAN, 113
VAWTER, 125
VERPLANCK, 125
VERTREES, 113
VIELLARD, 133
VINCENT, 155
VIOLETT, 56
VOGT, 14
VOLLENWEIDER, 71
VOWELL, 50
WACKER, 67
WADDILL, 122
WADDY, 50 189
WADE, 61 191
WAGGENER, 191
WAHL, 192
WAITT, 191
WAKEFIELD, 52
WALDEGRAVE, 39
WALDEN, 55
WALE, 23
WALKE, 148 159
WALKER, 12 107 125 151
WALL, 126 200
WALLACE, 76
WALLTON, 192 193
WALTERS, 113
WALTON, 75
WARD, 202
WARING, 29 107 193
WARNER, 201 202
WARREN, 28 84 147 195
WARTON, 195
WARWICK, 39
WASHINGTON, 51 63 115 141 202
WATERS, 4 64 141 195
WATHEN, 79
WATKINS, 49 149 168
WATSON, 1 25 95
WATTS, 26 165 189
WAUGH, 171
WAYBRIGHT, 198
WAYMAN, 124

www.ingramcontent.com/pod-product-compliance
Lightning Source LLC
Chambersburg PA
CBHW080419270326
41929CB00018B/3089